Lecture Notes in Computer Science

Edited by G. Goos, J. Hartmanis and J. van Leeu

Springer
Berlin
Heidelberg
New York
Barcelona
Hong Kong
London
Milan
Paris
Singapore
Tokyo

Hervé Debar   Ludovic Mé
S. Felix Wu (Eds.)

Recent Advances in Intrusion Detection

Third International Workshop, RAID 2000
Toulouse, France, October 2-4, 2000
Proceedings

Springer

Series Editors

Gerhard Goos, Karlsruhe University, Germany
Juris Hartmanis, Cornell University, NY, USA
Jan van Leeuwen, Utrecht University, The Netherlands

Volume Editors

Hervé Debar
France Télécom R & D
42 Rue des Coutoures, 14000 Caen, France
E-mail: herve.debar@francetelecom.fr

Ludovic Mé
SUPELEC, BP 28, 35511 Cesson Sevigne Cedex, France
E-mail: Ludovic.Me@supelec.fr

S. Felix Wu
University of California at Davis
Department of Computer Science, 2063 Engineering II
One Shields Avenue, Davis, CA 95616-8562, USA
E-mail: wu@cs.ucdavis.edu

Cataloging-in-Publication Data applied for

Die Deutsche Bibliothek - CIP-Einheitsaufnahme

Recent advances in intrusion detection : third international workshop ;
proceedings / RAID 2000, Toulouse, France, October 2 - 4, 2000.
Hervé Debar ... (ed.). - Berlin ; Heidelberg ; New York ; Barcelona ;
Hong Kong ; London ; Milan ; Paris ; Singapore ; Tokyo : Springer,
2000
    (Lecture notes in computer science ; Vol. 1907)
    ISBN 3-540-41085-6

CR Subject Classification (1998): K.6.5, K.4, E.3, C.2, D.4.6

ISSN 0302-9743
ISBN 3-540-41085-6 Springer-Verlag Berlin Heidelberg New York

Springer-Verlag Berlin Heidelberg New York
a member of BertelsmannSpringer Science+Business Media GmbH
© Springer-Verlag Berlin Heidelberg 2000
Printed in Germany

Typesetting: Camera-ready by author, data conversion by DA-TeX Gerd Blumenstein
Printed on acid-free paper   SPIN: 10722688   06/3142   5 4 3 2 1 0

Preface

Since 1998, RAID has established its reputation as the main event in research on intrusion detection, both in Europe and the United States. Every year, RAID gathers researchers, security vendors and security practitioners to listen to the most recent research results in the area as well as experiments and deployment issues.

This year, RAID has grown one step further to establish itself as a well-known event in the security community, with the publication of hardcopy proceedings. RAID 2000 received 26 paper submissions from 10 countries and 3 continents. The program committee selected 14 papers for publication and examined 6 of them for presentation. In addition RAID 2000 received 30 extended abstracts proposals; 15 of these extended abstracts were accepted for presentation. Extended abstracts are available on the website of the RAID symposium series, http://www.raid-symposium.org/. We would like to thank the technical program committee for the help we received in reviewing the papers, as well as all the authors for their participation and submissions, even for those rejected.

As in previous RAID symposiums, the program alternates between fundamental research issues, such as new technologies for intrusion detection, and more practical issues linked to the deployment and operation of intrusion detection systems in a real environment. Five sessions have been devoted to intrusion detection technology, including modeling, data mining and advanced techniques. Four sessions have been devoted to topics surrounding intrusion detection, such as evaluation, standardization and legal issues, logging and analysis of intrusion detection information. RAID will also host two panels, one on practical deployment of intrusion-detection systems where users of the technology will share their experience with the audience and one on the distributed denial of service attacks that generated a lot of attention in early 2000.

In summary, we hope that this very dense program and mix of practical and theoretical issues will satisfy the users of intrusion detection systems and encourage the researchers in the area to continue improving their technology.

October 2000

Hervé Debar
S. Felix Wu

Organization

RAID 2000 is hosted by and gratefully acknowledges the support of ONERA Centre de Toulouse.

Conference Chairs

Executive Committee Chair Marc Dacier (IBM Research, Switzerland)
Program Co-Chairs   Hervé Debar (IBM Research, Switzerland)
                        S. Felix Wu (North Carolina State University, USA)
Publication Chair   Ludovic Mé (Supélec, France)

Program Committee

Matt Bishop	University of California at Davis, USA
Dick Brackney	National Security Agency, USA
Rowena Chester	University of Tennessee, USA
Frédéric Cuppens	ONERA, France
Marc Dacier	IBM Research, Switzerland
Hervé Debar	IBM Research, Switzerland
Yves Deswarte	LAAS-CNRS and SRI-International, France
Terry Escamilla	IBM, USA
Deborah Frincke	University of Idaho, USA
Tim Grance	National Institute of Standards and Technology, USA
Ming-Yuh Huang	The Boeing Company, USA
Erland Jonsson	Chalmers University of Technology, Sweden
Sokratis Katsikas	University of the Aegean, Greece
Baudouin Le Charlier	Universite de Namur, Belgium
Ludovic Mé	Supélec, France
Abdelaziz Mounji	Swift, Belgium
Vern Paxson	ACIRI/LBNL, USA
Jean-Jacques Quisquater	Universite Catholique de Louvain, Belgium
Mark Schneider	National Security Agency, USA
Steve Smaha	Free Agent, USA
Peter Sommer	London School of Economics and Political Science, England
Stuart Staniford-Chen	Silicon Defense, USA
Peter Thorne	University of Melbourne, Australia
S. Felix Wu	North Carolina State University, USA
Kevin Ziese	Cisco Systems, USA

Additional Referees

Dominique Alessandri   IBM Research, Switzerland
Klaus Julisch   IBM Research, Switzerland
Andreas Wespi   IBM Research, Switzerland

Local Organization Committee

Frédéric Cuppens   ONERA, France
Claire Saurel   ONERA, France

Sponsoring Institutions

Alcatel
IBM
Internet Security Systems

Table of Contents

IDS Evaluation

Modeling

Better Logging through Formality

Applying Formal Specification Techniques to Improve Audit Logs and Log Consumers

Chapman Flack* and Mikhail J. Atallah**

CERIAS, Purdue University
1315 Recitation Bldg., West Lafayette, IN 47907-1315 USA
{flack,mja}@cerias.purdue.edu

Abstract. We rely on programs that consume audit logs to do so successfully (a robustness issue) and form the correct interpretations of the input (a semantic issue). The vendor's documentation of the log format is an important part of the *specification* for any log consumer. As a specification, it is subject to improvement using formal specification techniques. This work presents a methodology for formalizing and refining the description of an audit log to improve robustness and semantic accuracy of programs that use the log. Ideally applied during design of a new format, the methodology is also profitably applied to existing log formats. Its application to Solaris BSM (an existing, commercial format) demonstrated utility by detecting ambiguities or errors of several types in the documentation or implementation of BSM logging, and identifying opportunities to improve the content of the logs. The products of this work are the methodology itself for use in refining other log formats and their consumers, and an annotated, machine-readable grammar for Solaris BSM that can be used by the community to quickly construct applications that consume BSM logs.

Keywords: log, formal, specification, documentation, reliability, interoperability, CIDF, BSM, grammar

1   Introduction

Audit logs maintained by computing systems can be used for a variety of purposes, such as to detect misuse, to document conformance to policy, and to understand and recover from software or hardware failures. Any such application presumes a log consumer, software that can read and analyze the log, and

---

* Supported in part by an Intel Foundation Graduate Fellowship, by contracts MDA904-96-1-0116 and MDA904-97-6-0176 from Maryland Procurement Office, and by sponsors of the Center for Education and Research in Information Assurance and Security.

** Supported in part by Grant EIA-9903545 from the National Science Foundation, and by sponsors of the Center for Education and Research in Information Assurance and Security.

H. Debar, L. Mé, and F. Wu (Eds.): RAID 2000, LNCS 1907, pp. 1–16, 2000.

draw conclusions of interest about the state history of the system that produced the log.

Two requirements that apply to any log consumer are easily stated: the consumer should be able to read any sequence of the possible log records without failure, and any results computed (or conclusions drawn) should be correct (or justifiable). These requirements may not have the same weight in all applications. Some unreliability in a tool devised ad hoc to count uses of a certain software package, for example, may be tolerated as a practical matter.

Also, it may suffice for an ad hoc tool to skim the log for a very small fraction of its information content, as the use to which the information will be put is known in advance. However, initiatives like the Common Intrusion Detection Framework (CIDF)[14] place a renewed emphasis on exchanging event information among multiple agents, where one agent should not discard information another may need. CIDF's Common Intrusion Specification Language (CISL) is necessarily expressive enough to convey the semantic nuances of event records; that very expressiveness increases the pressure on any system that would translate logs into CISL not to miss or mistranslate those nuances, lest later analysis be led into error. In a production intrusion detection system, failures caused by incorrect handling of the input, or unsound conclusions resulting from semantic misunderstandings, may be costly. In unlucky cases, they may represent new, exploitable vulnerabilities introduced by the security tool itself.

This paper describes a way to reduce the risk, observing simply but centrally that the usual documentation accompanying a system that produces logs is also a partial *specification* for software that must consume those logs. Software engineering techniques for formalizing specifications can therefore be applied to find and purge ambiguities and inconsistencies, and reshape the document into one from which reliable log consumers can more readily and consistently be built. Opportunities to improve the log itself may be revealed in the same process.

The amount of attention devoted here to the mere task of reading a stream of data may be surprising to a reader who has not been immersed for some time in extracting meaning from audit logs of general purpose systems. The case that an audit log is a peculiarly complex stream of data, presenting subtle issues of interpretation, will be built in Sect. 4 with quantitative support in Sect. 6.

2   Contributions

Contributions of this work include artifacts of immediate use to the community, and suggestions with demonstrated potential to improve design of future audit producers and consumers.

- A grammar and lexical analyzer package for Sun's Basic Security Module[8] (BSM) audit data through Solaris 2.6. The package, requiring Java[3] and the ANTLR parser generator[11], produces a parser for BSM audit that can be rapidly extended with processing specific to an application. The parser is conservative: it may signal a syntax error on an undocumented BSM record that was not covered in our test data, but will not silently accept invalid input. Undocumented rules are readily added to the grammar as they are discovered. The package, available for educational and research purposes, has been used to speed development in one completed and several ongoing BSM-related projects.

– The BSM grammar in the package is extensively annotated, with hyperlinks from grammar rules to the corresponding pages of Sun documentation. While others working with BSM have undoubtedly noted some of the same ambiguous or misdocumented records that we have, and probably some not present in our test data, there has not always been a document available to the community and intended to detail such discoveries in one place.

– While grammars and parsing techniques arguably offer a natural approach to the reliable processing of structured information that auditing requires, they have been strangely often neglected in practice, as described in Sect. 4. Questions of practicality may have discouraged more widespread adoption. For example, while it is clear that audit records must be described by some grammar,[1] that observation does not alone guarantee a *tractably parsed* grammar. [4] Section 5.2 argues for more optimism, and this work demonstrates practicality and effectiveness on a widely-available, commercial audit format. At the same time, the complete grammar can be studied for useful insights such as which aspects of BSM logs are beyond the expressive power of, e.g. regular expressions.

– The requirement to draw justifiable conclusions, mentioned in Sect. 1, reveals that not only syntax but semantics must be captured. Semantic content is an, or possibly the, important thing to get right. Providing a grammar does not lay the issue to rest, but does help in two ways. First, Sect. 4 argues that the grammatical structure of the input cannot be ignored without sacrificing semantic information. Second, in a more cognitive than technical vein, without a concrete representation of the details to be resolved, promising discussions about audit content sometimes end up, to recycle Pauli, "not even wrong."

3 Audience

This paper assumes a familiarity with parsing concepts and some parser generating tool, such as might be acquired in an undergraduate compilers course. Examples will be in the notation of the ANTLR parser generator, similar enough to other tools' notations that the reader need not know ANTLR per se to follow the arguments, but may refer to [11] to pursue niceties that are tangential.

Examples of BSM event record formats will be presented and discussed. For the most part, these are records of UNIX system calls and the discussion may assume a familiarity with the operations and subtleties of the programming interface for UNIX or a similar operating system, and some of the ways those operations can be abused, such as might be expected in the intrusion detection

---

[1] They are produced by a Turing-equivalent machine.

community. Terms such as 'rules' and 'transition diagrams' familiar from rule-based (e.g. [10]) and state-based (e.g. [5]) intrusion detection efforts will be used freely. Sample BSM records, being binary rather than text, would add little to the perspicuity of the grammar examples they match, and such low level details play no role in the discussions. No specific familiarity with BSM will be required to follow the arguments, though the reader whose curiosity is piqued may refer to [8].

4   Other Approaches

It is not necessary to have a grammar to extract some useful information from an input stream. Various intrusion detection systems support BSM audit logs, and we obtained access to code or internals documentation to see how three of them do it.[2] ASAX[10], IDIOT[2], and USTAT[5] all skim information from BSM logs without concern for grammatical structure. This section will compare their approaches and examine some consequences. The critique is not intended to disparage these projects, which set out to shed light on other aspects of the intrusion detection problem and did so with acknowledged success. The consequences discussion will include some issues that apply to a grammar-based approach as well, and so should be considered in any audit project.

4.1   Canonical Form

All three systems have some notion of a canonical form into which the native BSM log is transformed as a preprocessing step. Their canonical forms are rather different in intent and reality from CISL. Where CISL sets out to allow heterogeneous applications across platforms to share event and analysis data and agree on their interpretation, the canonical forms of ASAX, IDIOT, and USTAT serve mostly to simplify porting of the tools themselves.

4.2   How the Log Is Processed

ASAX. In ASAX, most of the work of converting BSM to the "normalized audit data format" (NADF) is done in `conv_bsm.c`. Examination reveals a table, each row of which contains a BSM token ID, a base NADF field ID, and a pointer. There is a row for every BSM token type expected to occur; for tokens that can appear multiply in one event record (`arg`, for example), several rows are allocated. Before each BSM record is processed, the pointer is nulled in each row. Then, for each token in the record, if a row can be found that contains the token's ID and a null pointer, the first such row is updated to point to the token.

After the whole record has been read, the rows for token types that did not appear in the record still have null pointers, while rows for token types that

---

[2] We suspect the way these tools process the BSM input is typical, but there are certainly other tools that support BSM for which we did not obtain source code or sufficiently low-level documentation to make a determination.

appeared point to the corresponding tokens. Finally, in the order of appearance in the table, tokens are copied field-by-field to the NADF record. The final NADF record contains verbatim copies of the fields from the BSM record, but with padding to support aligned access, and reordered to match the order of token IDs in the table.

IDIOT. IDIOT's canonical form is slightly more abstracted from the underlying audit format than is NADF. IDIOT defines a set of attribute names and picks out field values of interest from BSM tokens as they are encountered, binding them to the corresponding IDIOT attributes. The mapping is done by a script that reads the line-oriented output of `praudit`, a Sun tool that renders the BSM data in readable text, one BSM token per line.

USTAT. USTAT also defines its own abstract event record, whose attributes (with a few exceptions) are bound to fields of BSM tokens as shown in Fig. 4.5 of [5], provided those tokens appear in the incoming event record.

4.3   Consequences

Invalid Input Detected Late or Not at All. A strategy of simply copying data from tokens as they appear, best seen in the ASAX source, will not detect ungrammatical input, such as an event header followed by an impossible sequence of tokens for that event. An invalid stream of native data can be silently transformed to an invalid stream in canonical form, leaving the problem to be detected in a later processing step, if at all.

Semantic Interpretation Left to Later Stages. The canonicalizers used by ASAX, IDIOT, and USTAT defer, to varying degrees, details of the native audit format to be handled by the later, ostensibly less platform-specific, stages of analysis. The situation is clearest in ASAX, whose canonical form is nothing more than the native form with fields reordered and padded for aligned access. The specific significance of information within the fields is left to be spelled out in RUSSEL, the language of ASAX rules. Dealing with native format issues in rules complicates porting those rules, even to other flavors of UNIX whose audit formats differ even though the system calls and their semantics are the same. Format idiosyncrasies of a given field or event must also be handled in each rule that involves the field or event, and a rule language may not have convenient facilities for functions or subroutines.[3]

IDIOT and USTAT take on more of the interpretation problem at the time of canonicalization, at least picking out certain fields of interest and mapping them into a set of attributes intended to be less platform specific. However, the

---

[3] It is possible in ASAX to isolate some format-specific processing in functions written in a traditional programming language, linked to ASAX, and invoked in RUSSEL rules.

combination of such selective inclusion of fields with disregard for grammatical structure can lead to loss of semantic content, as described next.

Lost Syntactic Cues to Meaning. Consider the BSM grammar rules in Fig. 1. To determine whether an `ioctl` system call was applied to a socket, an other non-file, a file descriptor with no cached name, or an ordinary good file descriptor requires careful consideration of what tokens appeared in the record. If a parser is used, subsequent analysis logic has only to look at the parse tree to determine which rule matched the input. Absent a parser, some analysis effort equivalent to deciding which rule would have matched is deferred to later processing stages. Again, in ASAX, the work can be done by RUSSEL rules that are tightly bound to the details of the native format, explicitly testing for the presence of certain fields or for distinctive field values.

```
IoctlGoodFileDescr
    : path (attr)? arg[2,"cmd"] arg[3,"arg"] ( arg[2,"strioctl:vnode"] )?
    ;
IoctlSocket
    : (socket)? arg[2,"cmd"] arg[3,"arg"]
    ;
IoctlNonFile
    : arg[1,"fd"] arg[2,"cmd"] arg[3,"arg"]
    ;
IoctlNoName
    : arg[1,"no path: fd"] ( attr )? arg[2,"cmd"] arg[3,"arg"]
      ( arg[2,"strioctl:vnode"] )* // have seen 0, 1, or 2 of these
    ;
```

Fig. 1. ANTLR grammar rules for a portion of a system call record. The parser's decision which rule to apply distills semantic content from a series of specific tests that would otherwise be left to later processing stages

In IDIOT or USTAT the situation is complicated by the mapping of native fields into canonical attributes. In Fig. 1, if the optional attribute and **vnode** arguments are absent, determining which of the last two rules to apply hinges on the text string of the first **arg** token. Because the text in an **arg** token is a constant string serving only as a syntactic cue, it is not copied to the canonical form used by IDIOT or USTAT. As a result, the semantic content conveyed in a parse of the native format cannot be recovered at all in IDIOT or USTAT, an example of the semantic sacrifice risked when grammatical structure is ignored.

Nonconservative Transformations. The problem of dangerous transformations must be considered in any audit project, grammar-based or not. However, the systems described in this section offer examples to illustrate this important issue.

IDIOT relies on Sun's `praudit` tool to preprocess the binary log format into a text representation. The transformations made by `praudit` go beyond representing the binary log. User and group IDs, for example, are presented as user and group names, and the transformation reflects the name-to-ID mapping in effect at the time `praudit` runs, not at the time of the audited event. That transformation can be disabled by a `praudit` option, but others cannot. IP addresses, for example, are displayed as domain names by `praudit`, a transformation that reflects the state of the Domain Name System[9] at the time the tool is run, not when the event was logged.[4]

The USTAT document in Sect. 4.1.2.6[5] describes another nonconservative transformation. BSM records often present path names in a non-canonical form such as `/etc/../usr/share`. USTAT's preprocessor, accordingly, includes a "filename correcting routine," the wisdom of which can be questioned on two grounds.[5] First, such a transformation cannot be said to conserve correctness without knowing the state of the affected file systems, including symbolic links and any cycles in the directory graph reflecting accidental or deliberate file system corruption at the time the event was logged. Second, the exact form of the path name appearing in the log reflects the kernel's construction of the path from a process root and working directory and any symbolic links encountered; it conveys part of how the event came to pass, and may have forensic value.

Audit records are often consulted in cases where the integrity of the system that produced those records is in doubt. It seems prudent, in transformations applied to those records after the fact, to avoid unnecessary assumptions about the state of the system that produced them. The same concern need not apply to transformations reliant on mappings that are widely known and independent of any single computer system. Those transformations, such as IP protocol numbers to the names of those protocols, may arguably be used wherever they would be useful.

4.4 Discussion

The intrusion detection systems just described all translate native BSM audit logs into some canonical form without looking at grammatical structure. They do so, however, by defining canonical forms that offer little semantic support to later analysis stages. The proposal by Bishop[1] is another example of such a canonical form. Where such a form is used, the authors of rules or transition diagrams must still account for what is meant *in the original native form* when, for example, a certain field is absent from a record. The rules, therefore, become platform specific.[6]

---

[4] A more fundamental, equally fatal, but less enlightening nonconservative transformation applied by praudit is the presentation of the log data in a delimited form with no escaped representation for occurrences of the delimiter in the data. This feature alone rules out any role for praudit in a reliable consumer of BSM logs.

[5] This transformation is also done by `praudit`.

[6] While this paper was in preparation, a portion of the EMERALD project[6], eXpert-BSM became available for review. Unfortunately, the distribution terms prohibit

Such lazy translation is not even an option if the target representation, like CISL, intends to convey the semantic nuances revealed by a careful parse of the original. A translator that overlooks or mistranslates those nuances will produce a false translation that may lead later analysis into error.

Finally, canonical or intermediate representations of audit data should be scrutinized for assumptions that would require nonconservative transformations during conversion. An example would be a canonical form that identifies machines by domain names, if IP numbers are used in the native form.

5   Appropriateness of a Grammar Approach

At least two objections may be considered to a grammar representation of a logging format.

5.1   Efficiency

Logs are voluminous and efficiency in their processing is important. Developers observing that constraint may lean toward ad hoc and handcrafted techniques and away from strict attention to grammatical structure. Section 4, however, showed that the price of parsing, if saved up front, must be paid later if the full information content is to be extracted from the input. In fact the price is paid with interest, as a single test and decision not made on the initial parse of the data may have to be duplicated in many rules that apply to the same records. It was not in the scope of this work to build otherwise-comparable intrusion detection systems and obtain a performance comparison, but these observations, coupled with the importance of reliability and maintainability, suggest that grammar techniques in audit processing should not be dismissed out of hand on efficiency grounds.

5.2   Applicability

The foregoing discussion breaks down unless it is reasonable to expect that audit logs can be described by grammars in the classes that enjoy efficient parsing algorithms.

A distinction must first be made, just as in the specification of programming languages. A grammar like that given in the Java specification[3] does not purport to describe the language "all semantically reasonable Java programs"; it describes the simpler language, "syntactically valid Java programs." The grammar, therefore, is a specification with a deliberately limited scope. Aspects of the language excluded from its scope fall into two broad categories:

---

reverse-engineering to discern just how the log is processed, but [7] presents some sample detection rules for this newer tool and here again, rules that describe attacks applicable to UNIX systems generally must be written to the specifics of the BSM format.

Unspecified Aspects. Some aspects of a language are not addressed by any part of the specification. For example, the Java grammar imposes no structure on a *methodBody* or other *block*, other than that it be some sequence of zero or more *blockStatements*. The statements themselves, and their subproductions, are explicitly specified, but it is considered beyond the scope of a language specification to characterize how those statements might be placed in meaningful blocks by programmers.

Aspects Specified Extragrammatically. Some details of the language are explicitly specified elsewhere. For example, Java's official grammar is Chapter 19 of the Java specification. Other chapters, in prose or grammar-like notation, contain requirements not embodied in the grammar itself, such as those for casts and parenthesized expressions, or field and method modifiers. Therefore, the grammar describes a superset of conforming programs, which must be culled after parsing by enforcing the extragrammatical requirements.

For Java, two factors contributed to the exclusion of these details from the grammar itself: the choice to provide a grammar no more complex than can be parsed left to right without backtracking and with only one token of lookahead, and the choice to adopt a C-like syntax, which includes constructs that cannot be parsed that way.

Minimizing Extragrammatical Requirements. The need for the second kind of scope restriction can be reduced by relaxing restrictions on the grammar to be provided. For example, ANTLR supports $LL(k)$ grammars for configurable k with predicates (a form of localized backtracking)[12], and comes with a $k = 2$ Java grammar that explicitly embodies requirements for casts, etc., that had to be left out of the official LALR(1) Java grammar.

If not constrained to perpetuate difficult features of an existing language, a designer can so craft a new language that a simple, efficiently parsed class of grammar is adequate to specify it, and few or none of its syntactic features need to be specified extragrammatically. The designer of a new audit logging format is in such a position.

Application to Audit Logs. The specification for an audit log, like that for a programming language, may be deliberately restricted in scope. While each individual event, and its subproductions, should be explicitly specified, the sequences in which events may appear in actual use of the system depend on user and program behavior, and their easy characterization *a priori* is unlikely. As with a block of "zero or more statements," the simple "zero or more events of any type" is a permissive superset of the expected event sequences and presents no difficulty in parsing.

The individual event records are produced by code that must execute when, and only when, the corresponding events take place. Necessary restrictions on the logging code (e.g. termination guarantees) limit its complexity and, with it, the complexity of the grammar required to describe the record, even if the format was not designed with a specific grammar class in mind. The commercial log format described in the next section was successfully described in ANTLR notation with 1-token lookahead for most choices. The predicates required at other choice points all amount to constant-depth additional local lookahead.

6   Formalizing the BSM Audit Format

This work began when a robust consumer for Sun's Basic Security Module (BSM) audit log format[8] was needed for another project. The existing documentation on the format was transcribed into a grammar notation. Before a parser could be generated to test the grammar against actual logs, it was necessary to modify the grammar to resolve all ambiguities detected by the parser generator. The grammar was then iteratively refined by generating a parser, running it on actual logs, and observing parse errors. A parse error could represent an error in the BSM documentation, or a fault in the Solaris log production code. It could be resolved for the next iteration by modifying either the grammar or the Solaris code. For this project, modifying the code was not an option, so all parse errors were resolved by modifying the grammar, leading ultimately to a grammar that describes closely the log that Solaris actually produces, even in instances that seem unintended.

The resulting grammar contains 327 named, nonterminal rules. Examination shows that the rules are associated in a straightforward manner with the 267 kernel and user event types and 41 token types found in the Solaris 2.6 system files, and follow the Sun documentation with only necessary departures. That is, the number of rules does not reflect an especially obfuscated grammar but, rather, an indication of the intrinsic complexity of the audit log alluded to in Sect. 1. By comparison, the example grammar supplied with ANTLR for the Java 1.1 programming language includes 64 such rules.

The remainder of this section will discuss selected examples of the flaws or ambiguities in BSM documentation or implementation that were detected by this methodology. The entire grammar, with annotations describing discrepancies, can be downloaded from http://www.cerias.purdue.edu/software/ with the other files needed to compile and run a working BSM parser. To print the grammar as an appendix would be impractical because of its size, and would sacrifice the hyperlinks that connect the grammar rules to the corresponding sections of Sun's BSM documentation.

6.1   Difficulties Detected by Static Analysis in Parser Generator

Non-LL(1) Constructs. Many of the ambiguities that were automatically detected simply reflected features of the BSM log format that cannot be recognized by an LL parser with one lookahead token; they were resolved by adding explicit lookahead at strategic places in the grammar. They do not reflect inherent ambiguity in the log format, but nevertheless are possible pitfalls for developers who attempt to develop a straightforward BSM consumer tool from the documentation without a parser generator's rigorous analysis.

Constructs Resolvable with Semantic Information. Compiling a naïve version of our BSM grammar will result in 16 warnings of ambiguity apparently inherent in the log syntax, any one of which would suffice to dash the hope of reliably processing BSM logs, whether by a conventional parser or by any other means. Although it is impossible in these cases to determine the correct grammar rule to apply from the sequence of BSM token types alone, they can be resolved by looking explicitly into the *values* carried by certain of those tokens, an operation known in ANTLR terms as a "semantic predicate." Specifically, a BSM 'arg' token contains a `data` field whose value is necessary and sufficient to resolve these 16 cases. The `data` values, which are constant character strings, are shown in the printed documentation, albeit without an explanation that they are essential at parse time to properly interpret the log. Both IDIOT and USTAT appear to discard these values in the conversion to canonical form, perhaps on the assumption that a token field whose value is constant does not convey essential information.

True Ambiguity. It may not be surprising, given the complexity of what BSM must log and the lack of formal analysis in its original design, that a few ambiguities remain. Instead of reflecting limitations of a particular parsing technique they are, if the BSM documentation is correct, inherent in the log format. Figure 2 is an example.

The description with two optional 'text' tokens followed by two mandatory ones leads to a formal ambiguity if an event record has exactly three text tokens following the header. It is clear in that case that one of the two optional text tokens is present, but the parser cannot determine whether it is the driver major number or the driver name. The ambiguity cannot be resolved, even with a semantic predicate, unless there is a way to tell decisively by looking at the text string whether it is a driver major number or a driver name. Perhaps the number is always a text string of only digits and the name must begin with a non-digit, but this should be stated in the BSM documentation if programs are expected to depend on it. Or, it may be that the documentation is mistaken in showing the number and name as being independently optional: perhaps it should be "[text text] text text" with the first two both there or both absent. If that is the case, the documentation should be corrected.

Without access to the intent of the BSM developers, the grammar was modified to embody the last interpretation, which is reasonable and conservative under the circumstances. It will work if the first two 'text' tokens are both present and if they are both absent. If an instance is encountered of the ambiguous case with one of the two present, a parse exception will be signaled, avoiding an undetected misinterpretation.

Event Name	Event ID	Event Class	Mask
AUE_MODADDMAJ	246	ad	0x00000800

Format:

```
header-token
[text-token]        driver major number)
[text-token]        (driver name)
text-token          (root dir.|"no rootdir")
text-token          (driver major number|"no drvname")
argument-token        (5, "", number of aliases)
(0..n)[text-token]      (aliases)
subject-token
return-token
```

Fig. 2. Description of a record from [8]

6.2 Difficulties Detected in Testing

After the statically-detectable problems were resolved, the grammar was repeatedly used to generate a parser. The parser was applied to a collection of 2.2 megabytes of BSM audit data obtained in-house and from other institutions, from SunOS and Solaris systems as recent as Solaris 2.6. Two general classes of discrepancy were detected between the BSM documents and the actual logs.

Undocumented Records. Some records were encountered in the sample logs that simply do not appear in the documentation. Corresponding rules were added to the grammar to allow the logs to be parsed. Fig. 3 is an example.

```
AUE_CONNECT
        : %AUE_CONNECT socket socket subj ret
        ;
```

Fig. 3. ANTLR grammar rule for an event record that appears in our sample logs but is not documented

Misdocumented or Misimplemented Records. Some records were encountered for event types that were documented, but parse errors were detected because the records did not conform to the published format. Fig. 4 is an example. So that the logs could be parsed, the affected grammar rules were changed from direct transcriptions of the documentation to reflect the records actually encountered.

Event Name	Program	Event ID	Event Class	Mask
AUE_su	/usr/bin/su	6159	lo	0x00001000

Format:
 	
`header-token`
 	
`text-token`   `(error message)`
 	
`subject-token`
 	
`return-token`				

Fig. 4. Description of a record from [8]. In actual audit logs examined in this work, the text and subject tokens appear in the reverse order

6.3   Difficulties Not Automatically Detected

Figure 5 illustrates a point where the published BSM documentation is incomplete, and hence the interpretation of a log record is not completely determined, but the formal method described in this work could not detect the problem. The problem was recognized, however, during the process of transcribing the documentation into a grammar, and the discipline of that process may have contributed to that recognition.

Two tokens are shown as optional: the file attributes for the source file, and the rename destination path. The rule is quite readily parsable, but has two suspicious features. First, the optional tokens are shown as *independently* optional, implying four possible record variants for the rename event. In actual logs, only two—both tokens present, both absent—have been observed. The documentation may be incorrect, but the methodology will not detect the problem. The rule as stated presents no parsing difficulty that would be detected in static analysis, and, if incorrect, it matches a superset of the records that can be encountered, so no parse error will be produced. Nevertheless, it should spur any conscientious developer of a log consumer to wonder exactly what should be inferred about the state of the audited system when each of the—as written—four variant forms is encountered.

The second suspicious feature is that the destination path is shown as optional at all. It is absent in our samples only when the file attributes are absent also, which seems to happen only when the source file is not found. The feature rename(2)

Event Name	Event ID	Event Class	Mask
AUE_RENAME	42	fc,fd	0x00000030

Format:

```
header-token
path-token        (from name)
[attr-token]         (from name)
[path-token]      (to name)
subject-token
return-token
```

Fig. 5. Description of a record from [8]. Why is the "to name" optional?

may be an artifact of some implementation detail within the rename system call. It might be worth changing, however. An intrusion detection system might recognize a certain intrusion attempt from a rename with a specific destination. Detection could be delayed if the intruder mistypes the source file name the first time, causing the recognizable destination path to be omitted from the record.

7   Methodological Recommendations

The ideal time to apply the ideas of this work would be during the design of the audit log format for a new system. A new log format can be designed to fall in a language class that is easily parsed with modest lookahead, and specification ambiguities detected by static analysis can be eliminated before implementation. Specification-driven tools can speed implementation and testing, and the annotated grammar can be provided as documentation.

The ideas can still be applied, however, when an existing log format is reviewed for possible improvement, and even in the simple development of tools to consume an existing format. In this less ideal setting, too late for the other formal-method benefits cited above, the technique has valuable potential for improved understanding of the log nuances and more thorough validation and verification of the software. It was applied in that way to BSM in this work, suggesting a methodology for similar projects. An existing audit format can be approached by iterating these four steps:

1. Prepare a grammar by transcription from whatever documents are available. As ambiguities are detected by the parser-generator's analysis, return to the documents, sample logs, experimentation, or system source code (if available)

to determine if any information present in the log can be used in explicit predicates to resolve the ambiguities. Also make note of constructs whose semantic significance is unclear to the human reviewer, even if not formally ambiguous.

2. When the grammar can be successfully compiled, apply the parser to a good sample of audit data and note any parsing diagnostics. Determine whether these represent flaws in the log documentation, the logging implementation, the grammar, or combinations of these. If this process is undertaken by a vendor, whatever needs to be corrected can be. Otherwise, options may be limited to suggesting fixes or documenting the issue and complicating the grammar.

3. Given a grammar that successfully describes the logs, scrutinize it for the semantic nuances of the rules. Choice points in the grammar always have semantic significance: because log records are produced by an automaton, the production of one of several forms of a record depends on and conveys information about the state of the system. An event record whose grammar rule shows three optional fields, for example, can make eight distinguishable statements about a particular event and the system state in which it occurred, beyond what is conveyed by field values. If the eight semantic nuances are not clear, return to documents, experiments, or source code until a satisfactory account of them can be made, or until the grammar rule can be tightened to imply fewer cases.

4. Update grammar, documentation, or code as necessary and possible, and repeat.

8   Future Work

– BSM and other auditing systems can have configuration options that control the inclusion or omission of certain optional fields in some records. Our grammar was tested on audit logs produced on systems with similar settings for those options. A single grammar could rapidly grow unwieldy if extended to accept the logs produced under all settings of the configuration options. *Environment grammars*[13] address the problem of parsing such classes of similar languages as efficiently as context-free languages, and could offer a cleaner solution.

As it happens, the difference between an environment-grammar parser and an ANTLR parser resides entirely in the analysis algorithms used during parser generation. The structures and features required at run time by a parser specified by an environment grammar are exactly those of a parser generated by ANTLR.

– The modest cost of careful parsing might be further discounted in a self-contained application where the exact information needed from the log is known in advance. For example, a self-contained intrusion detection system might compile its rule base together with the full log grammar, producing a parser that skims lazily where possible.

References

[1] Matt Bishop. A standard audit trail format. In *Proceedings of the 1995 National Information Systems Security Conference*, pages 136–145, Baltimore, Maryland, October 1995. 7

[2] Mark Crosbie, Bryn Dole, Todd Ellis, Ivan Krsul, and Eugene Spafford. IDIOT users guide. Technical Report TR-96-050, Purdue University, September 1996. 4

[3] J. Gosling, B. Joy, and G. Steele. *The Java Language Specification*. Addison-Wesley, 1996. 2, 8

[4] John E. Hopcroft and Jeffrey D. Ullman. *Introduction to Automata Theory, Languages, and Computation*. Addison-Wesley, 1979. 3

[5] Koral Ilgun. *USTAT: A Real-Time Intrusion Detection System for UNIX*. MS thesis, University of California, Santa Barbara, November 1992. 4, 5, 7

[6] SRI International. EMERALD website. http://www.sdl.sri.com/emerald/, April 2000. 7

[7] Ulf Lindqvist and Phillip A. Porras. Detecting computer and network misuse through the production-based expert system toolset (P-BEST). In *Proceedings of the 1999 IEEE Symposium on Security and Privacy*, Oakland, California, October 1999. 8

[8] Sun Microsystems. *SunSHIELD Basic Security Module Guide*. Sun Microsystems, 901 San Antonio Road, Palo Alto, California, Solaris 2.6 edition, 1997. Part Number 802-5757-10. 2, 4, 10, 12, 13, 14

[9] P. Mockapetris. Domain names – concepts and facilities. STD 13, ISI, November 1987. 7

[10] Abdelaziz Mounji. *Languages and Tools for Rule-Based Distributed Intrusion Detection*. D.Sc. thesis, Universitaires Notre-Dame de la Paix Namur (Belgium), September 1997. 4

[11] Terence Parr. ANTLR website. http://www.antlr.org/, February 2000. 2, 3

[12] Terence John Parr. *Obtaining Practical Variants of $LL(k)$ and $LR(k)$ for $k > 1$ by Splitting the Atomic k-tuple*. PhD thesis, Purdue University, August 1993. 9

[13] Manfred Ruschitzka. Two-level grammars for data conversions. *Future Generation Computer Systems*, pages 373–380, 1990. 15

[14] Brian Tung. Common intrusion detection framework. http://www.gidos.org/, November 1999. 2

A Pattern Matching Based Filter for Audit Reduction and Fast Detection of Potential Intrusions

Josué Kuri[1]*, Gonzalo Navarro[2], Ludovic Mé[3], and Laurent Heye[3]

[1] ENST, Department of Computer Science and Networks
Paris, France
kuri@enst.fr
[2] University of Chile, Department of Computer Science
Santiago, Chile
gnavarro@dcc.uchile.cl
[3] Supélec, Campus de Rennes, France,
Ludovic.Me@supelec.fr
Laurent.Heye@supelec.fr

Abstract. We present a pattern matching approach to the problem of misuse detection in a computer system, which is formalized as the problem of multiple approximate pattern matching. This permits very fast searching of *potential* attacks. We study the probability of matching of the model and its relation to the filtering efficiency of potential attacks within large audit trails. Experimental results show that in a worst case, up to 85 % of an audit trail may be filtered out when searching a set of attacks without probability of false negatives. Moreover, by filtering 98 % of the audit trail, up to 50 % of the attacks may be detected.

1 Introduction

Research in intrusion detection has emerged in recent years as a major subject in the computer security field because of the difficulty of ensuring that information systems are free from security flaws. Computer systems suffer from security vulnerabilities regardless of their purpose, manufacturer or origin. It is both technically hard and economically costly to ensure that systems are not susceptible to attacks.

Two approaches have been proposed to address the problem: *anomaly detection* (see for example [1,2]) and *misuse detection* (see for example [3]). The former suggests that user's activity in the system can be characterized so that a profile of "normal utilization" of the system is established and excursions from this profile are flagged as potential intrusions, or attacks in a more general sense. The latter assumes that attacks are well-known sequences of actions, called *scenarios* or *attack signatures*, and that the activity of the system (in the form of

---

* Partially supported by CONACyT grant #122688.

H. Debar, L. Mé, and F. Wu (Eds.): RAID 2000, LNCS 1907, pp. 17–27, 2000.

logs, network traffic, etc.) may be audited in order to determine the presence of such scenarios in the system.

Anomaly detection leads to some difficulties: a flow of alarms is generated in the case of a noticeable systems environment modification and a user can slowly change his behavior in order to cheat the IDS. On the other hand, misuse detection becomes an increasingly demanding task in terms of semantics and processing, as more sophisticated attacks are discovered every day (which implies an increasing number of sophisticated scenarios to search for in audit trails). These challenges have lead to a research trend aimed to a simplified representation of the problem in order to improve performance and efficiency of detection. In the short term, effective intrusion detection systems will incorporate a number of techniques rather than a "one-strategy-fits-all" approach. The greater the variety of available tools is, the better the IDS is.

In this spirit, we introduce an original intrusion detection model inspired by the misuse detection approach. Its main goal is to provide an intrusion detection system for *fast* detection of *potential* attacks rather that accurate (i.e., exhaustive) detection of actual attacks. The results of such a detection (i.e., filtered audit trails, in which attacks may be present) would be used in turn as input for a more accurate detection algorithm. This idea was already at the root of the G^{A}sSA$_T$A IDS, which use a genetic algorithm with this aim in view [4].

We formalize a concrete instance of the misuse detection problem as a pattern matching problem which permits very fast searching of potential attacks. We then study the statistics of this model and their relation to filtering efficiency of potential attacks in the resulting system.

Section 2 explains our proposed intrusion detection model and the constraints of the problem. Section 3 gives analytical and experimental results on the probability of matching. Section 4 presents our testing system and experimental results. Finally, conclusions and future works are presented.

2   Intrusion Detection as a Pattern Matching Problem

In general terms, the misuse detection problem is to detect the existence of *a priori* known series of events within the traces of activity of a system to protect.

Traces widely differ in their origin, form and content, depending on the type of potential attacks that they attempt to cover. For example, traces in the form of network traffic collected by a firewall or a sniffer may be used to detect wellknown attacks to implementations of a TCP/IP protocol stack. Another example are the logs of commands typed by users of a multi-user computer. In both cases, traces may be collected at a single place (e.g., an ethernet segment, a host computer) or at multiple locations simultaneously. We consider the detection of attacks using logs (audit trails) of commands typed by users of a distributed computer system. In this context, attacks appear to be typically short sequences of no more than 8 commands.

We propose to model the misuse detection problem as a pattern matching problem in the following way: auditable commands in the system can be seen

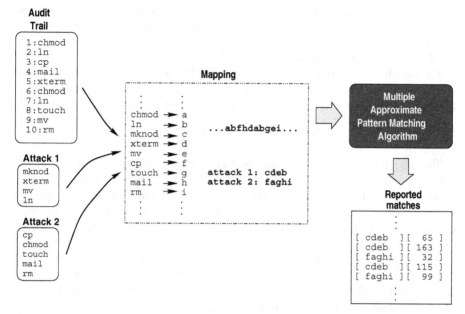

Fig. 1. Attack signature searching as a multiple approximate pattern matching problem

as letters of an alphabet Σ and the audit trail as a large *string* of letters in Σ (i.e., the text). The sequences of events representing attacks to be detected are then *substrings* (i.e., patterns) to be located in the main *string*. Since attackers may introduce spurious commands among those that represent an actual attack in order to disperse their evidence, a limited number of spurious letters must be allowed when searching the pattern. We are interested in simultaneously searching a *set* of patterns. Thus, the misuse detection problem can be regarded as a particular case of the *multiple approximate pattern matching problem*, where *insertion* in the pattern is the only allowed edit operation. Figure 1 illustrates our proposed model to map the misuse detection problem as a multiple approximate pattern matching problem. The set of commands in the audit trail and attack signatures is translated into letters of Σ. The resulting string and patterns are passed to a multiple approximate pattern matching algorithm which in turn searches for the occurrences of substrings in the main string. Matches represent potential attacks in the audit trail.

We formalize the above problem as follows: Our text, $T_{1..n}$, is a sequence of n characters from an alphabet Σ of size σ. Our patterns, $P^1 \ldots P^r$, are (short) sequences of characters from Σ. Let us consider such a pattern $P_{1..m}$ of length m. We want to report all the text positions that match P, where at most k insertions between characters of P are allowed in its occurrence in T. We call $\alpha = k/m$ the "error level".

Our problem can be modeled using the concept of *insertion distance*. The insertion distance from a to b, denoted $id(a, b)$, is the number of insertions necessary to convert a into b. We say that $id(a, b) = \infty$ if this is not possible. Clearly, $id(a, b) = |b| - |a|$ if a is a subsequence of b, and ∞ otherwise.

We search for the pattern P in a text T allowing insertions. At each text position $j \in 1..n$ we are interested in the minimum number of insertions needed to convert P into some suffix of $T_{1..j}$. This is defined as

$$lid(P, T_{1..j}) = \min_{j' \in 1..j} id(P, T_{j'..j}) .$$

The search problem can therefore be formalized as follows: given $P^1 \ldots P^r$, T and k, report all text positions j such that $lid(P^i, T_{1..j}) \leq k$ for some $i \in 1 \ldots r$.

In [5], two different multipattern search algorithms specifically tailored for this pattern matching problem are presented. They are based on "bit-parallelism", a technique to represent the state of the search using the bits of a computer word of w bits (typically $w = 32$ or 64). The basic algorithm takes $O(nm \log(k)/w)$ time to scan the text for one pattern. A first multipattern search algorithm is $O(nr(1 + \alpha)^{1+\alpha}/(\sigma \alpha^{\alpha}))$, which is better than r applications of the basic algorithm whenever $\alpha < (\sigma/e) - 1$. A second multipattern search algorithm takes $O(nr \log(m + k)/w)$ time and is useful for $\alpha < (\sigma/m) - 1$.

It is shown in [5] that the algorithms can achieve impressive scanning speeds in practice. For example, they show the case of 4-letters patterns searched allowing 4 insertions, which is a case of interest in intrusion detection applications. On a Sun Enterprise 450 server, these algorithms allow searching for 100 patterns at a rate of 4 megabytes per second.

The focus of this paper lies in the probabilistic model for the occurrences of patterns in text when insertions are allowed, and its relation to the problem of false detection of nonexistent attacks (i.e., "false positives") and misdetection of existing attacks (i.e., "false negatives"). By characterizing this relation, the optimal filtering efficiency of the model may be determined.

3   Probability of Matching

We start by giving an upper bound on the matching probability of a random pattern of length m at a random text position, with up to k insertions. Consider a random text position j. The pattern P appears with k insertions at a text position ending at j if and only if the text window $T_{j-m-k+1..j}$ contains the m pattern letters in order. The window positions that match the pattern letters can be chosen in $\binom{m+k}{m}$ ways. Those letters are fixed but the other k can take any value. Therefore the probability that the text window matches the pattern with k insertions is at most

$$\binom{m+k}{m} \frac{\sigma^k}{\sigma^{m+k}} = \binom{m+k}{m} \frac{1}{\sigma^m} \tag{1}$$

where we are overestimating because not all the selections of window positions give different windows. For instance the pattern `"abcd"` matches in text window "abccd" with $k = 1$ in two ways, but only one text window should be counted. In particular, our overestimation includes the case of $k' < k$ insertions, which is obtained by selecting the first $k - k'$ characters of the text window as insertions and distributing the k' remaining insertions in the remaining text window of length $m + k'$.

An asymptotic simplification (for large m and $\alpha = k/m$ considered constant) of the cost can be obtained using Stirling's approximation to the factorial $m! = (m/e)^m \sqrt{2\pi m}(1 + O(1/m))$:

$$\left(\frac{(1 + \alpha)^{1+\alpha}}{\sigma \alpha^\alpha} \right)^m \tag{2}$$

which, as α moves from zero, grows from $1/\sigma^m$ to 1. To determine where the probability reaches 1, we require that $\sigma \alpha^\alpha \leq (1 + \alpha)^{1+\alpha}$, i.e., $\sigma \leq (1 + \alpha)(1 + 1/\alpha)^\alpha$. A sufficient condition can be obtained by noticing that $1 \leq (1+1/\alpha)^\alpha \leq e$, and therefore $\alpha \geq (\sigma/e) - 1$ suffices.

This means that a model based on insertions can be useful only if we keep k reasonably low, i.e., $k < m((\sigma/e) - 1)$. However, this is a pessimistic analytical model that needs experimental verification.

We test experimentally the probability that a random pattern matches at a random text position. We generated a random text and 100 random patterns for each experimental value shown. Figure 2 (left) shows the probability of matching in a text of 3 Mb for a pattern with $m = 300$, where pattern and text were randomly generated over an alphabet of size $\sigma = 68$. The reason to choose such a long pattern is given shortly.

As can be seen, there is a k value from where the matching probability starts to grow abruptly, moving from almost 0 to almost 1 in a short range of values. This phenomenon is sharp enough to make this k value the most important parameter governing the behavior of the algorithm. We call k^* this point, and $\alpha^* = k^*/m$ the corresponding error level.

On the right part of figure 2 we have shown this limiting α^* value for different pattern lengths, showing that α^* tends to a constant for large m, despite that it is smaller for short patterns. The fact that α^* tends to a constant limit when m grows motivated us to use $m = 300$ to show the process at a stable point. On the other hand, it must be noted that the limit is much lower for short patterns than its asymptotic value, and therefore the exact combinatorial formula of Eq. (1) should be preferred, leaving Eq. (2) just as a conceptual tool to understand how the process behaves in general.

Finally, we show in figure 3 how the alphabet size σ affects the α^* value. As can be seen, the curve looks as a straight line, where least squares estimation yields $\alpha^* = (\sigma/1.0856) - 0.8878$. Again, this corresponds to long patterns, while the real values for short patterns should be obtained from the exact formula.

All this matches our analytical results in the sense that (a) there is a clear error level α^* where the matching probability goes almost from 0 to 1; (b) this point does not depend on m asymptotically; and (c) it depends on σ linearly as predicted by the analysis ($\alpha^* = (\sigma/e) - 1$) except because the e has been

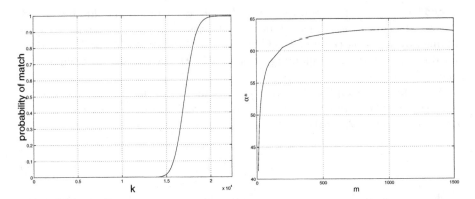

Fig. 2. On the left, matching probability for increasing k values and fixed $m = 300$. On the right, the α^* limit as m grows

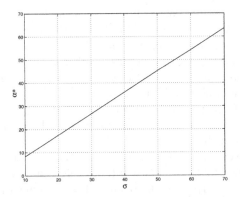

Fig. 3. The α^* limit as σ grows

changed to about 1.09. Interestingly, this is similar to the result obtained for the k differences problem in [6,7] when relating their analytical predictions ($\alpha^* = 1 - e/\sqrt{\sigma}$) with the experiments ($\alpha^* = 1 - 1.09/\sqrt{\sigma}$) and shows a consistent behavior of the pessimistic analytical model used in both cases.

4   Experimental Results

We experimentally studied how the probabilistic model of string matching allowing insertions relates to the problem of false negatives and positives. Our interest is to determine how α^* relates to the ratio between false negatives and positives and the total number of reported attacks and, consequently, to the filtering efficiency of the model.

The experimental input data consists of an audit trail and an attack database. Both of them are very simple. The audit trail was collected using the $G^A_SSA_TA$

IDS in a real environment. The format of events given to G^{A}sSA$_T$A is for the moment an extension of the one proposed in [8]:

```
#S#version=suntrad5.6#system=SOLARIS#deamon=system#ahost=amstel#no=28#
event=AUE_EXECVE#date=2000.3.14@14.29.41#program=/var/audit/ls#
file=/var/audit/ls#euid=root#egid=other#ruid=root#rgid=other#pid=13949#
error=-1#return=KO#E#I#

#S#version=suntrad5.6#system=SOLARIS#deamon=system#ahost=lancelot#no=29#
event=AUE_EXECVE#date=2000.3.14@14.29.41#program=/usr/bin/ls#
file=/usr/bin/ls#arg=ls,-als#euid=root#egid=other#ruid=root#rgid=other#
pid=13949#error=0#return=OK#E#I#
```

The attack database consists of attacks signatures with the following format:

```
>>> Attack_login
rule1
rule1
rule1
>>> Attack_file_creation
rule2
>>> Attack_ps_cmd
rule3
rule7
```

Rules are defined in the following way:

```
rule1 ::= ( (event=AUE_login)||(event=AUE_rlogin) ) && (return=KO) ;
rule2 ::= (event=AUE_CREAT) && ( (file co ls)||(file co cd) ) ;
rule3 ::= (event=AUE_EXECVE) && (program=/usr/bin/ps) ;
rule4 ::= (event=AUE_EXECVE) && (program co crack) ;
rule5 ::= (event=AUE_su);
```

where the co operator stands for "contains".

The audit trail and attack signatures are translated into a pattern matching representation in three steps. First, a different letter is assigned to each rule (e.g., rule1 = 'a'). Attack signatures are then translated into patterns by mapping their rules to the corresponding letters. Finally, the audit trail is scanned and its events are matched against the rules. Events which match more than one rule are assigned the corresponding letters. Events which do not match a rule are assigned arbitrary letters. The final string is constructed by concatenating the sequence of letters corresponding to matches of rules and the arbitrary letters.

We used an audit file of 24,847 events and studied three different series of actions[1]:

---

[1] These are not really attacks, but it makes no difference from the algorithmic point of view.

Table 1. Main parameters for the three search patterns

Attack	m	Occs.	Prob. letter	Nec. k	Max. k	Fract. of text
Chained who	4	4	0.004382	225	500	8.21%
Sensitive commands	10	2	0.007187	580	620	14.50%
Chained whois	4	1	0.001402	1425	1570	5.74%

Chained who: represented as a pattern of four events of a `"who"` command. The probability of the corresponding letter in our audit file is 0.004382 and there are four real attacks of this kind in the audit file.

Sensitive commands: represented as a pattern of ten events of any command in the set { `"last"`, `"ps"`, `"who"`, `"whois"` }. The probability of the corresponding letter in our audit file is 0.007187 and there are two real attacks of this kind in the audit file.

Chained whois: represented as a pattern of four events of a `"whois"` command. The probability of the corresponding letter in our audit file is 0.001402 and there is one real attack of this kind in the audit file.

We have searched the three patterns in our audit file allowing an increasing number of insertions k. Our goal is to determine the effectiveness of the proposed filtering algorithm[2]. That is: how much text is it able to filter out in order to retrieve what fraction of the real attacks that occur in the audit file?

By applying the analytical predictions of Section 3 to our real data, we computed the maximum k value for which the matching probability does not reach 1 (recall that the model is pessimistic). To compute that maximum value, we have used the most precise formula (Eq. (1)) for the matching probability. Given that the text is biased we have replaced $1/\sigma^m$ by p^m, where p is the relative frequency of the letter that forms the pattern (all the attacks are repetitions of a single letter, otherwise we can just multiply the probabilities of the participating letters).

Together with the maximum k recommended by the model we have computed the fraction of the text that the filter selects (for that k) as a candidate for further evaluation. This is simply the $m+k$ characters preceding every match, avoiding to count multiple times the overlapping areas.

Table 1 shows that using the maximum k recommended by the model selects just 6% to 15% of the text to be processed by a more costly algorithm. Moreover, we show in the column of "necessary k" the minimum k value that is necessary to detect all the attacks present in the audit file. This turns out to be below (and

---

[2] The text that our filter is not able to discard has to be processed by a more sophisticated algorithm in order to determine the presence of a real attack. As those algorithms are much slower than our pattern matching based approach, the effectiveness of the filter is crucial.

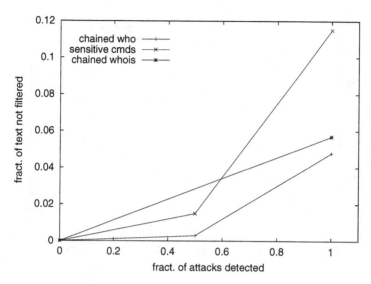

Fig. 4. Fraction of attacks detected versus fraction of text left for further processing

generally close to) the maximum k recommended by the model. Therefore, the model can be used to obtain a good estimator of the k value to use in order to detect all the real attacks. Of course, it is also possible to use specific knowledge of the application to determine the appropriate k.

Regarding the false negatives, we evaluated, for our three particular patterns, the fraction of text filtered as a function of the fraction of attacks detected (see figure 4). As can be seen, the curve is concave, which suggests that considering a very small fraction of the text permits to detect most of the attacks. For example, with a k value that leaves just 2% of the text for further evaluation we get 50% of the attacks (and thus 50% of false negatives). We have here a way to balance the false negatives rate and the speed of detection. Of course, in many cases, no false negative is required. In that situation, the value of k determined by the model is an upper bound of the value to be used for the corresponding pattern.

Regarding the false positives, we studied the evolution of the number of matches as a function of k for the three patterns (se figure 5). Of course, for some patterns, using a too large k value leads to many false positives. Let's note that these false positives may be discarded by the more accurate detection algorithm which may analyse the output of our pattern matching mechanism (recall that we give a part of the trail containing a *potential* attack). To limit false positives without allowing false negatives, the value of k determined by the model appears as a near-optimum.

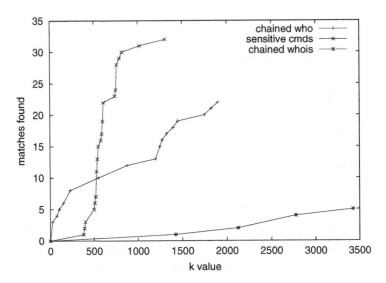

Fig. 5. Number of matches found as a function of k

5   Conclusions and Future Work

We have addressed a performance problem in intrusion detection. The problem is that the algorithms that accurately detect attacks in audit trails are complex and slow, and therefore can not cope with huge amounts of data that are generated when a system or a network is monitored.

We have presented a pattern matching based filter for intrusion detection. The idea is that, despite that it may be difficult and slow to determine that an attack has occurred, it is possible to quickly determine that there is no attack in large portions of the audit trail.

The pattern matching model is based on the concept of *insertion distance*, where the attack is seen as a sequence of letters (events) and the algorithms detect the text portions where all the events of the attack appear in order within a window of k other events. Recent pattern matching algorithms [5] specialized for this problem are able to spot the suspicious areas of the audit trail by scanning millions of events per second. In this way, the pattern matching algorithm quickly *filters out* a large portion of the text, leaving the rest to be examined by a more sophisticated (and slower) algorithm.

We have presented an analytical model and preliminary experimental results about the fitness of the insertion distance model to detect attacks in a real application. We have shown that the k value predicted by the model is large enough to detect virtually all the relevant attacks, yet it still filters out most of the text (85% to 94%). This means that only 6% to 15% of the original text needs to be analyzed by a more sophisticated algorithm. Moreover, we have shown that most of the attacks are indeed found with a much smaller k value, so that speed can be traded for precision. For example, leaving just 2% of the text to examine we were able to detect 50% of the attacks. An optimal value for k can be found which minimizes false negatives and false positives for groups of patterns with specific characteristics.

Some work to undergo to improve the proposed approach follows.

Further experiments with larger and more realistic data sets must be carried out in order to provide more accurate estimations of the filtering efficiency.

The algorithm is assumed to take a random text with uniform distribution as input, which is not the case of our converted audit trails. The study of the implications of that fact is to be done.

Our experiments were conducted off-line. We now need to conduct some on-line experiments. In that context, the efficiency of the mapping process will have to be studied with care.

To conclude, the proposed approach was used for misuse detection. It could be also used for anomaly detection. The algorithm may then be used to verify that a process behaves as during a training period, as proposed by [9].

References

1. J. P. Anderson. Computer security threat monitoring and surveillance. Technical report, James P. Anderson Company, Fort Washington, Pennsylvania, April 1980. 17

2. Teresa F. Lunt. A survey of intrusion detection techniques. *Computers and Security*, 12, 1993. 17

3. T. D. Garvey and T. F. Lunt. Model-based intrusion detection. In *Proceedings of the 14th National Computer Security Conference*, October 1991. 17

4. Ludovic Mé. Gassata, a genetic algorithm as an alternative tool for security audit trails analysis. In *First international workshop on the Recent Advances in Intrusion Detection*, 1998. 18

5. J. Kuri and G. Navarro. Fast multipattern search algorithms for intrusion detection. Technical Report TR/DCC-99-11, Dept. of Computer Science, Univ. of Chile, December 1999. To appear in *7th International Symposium on String Processing and Information Retrieval (SPIRE'00)*, IEEE CS Press. 20, 26

6. R. Baeza-Yates and G. Navarro. Faster approximate string matching. *Algorithmica*, 23(2):127–158, 1999. 22

7. G. Navarro. *Approximate Text Searching*. PhD thesis, Dept. of Computer Science, Univ. of Chile, December 1998. Technical Report TR/DCC-98-14. ftp://ftp.dcc.uchile.cl/pub/users/gnavarro/thesis98.ps.gz. 22

8. M. Bishop. A standard audit log format. In *Proceedings of the 19th National Information Systems Security Conference*, pages 136–145, October 1995. 23

9. P. D'haeseleer, S. Forrest, and P. Helman. An immunological approach to change detection: Algorithms, analysis and implications. In *Proceedings of the 1996 IEEE Symposium on Research in Security and Privacy*. IEEE Computer Society, IEEE Computer Society Press, May 1996. 27

Transaction-Based Pseudonyms in Audit Data for Privacy Respecting Intrusion Detection*

Joachim Biskup and Ulrich Flegel

University of Dortmund
44227 Dortmund, Germany
{Joachim.Biskup,Ulrich.Flegel}@ls6.cs.uni-dortmund.de

Abstract. Privacy and surveillance by intrusion detection are potentially conflicting organizational and legal requirements. In order to support a balanced solution, audit data is inspected for personal data and identifiers referring to real persons are substituted by transaction-based pseudonyms. These pseudonyms are constructed as shares for a suitably adapted version of Shamir's cryptographic approach to secret sharing. Under sufficient suspicion, expressed as a threshold on shares, audit analyzers can perform reidentification.

Keywords: privacy, anonymity, pseudonymity, audit analysis, intrusion detection, secret sharing, purpose binding

1 Introduction

Recent trends in computing and communication demand for two potentially conflicting requirements, namely surveillance and privacy. Surveillance is necessary in order to guarantee secure services to the parties involved, even in the presence of attacks against suboptimal security mechanisms. It is based on audit data about the activities of entities within a computing system. Since parts of such data can be associated with real persons, audit data contain personal data.

Privacy, or more specifically informational self-determination, confines the processing of personal data, as regulated by the pertinent legislation. Among its basic principles, we find the need of either the data subject's informed consent on or the legal or contractual necessity of processing the personal data and, accordingly, a strict purpose binding for collecting, processing and communicating personal data. Pseudonymization, hiding the association between the data and real persons, can help to avoid confinements, as far as the original goals can be still achieved.

Obviously, there are conflicts and tradeoffs among surveillance and privacy, and among audit analysis and pseudonymity, which have to be appropriately solved in a balanced way, both on the organizational level and by the technical

---

* The work described here is currently partially funded by Deutsche Forschungsgemeinschaft under contract number Bi 311/10-1.

H. Debar, L. Mé, and F. Wu (Eds.): RAID 2000, LNCS 1907, pp. 28–48, 2000.

mechanisms. In fact, there are even acts dealing with aspects of surveillance and privacy in the same context.

In this paper we provide an in-depth study of the problem to employ pseudonyms in audit data, as already sketched above. And we propose a widely applicable solution to be used in the framework of intrusion detection systems (IDS). Basically, our solution comprises the following features:

- Audit services are supposed to be under the primary control of the personal data protection official (PPO) who is trusted by the user, on behalf of which the event generating component is operating.
- The audit services, either by themselves or by appropriate extensions, forward sensitive audit data to remote analyzers only if that data is required to detect harmful behavior of the involved entities.
- Pseudonymizers are implanted just behind the standard audit services, or their extensions, respectively, and are still under the primary control of the same PPO, though the analyzers have to assign (or to enforce) some restricted trust in them.
- The pseudonymizer inspect standard audit data, and they substitute identifiers by carefully tailored pseudonyms. Exploiting Shamir's cryptographic approach to secret sharing, these pseudonyms are actually shares, which can be used for reidentification later on, if justified by sufficient suspicion.
- Sufficient suspicion is defined by a threshold on weighted occurrences of potentially harmful behavior, and, accordingly, by a threshold on shares belonging together. Exceeding such a threshold results in the ability to reveal the secret, i.e. to recover the identity behind the pseudonyms.
- Thus the analyzers, holding the pseudonymized audit data including the shares, can reidentify the data if and only if the purpose of surveillance requests to do so.
- Since shares are mixed together, we have to take precautions that shares are not inappropriately combined leading to blame innocent persons.

Our approach follows the paradigm of multilaterally secure systems that take into account security requirements of all involved parties and balance contrary interests in an acceptable way [1]. Conventional approaches to securing audit prioritize the protection of interests of IT systems owners, emphasizing accountability, event reconstruction, general and security related problem and damage assessment and last but not least deterrence. On the other hand, also the interests of other parties are affected, in particular unobservability, anonymity and unlinkability, since audit analysis deals with personal data including but not limited to activity subjects, objects and their owners, results, origin and time.

Once audit data is available in a processible form, it is hard to enforce accountability of processing, for it can be performed on copies of the data externally to the domain under control. The high complexity, composability and short life cycles of todays IT systems render the application of available verification techniques to these systems impractical. It is exceedingly difficult to rule out that an IT system does not contain a trojan horse. It is therefore insufficient to legally prohibit activities necessary for large-scale surveillance. In fact, there is an increasing demand for technical enforcement of privacy principles, reflected by emerging approaches for various applications (see also [2]). In our context, pseudonymization is the tool to do so.

The rest of the paper is organized as follows. First we review the European legislation (Sect. 2), identify the paradigms regarding pseudonymization (Sect. 3) and survey related approaches (Sect. 4). Then we present our approach in more detail, specifying the audit architecture (Sect. 5) and the application of secret sharing to pseudonymization (Sect. 6). We conclude with an outlook on issues for further investigation (Sect. 7).

2   European Legislation

As summarized in consideration (1) in [3] the objectives of the European Community (EC) include "ensuring economic and social progress by common action to eliminate the barriers which divide Europe, encouraging the constant improvement of the living conditions of its peoples, preserving and strengthening peace and liberty and promoting democracy on the basis of the fundamental rights recognized in the constitution and laws of the Member States and in the European Convention for the Protection of Human Rights and Fundamental Freedoms". Accordingly IT systems must respect the right to privacy (see consideration (2) in [3]). From Articles 25 and 26 in Chapter IV "Transfer of Personal Data to Third Countries" and from Article 4 derives the relevance of the directive and the respective national laws for third countries regarding export and processing of personal data from and on EC territory, respectively.

2.1   Fundamental Principles for the Protection of Personal Data

While the directive amalgamates different traditions in dealing with protection of personal data, we rather work out the fundamental principles in a discourse on relevant German law. Important fundamental principles can be found in a sentence [4] of the German Constitutional Court ("Bundesverfassungsgericht"), which postulates the informational self-determination. Collecting and processing personal data without consent of the data subject constitutes a restriction of the data subject's right on informational self-determination. Such restrictions require a statutory foundation meeting two criteria: the first implies that prerequisites and scope of restrictions are clearly identifiable, but more importantly, restrictions are limited to the amount strictly *necessary to achieve the objectives* supporting the restrictions. The scope and nature of personal data being considered is determined by the objective and the resulting restrictions. As the sentence emphasizes, the *sensitivity* of data depends not merely on its nature, rather on the pursued *objective* and on its *linkability* and *processibility*.

Accordingly, measures which restrict the data subject's ability of informational self-determination, such as audit and audit analysis do, must be *adequate, relevant and not excessive* (read *minimal*) with respect to the goals, which are *proportional* with respect to the audit data sensitivity. The principles of *data avoidance* and *data reduction* derive from this fundamental principle of *necessity*. To fix sensitivity, the *objectives are fixed* beforehand, and consequently the nature and scope of data being collected as well as the nature of processing results (analysis) have to be fixed. This fixation is a fundamental privacy principle and henceforth is referred to as *purpose binding*.

2.2   Instruments for the Enforcement of Privacy

From some important European and German directives, acts, ordinances and sentences [5, 4, 6, 3, 7, 8, 9, 10] and [11] we isolated common instruments for the protection of personal data. We found many of the instruments to be relevant for audit analysis. The most important ones are summarized in the following. There are several claims concerning the *data quality*. Here we subsume the fundamental principles of *necessity* and *binding to a legal purpose* and the derived demand for *data avoidance* and *data reduction*. We can avoid personal data by not collecting it in the first place or by anonymizing it. The German TDDSG, [7], Article 2, explicitly allows profiling of teleservice users only under the condition that pseudonyms are used and prohibits correlating profiles with personal data of the data subject. Data reduction can be achieved by discarding personal data as soon it is not needed anymore for the purpose, or by specifying *mandatory timeouts* for data disposal.

Apart from several exceptions, processing personal data is legitimate only when the data subject has unambiguously given his *consent*. Systems therefore must be able to request and store freely given, specific and informed indication of his wishes by which the data subject signifies his agreement. Controllers are obliged to inform data subjects before, or notify them after collection, respectively, about certain facts and rights. This can partly be carried out by the system. Data subjects have the right to choose *acting anonymously* within a system, unless laws collide. Referring to the instruments of information and notification, the data subjects must be enabled to make informed decisions regarding their options. *Default settings* should choose the maximum achievable anonymity and settings should allow for *differentiation of various transaction contexts*. Systems need to be designed such that data subjects are not subject of solely automatic decisions producing legal effects concerning them. See [3], Article 15 for details.

The controller must implement appropriate technical and organizational measures to protect personal data having regard to the state of the art and the cost of their implementation, ensuring a level of security appropriate to the risks represented by the processing and the nature of the data [3], Article 17.

Some regulations apply directly to audit analysis for the purpose of misuse and anomaly detection. For example, the German Data Protection Act [5], §14(4), §31 and its forthcoming amendment [6], §14(4), §31 include explicitly a strict purpose binding for IDS. While the act in force [5], §19(2), §33(2)2, §34(4) allows refusing data subjects to access IDS related personal data concerning them, the draft amendment [6], §19(2), §33(2)2, §34(4) does so only under the condition that the access generates an inappropriate effort. One could still try to apply §19(4)3 and §33(2)3, respectively.

In the EC directive [11] processing of traffic and billing data is allowed for persons handling fraud detection. In the German ordinance [8] based on act [9] the carrier and the provider of telecommunication services may analyze one month worth of the call database to pick suspicious calls [8] (2). They may then collect an analyze customer and call data relating to aforementioned suspicions [8], (1) 2. If it is necessary in a given instance, message content may be collected and analyzed [8] (4). The responsible supervisory authorities and the data subjects must be notified of any analysis of the complete database or of message content.[8] (3). A recent amendment [10] reduces the obligatory notification to establishing and modifying an analysis system and increases aforementioned time period from one to six months.

3   Paradigms Regarding Pseudonymization

Multilaterally secure systems balance interests of various actors. Henceforth we call representatives of the system's owners, also responsible for the system's security, system security officers (SSO). To balance their power against privacy interests of users, they sometimes would have to cooperate with personal data protection officials (PPO).

An entity is called anonymous if an attacker cannot link its identity with its role or activities within an anonymity group. While unlinking events from identities by means of pseudonymization as a kind of (reversible) data avoidance is just one method among others for achieving anonymity, we focus on pseudonymization here. Most data protection acts demand a reasonable strength of anonymity in consideration of the effort required by an attacker and of the risk represented by the processing and nature of the data. We consider some criteria determining the strength of anonymity achieved.

The *attacker model* specifies against whom anonymity is achieved, and whether it persists if any parties, participators or not, compile and correlate information. A related design decision is *when* to pseudonymize. Personal data shall be pseudonymized before entering domains monitored by adversaries. The earlier collected data is pseudonymized, the larger hostile domains can be handled.

The existence of an instance with the ability for *reidentification* is an important factor influencing strength of anonymity. The answer is affected by the choice of *method* for pseudonymization as well as *who* introduces pseudonyms. Both determine the participant(s) needed to cooperate for reidentification. Reidentification should be independent from the anonymous entities but be infeasible for adversaries. Note that an IDS and associated personnel (SSOs) is regarded as adversary to the entities' privacy, therefore necessitating IDS being constructed in a way either requiring technically enforced cooperation of PPOs or analysis and results being exclusively confined to the purpose of intrusion detection. In absence of techniques enforcing such a kind of restriction to a purpose, one can scrutinize and certify the functionality of the implemented audit analysis component. Our contribution offers a method for technical enforcement of purpose binding.

Parameterization influencing reidentification as well as quantity and quality of profiling should be transparently coordinated with all involved parties or their representatives. Accordingly audit analysis needs to be carried out on pseudonymized data. Another conclusion demands strictly separating domains controlled by IDS and associated personnel from domains where personal data is processed in the clear. Appropriate organizational as well as technical measures need to be taken and made transparent to all involved parties or their representatives.

Another indicator for the strength of anonymity is the cardinality of the *anonymity group*. An attacker should experience greater losses than gains when damage by reidentification is done to all members of the anonymity group instead of just one entity. The cardinality of the anonymity group is bounded by the range of valid values for the features being pseudonymized. In addition utilizing a bijection as pseudonymization method is insecure for scarce anonymity group populations. In that case it seems advisable choosing an injection.

One more pertinent criterion is the *linkability* of activities with the same person. The selection of *what* features being pseudonymized and the class of pseudonyms being utilized substantially influence linkability. For a discussion about user identifying features and which features to pseudonymize refer to [12]. Note that design has to consider the degree of linkability required by the audit analysis method. If certain data cannot be analyzed in pseudonymous form, strength of anonymity needs to be traded off against quality of analysis.

An entity has one identity but may use one or more pseudonyms. We consider various classes of pseudonyms differentiated by reference and achieving increasing degrees of anonymity [13]: *Entity-based pseudonyms* may be *public* or *non-public* or *anonymous*. *Role-based pseudonyms* can be *relation-based* or *transaction-based*.

Finally we always have to keep in mind, that we don't need to pseudonymize data we don't collect. Consequently audit shouldn't collect and permanently store data not strictly necessary for the purpose of analysis, eg. intrusion detection. Another general point is that false positives are not only a nuisance for site security officers (SSO), they are also affecting the users' privacy due to undesirable reidentifications [14, 15]. We therefore propose the following framework for reidentification handling:

Each reidentification is audited with the respective reason including information available and necessary for an SSO to investigate the validity of the reidentification. Such investigations may encompass taking note of statements about certain aspects of user behavior. Such statements most certainly are sensitive personal data. The SSOs should be technically restricted to reception of statements about aspects of behavior seeming to be responsible causes for the anomaly to be investigated. On grounds of the investigation results an SSO decides whether the affected user can be informed about the reidentification without compromising security. This would be the case for false alarms. In case the results raise suspicion that it would be advantageous not to inform the user, the SSO would mark the reidentification audit record as deferred and would have to document the reason associated with the record. The PPOs could be notified when an SSO defers a reidentification record and they must be able to contemporarily review all deferred records together with the respective reasons. PPOs thus can attend to their control function and could solve conflicts resulting from SSO misbehavior externally to the system. Many parts of the framework could be enforced by the design of the IDS.

4   Related Approaches

We evaluated four related approaches: the *Intrusion Detection and Avoidance* system (IDA) [16, 17, 12], the *Adaptive Intrusion Detection* system (AID) [18, 19, 12, 20, 21], a Firewall audit analyzer (FW) [14, 15], and the *Aachener Network Intrusion Detection Architecture* (ANIDA) [22], as well as our approach *Pseudonymizer with Conditional Reidentification* (Pseudo/CoRe).

We used several criteria, derived from the paradigms above, to capture the privacy properties of the systems. Table 1 shows, whether the systems have special provisions for *data avoidance* and *data reduction*, whether a part of the system architecture itself enforces the *separation of domains* under control of SSOs or PPOs, respectively. We denote the class of *pseudonyms* in use and how *cumulation* of information regarding entity-based or relation-based pseudonyms is limited, and which *method* is applied for generating pseudonyms, whether there are explicit *identity mapping* data structures and whether they are available to the SSO in protected form, whether pseudonyms are *introduced* locally on the machine, where the audit is generated, or elsewhere. Regarding after which point of the activity flow audit data is *pseudonymized* allows to infer in which domains it remains unprotected. It is furthermore important to know, whether a system pseudonymizes merely directly identifying *features* or also other potentially identifying features, if the analysis establishes *linkability* of activities via pseudonyms or other features, and whether *access control* in the monitored system is based on identifying features. An extremely important area is the *reidentification* handling: whose *cooperation* is required for an SSO to reidentify an entity, and which entity ensures the *binding* of reidentification to the *purpose* of intrusion detection. If an SSO requires no cooperation from a PPO or her technical representative, then it is of utter importance, that there are technical provisions for purpose binding, controlled by a PPO. There are two cases in AID, the first concerning real-time intrusion detection, the second relating to after-the-fact review of archived audit records.

5   Audit Architecture

Most modern operating systems offer similar audit components. No matter whether audit data is generated using AIX, BSDs, HP-UX, Linux, Solaris, Win-

Table 1. An overview of the privacy properties of related approaches. '%' denotes unavailable information, '()' brackets indicate the controlling entity, 'n.a.' means not applicable

criteria	IDA	AID	FW	ANIDA	Pseudo/CoRe
data reduction	no	no	no	anomaly filter	n.a.
data avoidance	no	no	no	client IP	n.a.
features	subjects	identifying features	subjects, hosts	subject	configurable
pseudonyms	entity	entity	entity	relation/transaction	transaction
cumulation limitation	rekeying	rekeying	remapping	no need	no need
method	symmetric encryption	symmetric encryption	sequence numbers, NAT	%	secret sharing
introducer	local	local	local	TTP	local
pseudonymization	in reference monitor	after Solaris BSM `auditd`	after firewall audit	after TTP login	after e.g. `syslogd`
analysis linkability	pseudonyms	pseudonyms	pseudonyms	group IDs	n.a.
access control on	pseudonyms	identities	identities	group IDs	identities
identity mapping	implicit, SSO	implicit, SSO	unprotected, SSO	%, TTP	random. encrypted, SSO
reidentification	manually	automatic	manually	%	automatic
cooperation	PPO	none / PPO	none	TTP (PPO)	none
purpose binding	PPO	analyzer (SSO)/PPO	no	PPO	pseudonymizer (PPO)
domain separation	no	no	no	yes	yes

dows NT or another operating system, the identity of the acting subject is part of the information being recorded [23, 24]. In particular operating systems designed for compliance with the Trusted Computer System Evaluation Criteria (TCSEC) [25, 26] or the Common Criteria (FAU_GEN1.2 and FAU_GEN2) [27] have to provide audit information identifying a security relevant event's originator.

To substantiate placement of a pseudonymizer we chose Unix/Solaris as an exemplary platform. Figure 1 depicts an abstraction of components relevant for auditing at kernel and user level. Basically we find two auditing situations. Some audit streams go directly into dedicated files, others are funneled through central service points, `syslogd` and `auditd` respectively, adding certain supplementary information before merging and/or distributing the streams.

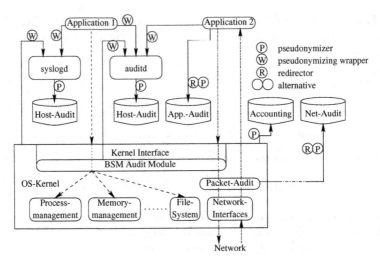

Fig. 1. Solaris audit facilities and placement opportunities for pseudonymizer components

The audit daemon `auditd` is part of the SunSHIELD Basic Security Module (BSM) [28] which is included with Solaris starting with release 2.3. BSM is intended to supplement Solaris for TCSEC C2 compliance and is not activated by default. Audit events may be delivered to `auditd` by the kernel and by user level applications.

BSM Kernel level events comprise system calls (see 'Application 1' in Fig. 1) which allow for potentially security sensitive actions. A few select user level applications included in the Solaris release emit events via `auditd`, such as some local and remote login services, `passwd`, `inetd`, `mountd`, etc.

As `auditd`, also `syslogd` collects event records from kernel and user level sources. Mostly optionally `syslogd` also accepts remotely generated event records at UDP port 514. For management purposes *syslog* also handles event classes differentiating event sources and event priorities, referred to in *syslog* parlance as *facilities* and *severity levels* respectively. The event to class mapping is determined by the event sources. `syslogd`'s behavior concerning incoming events is configurable wrt. the events' classification and priority. Events can be ignored, sent to files, devices, named pipes, remote hosts or to the console for selected or all users. Except for the event header the record format is determined by the event source.

We differentiate three categories of input data for audit analysis: *Host-based* data is derived from sources internal to individual hosts, including some types of events concerning networking, *network-based* data derives from network associated sources, and *out-of-band* data is derived from other sources. While expanding on different data categories is helpful for classifying audit analysis (eg. intrusion detection) systems [29, 30], we were interested in covering with one non-invasive approach to pseudonymizer placement as many existing sources as possible.

All mentioned event data categories are represented in Fig. 1. Host-based data is collected in storage components labeled 'Host-Audit', 'Accounting' and 'App.-Audit' for application audit. The respective sources are applications and the kernel including the BSM audit module and the accounting component. Network-based data also is extracted in a kernel module, in our case using *ip filter* [31]. The packet audit data path in Fig. 1 actually is a simplified illustration. *ip filter*, as commonly set up, sends audit events via `ipmon` to `syslogd`. The data path of other suitable products may vary. Acquisition of out-of-band data is usually implemented by means of applications querying other sources, they are thus represented in Fig. 1 by applications.

5.1   Choosing an Audit Format for the Prototype

For our first prototype we chose to support the *syslog* audit format. The available audit facilities use various event record formats. For our prototype we wanted to initially support the record format featuring the widest applicability and the least limitations. There have been proposed some common audit formats [32, 33, 34] and many IDS use their own canonical format, but in the past these formats have not been taken up on a large scale. Event sources using their own audit files either use a format similar to *syslog* or an own record format. In the first case, we treat them as we treat all *syslog* clients. Implementing a prototype specialized to handling the latter case would limit applicability substantially. Accounting monitors the utilization of shared system resources. Its record format is very similar on all Unixes, involving low recording overhead. An audit record is emitted after the respective event terminates, resulting in accounting records for daemon processes normally being withheld. Thus accounting will not generate privacy problems for networked service clients, but sensitive information regarding local users is recorded. The sensitivity of network packet audit data depends on their content's detail level. When network packets contain external knowledge or application level data, pseudonymization of packet audits should be considered. As mentioned above, TCSEC C2 audit record formats vary between implementations of diverse vendors. Tailoring the prototype to BSM audit records would limit its applicability. Anyhow TCSEC C2 audit implementations, particularly Sun's BSM, are quite popular with host-based IDS, which potentially can impair the privacy of users associated with a login session.

Last but not least the centralized *syslog* audit facility is widely utilized by the kernel and by user level applications for auditing, owing to its uniformity and availability in all significant Unixes. It has its uses in troubleshooting and limited manual intrusion detection. While only serious actions of users associated with a login session appear in *syslog* events, many network services audit via *syslog* with varying levels of detail. TCP wrappers on hosts with huge login user populations, busy web sites and mail exchangers can generate remarkable amounts of audit records containing personal data.

5.2   Embedding Pseudonymizers

Providing pseudonymization directly at the source of audit events, namely in the kernel or user level applications, does not scale well, for all event sources would have to be modified. Then event data should be pseudonymized somewhere on its way from the event source to the event sink, but before it enters domains controlled by expected adversaries. It is thus in most cases not sensible to integrate pseudonymization with the event sink (audit file or audit analyzers).

For auditing by means of both, `auditd` and `syslogd`, system call interfaces are provided. Using wrappers for the appropriate auditing system calls, pseudonymization of audit data can be performed before the data enters the daemons. Another solution is anchoring pseudonymization directly in the daemon code. While these approaches are feasible for Solaris, as its source code is available, this may not be the case for other platforms.

A third approach is pseudonymizing the output event streams of `auditd` and `syslogd`. This can be achieved rather directly by having the daemons audit into pipes than indirectly via temporary files as depicted in Fig. 2.

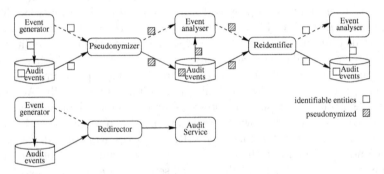

Fig. 2. A pseudonymizer and a redirector

This solution is also applicable to sources emitting events directly to files without using central auditing services. For manageability and technical reasons it can be profitable to further audit centralization. If we wanted 'Application 2' in Fig. 1 to audit to `syslogd` instead of the 'App.-Audit' file, we needed a redirector as in Fig. 2, which picks up the audit stream as the pseudonymizer does, and uses the *syslog* call interface to deposit the events. In case an application executes accesses on its audit files beyond appending events, the redirector could only be used by indirection via files. Those files shouldn't be pruned while the application might revisit old contents.

5.3   Pseudonymizing *syslog*-Style Audits

The pseudonymizer shall receive the input audit records from `syslogd` and while pseudonymizing shall be able to differentiate audit records belonging to different event types, cluster audit records belonging to the events that always occur conjointly, associate events with different attack scenarios, and prioritize events within an attack scenario.

The pseudonymizer accomplishes these requirements based on knowledge provided by its administrator, preferredly a PPO. He specifies the syntax of event types and related features as well as memberships of event types in event type clusters. For brevity we will subsequently abstract clustered event types into a new event type containing the same information, particularly the same features, as the cluster members. PPOs, reasonably in collaboration with SSOs, specify which events occur in which attack scenario and the priority of their features' contribution to the attack. The same knowledge is made available to reidentifiers.

In order to pseudonymize *syslog* audit records, we have to analyze and parse the respective format. Parsing is based on recognizing some basic concepts, which are defined as follows. Recognition of concepts is based on the evaluation of syntactical context, eg. by means of regular expressions for pattern matching.

```
Oct 20 20:48:29   pony   identd[22509]: token TWpldDmO2sq65FfQ82zX == uid 1000 (deedee)
```

The first framed field in the record above specifies the *time and date* when `syslogd` handled the record, which is the symptom of an event having occurred in an application process which resides on the *host* denoted by the other framed field. For the sake of presentation, we will henceforth omit time/date and host fields from audit records. The framed fields in the record below specify the name of the *facility* and optionally the facility's *process ID*. Facilities can be applications or kernel components.

```
identd [ 22509 ]: token TWpldDmO2sq65FfQ82zX == uid 1000 (deedee)
su : BAD SU deedee to root on /dev/ttyp1
```

The *event type context* (framed below) of a record uniquely specifies a type of event specific to a given facility. We define an *event type* as a combination of a facility and an event type context.

```
identd[22509]: token  TWpldDmO2sq65FfQ82zX  == uid  1000 (deedee)
su:  BAD SU  deedee to root  on  /dev/ttyp1
```

An audit record of a specific event type may contain a number of *features* identifying entities. Features like user IDs or user names may directly identify entities; others may be indirectly identifying features [12]. Below some identifying features are framed.

```
identd[22509]: token TWpldDmO2sq65FfQ82zX == uid  1000  ( deedee )
su: BAD SU  deedee  to  root  on  /dev/ttyp1
```

A *feature type* is uniquely specified by its *feature type context*, which is specific to the event type of the audit record. We define a *feature type* as a combination of an event type and a feature type context. Each feature is understood as an instance of a feature type. Below the context of the feature 1000 of the type 'identd token user ID' is framed.

```
identd[22509]: token TWpldDmO2sq65FfQ82zX == uid 1000 ( deedee)
```

The basic idea of our approach is cryptographically enabling reidentification if an entity has caused at least as many possibly attack related events as specified by a threshold. Since various attack methods produce differing numbers of audit records of various event types, we allow for the grouping of event types, and for assignment of an own threshold t_g to each group. It may be the case that different feature types of an event type contribute with a specific weight to different attack scenarios. We therefore actually assign *feature types* to *groups* I_g, which represent the different attack scenarios A_g. In addition we assign a weight function $w_{fg}()$ to each feature type f, representing the priority of f's specific contribution to A_g.

The knowledge about event types and attack scenarios is thus represented by triplets $\langle f, I_g, w_{fg}() \rangle$ per each feature type f. Each triplet expands to a 5-tuple:

$$\langle \text{facility, event type context, feature type context}, I_g, w_{fg}() \rangle$$

There may be multiple occurrences of the identity of the same entity in different feature types of one or more audit records. We thus can associate the same entity, though not the same feature type, with different attack scenarios. As a result, pseudonyms of a specific entity, which are delivered from the same I_g, contribute to the same attack scenario and therefore contribute to reach t_g. This is not the case for pseudonyms of a specific entity, which are delivered from different I_g's.

The tuples defined above form a tree with a virtual root connected to all specified facilities. Each facility is connected to the event type contexts contained in tuples with the same facility. Likewise each event type context is connected to all feature type contexts contained in tuples with the same facility and event type context. I_g and $w_{fg}()$ are stored with their respective feature type context. For an incoming audit record the pseudonymizer determines in the tree the matching facility. Next, in the subtree of the matched facility the matching event type context is determined. Finally, the matching feature type context is determined in the subtree of the event type.

The pseudonymizer performs an *identity update*. It isolates the feature or identity, respectively, retrieves the data structure denoted by I_g and checks, whether the identity is already a member of I_g. In case it is not, an entity entry for the identity is allocated and initialized in I_g. Finally it generates $w_{fg}()$ pseudonyms for the identity and in the audit record replaces the identity by the generated pseudonyms. The higher the priority of a specific feature type's contribution to A_g, according to $w_{fg}()$, the more pseudonyms are generated for the identity.

Similarly proceeding, reidentifiers can relate incoming pseudonyms with their respective I_g.

6   Applying Secret Sharing to Pseudonymization

The basic idea of our approach is to have a pseudonymizer, acting as representative of the anonymity group of all its clients, split an identifying feature id_{i_g} into as many pseudonyms as are needed to pseudonymize audit records containing id_{i_g}, at maximum[1] $P-1$ pseudonyms. The pseudonyms shall have the property, that given any t_g, but not less, pseudonyms of id_{i_g} taken from pseudonymous audit records, a reidentifier is able to recover id_{i_g}. Secret sharing schemes are suitable to fulfill these requirements.

For our purposes we exploit Shamir's threshold scheme, as described in detail in [35] with some modifications. Shamir's threshold scheme has some desirable properties: it is perfect, ideal and it does not rely on any unproven assumptions. New shares can be computed and issued without affecting preceding shares, and providing an entity with more shares than others, bestows more control upon that entity.

6.1   Deviations from Shamir's Threshold Scheme

Owing to different conditions of deployment of Shamir's threshold scheme, we make some modifications with regard to its application. Firstly, in our scenario we don't have a group of participators, of which each confidentially receives and stores one or more shares, until some of them pool t_g shares for secret recovery. Instead, we have one or more reidentifiers, each of them receiving *all* shares. A reidentifier is always in the position to recover the secret, which is the identity id_{i_g} associated with a polynomial $p_{i_g}(x)$, as soon as it received t_g compatible shares, which are the pseudonyms of id_{i_g}. Additionally, since from the point of view of the pseudonymizer all reidentifiers are potential adversaries, the confidentiality requirements regarding shares cease to apply.

While in conventional applications of secret sharing schemes it is feasible to estimate the number of shares preliminarily to be issued, the same is impractical in our scenario, for it is unknown which identities in the near future will require pseudonym generation. We thus take a stepwise approach to the choice of x-coordinates and to share generation, and we distribute $p_{i_g}(x)$ paired with its x. We have to preclude linkability wrt. the x-coordinates of shares within a group of feature types. Accordingly we choose unique x-coordinates for shares of identities being member of the same I_g.

Normally certain products of pairwise combinations of the x-coordinates of shares pooled for secret recovery can be precomputed and issued to the participants in order to improve the performance of secret recovery using Lagrange interpolation. Since this optimization is impractical in our stepwise approach, we do not use it.

---

[1] The secret sharing scheme we apply operates over $GF(P)$.

6.2   Mapping Secrets to Identities

As the assignment of identities to different feature type groups I_g and respective thresholds t_g is just a matter of applying rules specified by an administrator (see Sect. 5.3), for our forthcoming discussion we regard a given I_g and omit the index g wherever applicable. In our approach we do not share identities directly. Instead we assign a unique secret wrt. I to each identity and are going to share this secret. For reidentification after secret recovery we need a function (or table) that maps secrets to identities, and in doing so, fulfills some basic security requirements:

- Since the SSOs using the reidentifier need to control the host on which the reidentifier operates, and since SSOs in our attacker model are potential adversaries, we cannot rely on the Unix operating system to protect the confidentiality of the mapping. The function has to provide itself for its confidentiality.
  In its basic version the mapping from secrets to identities is accomplished by storing cryptograms of the identities, regarding the decryption key k_i as the secret, matching the encryption key $\tilde{k}_i$, pseudo-randomly chosen and unique wrt. I. After an identity update (see Sect. 5.3), I is to be made available to the reidentifiers.
- Once reidentified, an identity shall not be indefinitely linkable to forthcoming events caused by the respective entity. We have to trade off the anonymity of entities against the linkability of events. Since linkability is required by audit analysis to some degree, we carefully have to trade off anonymity against accountability. Other parameters include but are not limited to performance and storage requirements for handling growing numbers of shares and limitations to the number of issueable shares, and the performance penalty imposed by limiting measures as well as their consequences.
  To limit linkability we change the mapping after expiry of an *epoch*. During an epoch, identities are not deleted from the mapping. After expiry the mapping is discarded and rebuilt on demand during the next epoch. Alternatively appropriate rekeying of all identities could be performed.

6.3   The Mismatch Problem

Provided the pseudonymizer issues shares for id_i as unmarked pairs $\langle x, p_i(x) \rangle$, then a reidentifier cannot determine which shares within a group I belong to the same identity, unless it tries to recover an identity from each combination of t shares.

While 'blindly' choosing combinations of t shares, a reidentifier will not always draw t shares stemming from the same polynomial. Consider a reidentifier, which, as depicted in Fig. 3, chooses three shares stemming from three different polynomials p_2, p_3 and p_4. The solution p^* of the linear equations in this case matches in $s^* = p^*(0)$, the secret of p_1. If the reidentifier recovers the respective identity id_1, correct accountability could not be established. Accordingly, if the solution of a combination of t shares matches a secret s_i in I, it is denoted as a *valid match* if all shares are *compatible*, i.e. stem from the same polynomial p_i, otherwise it is called a *mismatch*.

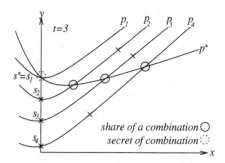

Fig. 3. A mismatch: the solution s^* of a combination of t shares, not all stemming from the same polynomial, matches a secret s_1, though it should not

6.4   Tackling the Mismatch Problem

A straightforward approach to the mismatch problem discussed in Sect. 6.3 is to supply reidentifiers with information enabling them to determine, whether two shares stem from the same polynomial. One, but not the best, method to accomplish this is marking all shares stemming from the same polynomial p_i, and thus from the same identity id_i within I, with an identical label.

This approach has a weakness concerning the unlinkability of audit records. Audit records caused by the same identity in a feature type group I, are linkable wrt. to the labels, even before t pseudonyms have been issued. In other words: if we always mark them, we have relation-based, not transaction-based pseudonyms. Subsequently we suggest and compare three further approaches to mismatch handling avoiding this problem.

Mismatch Avoidance by Deferred Marking. Instead of immediately letting reidentifiers know which shares are compatible, we can defer this information until t compatible shares have been issued. Before this condition holds, reidentifiers can't recover the respective secret, anyway.

Mismatch Avoidance without Marking. Instead of marking shares, the pseudonymizer can take precautions, altogether avoiding the occurrence of mismatches. To enable the pseudonymizer and reidentifier to check for matching combinations of t shares, we have to provide a verifier with each entity in I. In its basic version, a verifier is just the value of a secure one-way hash function of the secret, e.g. a message digest. Before issuing a share, the pseudonymizer checks, if all combinations of t incompatible shares, each including the new share, are free of mismatches. If a mismatch is found, the share is discarded and another one is chosen and tested. Since the reidentifier cannot look at the labels to find compatible shares, it has to test if any combination of t shares matches, each including the incoming share.

Mismatch Verification without Marking. We have to keep in mind, that pseudonymizer always need to reside on production machines to be able to protect the user's privacy. It is thence imperative to minimize the performance penalty imposed upon the machine by the pseudonymizer. Reidentifiers instead could use dedicated machines. We can modify the aforementioned mark-free approach by not having the pseudonymizer avoid mismatches, but having the reidentifier verify matches with the pseudonymizer's help. The pseudonymizer in this case takes no precautions to avoid mismatches and just issues unmarked pseudonyms. As in the approach above, the reidentifier 'blindly' searches for matching combinations of t pseudonyms. It then verifies the validity of a match by providing the ppseudonymizeeudonymizerseudonymizer with I, the share-combination, a nonce and the secure one-way hash value of the concatenation of the nonce and the matching solution. The peudonymizerseudonymizer accepts the query if the nonce is fresh, searches the data structure denoted by I for the appropriate entity, and uses the respective polynomial to test whether the supplied shares are compatible.

In Table 2 we give a brief overview of all approaches. The rows refer to the properties being compared: *privacy* refers to the linkability of audit records from an entity in a specific attack scenario before t shares have been issued. If records are unlinkable, we assign a '+'; if *offline validation* can be implemented, a '+' is assigned; the other rows denote the *performance penalty* imposed by the pseudonymizer 'P' and the reidentifier 'R', respectively. It can be seen, that the approach *mismatch avoidance by deferred marking* has the most desirable properties.

Table 2. A comparison of all proposed mismatch handling approaches

	avoidance by marking	avoidance by deferred marking	avoidance no marking	verification no marking
privacy	−	+	+	+
offline validation	+	+	+	−
performance penalty P	+ low	+ low	− high	+ low
performance penalty R	+ low	+ low	− high	− high

6.5 Enhanced Mapping Requirements

Hitherto we regarded reidentifiers as potential adversaries and equated them with other attackers. In some environments it might be profitable to form further obstacles for attackers being no reidentifiers.

When using differentiated protection areas, initially we perform a secure key exchange, such that both, pseudonymizer and reidentifier, know an encryption key $\tilde{k}_e$ and an optional symmetric key k_v. The reidentifier knows the respective decryption key k_e. Secrets being shared then are not defined as the keys k_i needed for decrypting the identity cryptograms. Instead, k_i is encrypted under $\tilde{k}_e$ to form a secret. In case no labels are used, verifiers not merely are the one-way hash value of the secret, but the value of a keyed one-way hash-function under k_v, applied to the secret. Note, that the effect of using k_v is insignificant, since an attacker who is unaware of k_e, in any case is unable to decrypt the identities.

Since we use a kind of transaction-based pseudonyms, it would be advantageous to hide the number of actually involved entities, in order to make it harder for an adversary to apply external knowledge. This cannot be achieved under immediate marking for mismatch handling. In a nutshell, we introduce dummy entries in I, which are treated like entries for real identities, except that they are annotated as dummies.

7 Open Issues and Further Research

There are a number of promising areas for future research related to our approach. Regarding anonymity we are interested in further methods for reducing the granularity of reidentifications, as well as potential benefits and required properties of dummy audit records.

In addition we will focus on intrusion detection related issues. Our approach is extendible to allow associating a specific feature type with more than one group, which may be needed for attack modeling. Additionally we may consider extending a priori knowledge rules by a condition to differentiate internal and external instances of feature types. This would allow us to provide different thresholds and weights for internal, and external identities, respectively.

Another promising area is the derivation of pseudonymization parameters from attack contexts extracted from knowledge data in intrusion detection systems. Exploiting secret sharing access structures for modeling the weight functions $w_{fg}()$ seems auspicious. Other directions worth investigating are adaptation of the cardinality of anonymity groups to the attention level of the analysis component, linkability and other issues concerning epoch transition.

Further investigation is required considering one or more adversaries coordinating the attack over several machines and user accounts. A single attacker using accounts of identical names on several machines could be handled by a centralized pseudonymizer. In case different user accounts act in concert, correlation must be carried out using features other than account names, as in non-pseudonymous intrusion detection. Existing techniques, such as connection fingerprinting, would have to be extended for pseudonymity.

A final area of investigation is the complementation of audit pseudonymization with detectability of integrity loss. This might be achieved by marrying our approach with the one of Schneier and Kelsey [36, 37].

References

[1] Kai Rannenberg, Andreas Pfitzmann, and Günther Müller. It security and multilateral security. In Müller and Rannenberg [38], pages 21–29. 29

[2] Joachim Biskup. Technical enforcement of informational assurances. In Sushil Jajodia, editor, *Proceedings of the 12th international IFIP TC11 WG 11.3 Working Conference on Database Security*, pages 17–40, Chalkidiki, Greece, July 1998. IFIP, Kluwer Academic Publishers. 30

[3] Directive 95/46/EC of the European Parliament and of the Council of 24 october 1995 on the protection of individuals with regard to the processing of personal data and on the free movement of such data. Official Journal L 281, October 1995. http://europa.eu.int/eur-lex/en/lif/dat/1995/en_395L0046.html. 30, 31

[4] Erster Senat des Bundesverfassungsgerichts.   Urteil vom 15. Dezember 1983 zum Volkszählungsgesetz - 1 BvR 209/83 u.a. (in German).   *Datenschutz und Datensicherung*, 84(4):258–281, April 1984. http://www.datenschutz-berlin.de/gesetze/sonstige/volksz.htm.   30, 31

[5] Federal data protection act. In *Bundesgesetzblatt*, page 2954 ff. December 1990. http://www.datenschutz-berlin.de/gesetze/bdsg/bdsgeng.htm. 31

[6] Bundesministerium   des   Inneren.   Entwurf   zur   Änderung des   BDSG   und   anderer   Gesetze   (in   German),   July   1999. http://www.datenschutz-berlin.de/recht/de/bdsg/bdsgbegr.htm, http://www.datenschutz-berlin.de/recht/de/bdsg/bdsg0607.htm. 31

[7] Bundesministerium für Bildung, Wissenschaft, Forschung und Technologie. Federal act establishing the general conditions for information and communication services — information and communication services act. *Federal Law Gazette I*, 52:1870, June 1997. http://www.iid.de/iukdg/gesetz/iukdgebt.pdf. 31

[8] Federal Ministry of Posts and Telecommunications. Telecommunications carriers data protection ordinance. *Federal Law Gazette I*, page 982, July 1996. http://www.datenschutz-berlin.de/gesetze/medien/tdsve.htm. 31, 32

[9] Der   Deutsche   Bundestag.   Telecommunications   act,   July   1996. http://www.datenschutz-berlin.de/gesetze/tkg/tkge.htm. 31, 32

[10] Entwurf einer Telekommunikations-Datenschutzverordnung (TDSV) (in German), 1999 December. http://www.hansen-oest.de/Dokumente/dsv-e-9912.pdf. 31, 32

[11] Directive 97/66/EC of the European Parliament and of the Council of 15 december 1997 concerning the processing of personal data and the protection of privacy in the telecommunications sector. Official Journal L 024, January 1998. http://europa.eu.int/eur-lex/en/lif/dat/1997/en_397L0066.html. 31, 32

[12] Michael Sobirey, Simone Fischer-Hübner, and Kai Rannenberg. Pseudonymous audit for privacy enhanced intrusion detection. In L. Yngström and J. Carlsen, editors, *Proceedings of the IFIP TC11 13th International Conference on Information Security (SEC'97)*, pages 151–163, Copenhagen, Denkmark, May 1997. IFIP, Chapman & Hall, London. 33, 34, 39

[13] Birgit Pfitzmann, Michael Waidner, and Andreas Pfitzmann. Rechtssicherheit trotz Anonymität in offenen digitalen Systemen (in German). *Datenschutz und Datensicherheit*, 14(5-6):243–253, 305–315, 1990. 33

[14] Emilie Lundin and Erland Jonsson. Privacy vs intrusion detection analysis. In *Proceedings of the Second International Workshop on the Recent Advances in Intrusion Detection (RAID'99)* [39]. 33, 34

[15] Emilie Lundin and Erland Jonsson. Some practical and fundamental problems with anomaly detection. In *Proceedings of NORDSEC'99*, Kista Science Park, Sweden, November 1999. 33, 34

[16] Simone Fischer-Hübner and Klaus Brunnstein. Opportunities and risks of intrusion detection expert systems. In *Proceedings of the International IFIP-GI-Conference Opportunities and Risks of Artificial Intelligence Systems ORAIS'89*, Hamburg, Germany, July 1989. IFIP. 34

[17] Simone Fischer-Hübner. *IDA (Intrusion Detection and Avoidance System): Ein einbruchsentdeckendes und einbruchsvermeidendes System (in German)*. Informatik. Shaker, first edition, 1993. 34

[18] Michael Sobirey. Aktuelle Anforderungen an Intrusion Detection-Systeme und deren Berücksichtigung bei der Systemgestaltung von AID^2 (in German). In Hans H. Brüggemann and Waltraud Gerhardt-Häckl, editors, *Proceedings of Verläßliche IT-Systeme*, DuD-Fachbeiträge, pages 351–370, Rostock, Germany, April 1995. GI, Vieweg. 34

[19] M. Sobirey, B. Richter, and H. König. The intrusion detection system AID – Architecture and experiences in automated audit trail analysis. In P. Horster, editor, *Proceedings of the IFIP TC6/TC11 International Conference on Communications and Multimedia Security*, pages 278–290, Essen, Germany, September 1996. IFIP, Chapman & Hall, London. 34

[20] Michael Sobirey. *Datenschutzoruientiertes Intrusion Detection (in German)*. DuD-Fachbeiträge. Vieweg, first edition, 1999. 34

[21] Michael Meier and Thomas Holz. Sicheres Schlüsselmanagement für verteilte Intrusion-Detection-Systeme (in German). In Patrick Horster, editor, *Systemsicherheit*, DuD-Fachbeiträge, pages 275–286, Bremen, Germany, March 2000. GI-2.5.3, ITG-6.2, ÖCG/ACS, TeleTrusT, Vieweg. 34

[22] Roland Büschkes and Dogan Kesdogan. Privacy enhanced intrusion detection. In Müller and Rannenberg [38], pages 187–204. 34

[23] Terry Escamilla. *Intrusion Detection: Network Security Beyond the Firewall*. Wiley Computer Publishing. John Wiley & Sons, Inc., first edition, 1998. 35

[24] Katherine E. Price. Host-based misuse detection and conventional operating systems' audit data collection. Master's thesis, Purdue university, December 1997. 35

[25] National Computer Security Center. US DoD Standard: Department of Defense Trusted Computer System Evaluation Criteria. DOD 5200.28-STD, Supercedes CSC-STD-001-83, dtd 15 Aug 83, Library No. S225,711, December 1985. http://csrc.ncsl.nist.gov/secpubs/rainbow/std001.txt. 35

[26] National Computer Security Center. Audit in trusted systems. NCSC-TG-001, Library No. S-228,470, July 1987. http://csrc.ncsl.nist.gov/secpubs/rainbow/tg001.txt. 35

[27] Common Criteria Implementation Board, editor. *Common Criteria for Information Technology Security Evaluation — Part 2: Security functional requirements, Version 2.1*. Number CCIMB-99-032. National Institute of Standards and Technology, August 1999. http://csrc.ncsl.nist.gov/cc/ccv20/p2-v21.pdf. 35

[28] Inc. Sun Microsystems. *Solaris 2.6 System Administrator Collection*, volume 1, chapter SunSHIELD Basic Security Module Guide. Sun Microsystems, Inc., 1997. 36

[29] Rebecca Gurley Bace. *Intrusion Detection*. Macmillan Technical Publishing, first edition, 2000. 36

[30] Hervé Debar, Marc Dacier, and Andreas Wespi. Towards a taxonomy of intrusion-detection systems. Technical Report 93076, IBM Research Division, Zurich Research Laboratory, 8803 Rüschlikon, Switzerland, June 1998. 36

[31] Darren Reed. Ip filter. `http://coombs.anu.edu.au/ avalon/ip-filter.html`, 1999. 37

[32] Stephen E. Smaha. svr4++, A common audit trail interchange format for Unix. Technical report, Haystack Laboratories, Inc., Austin, Texas, October 1994. Version 2.2. 37

[33] Matt Bishop. A standard audit trail format. In *Proceedings of the 18th National Information Systems Security Conference*, pages 136–145, Baltimore, Maryland, October 1995. 37

[34] Stefan Axelsson, Ulf Lindquist, and Ulf Gustafson. An approach to unix security logging. In *Proceedings of the 21st National Information Systems Security Conference*, pages 62–75, Crystal City, Arlington, VA, October 1998. 37

[35] Douglas Robert Stinson. *Cryptography — Theory and Practice*, chapter Secret Sharing Schemes, pages 326–331. Discrete mathematics and its applications. CRC Press, first edition, 1995. 41

[36] Bruce Schneier and John Kelsey. Cryptographic support for secure logs on untrusted machines. In *Proceedings of the First International Workshop on the Recent Advances in Intrusion Detection (RAID'98)*, Lovain-la-Neuve, Belgium, September 1998. IBM Emergency Response Team. `http://www.zurich.ibm.com/~dac/Prog_RAID98/Table_of_content.html`. 46

[37] John Kelsey and Bruce Schneier. Minimizing bandwidth for remote access to cryptographically protected audit logs. In *Proceedings of the Second International Workshop on the Recent Advances in Intrusion Detection (RAID'99)* [39]. 46

[38] Günter Müller and Kai Rannenberg, editors. *Multilateral Security in Communications*. Information Security. Addison Wesley, first edition, 1999. 46, 47

[39] Purdue University, CERIAS. *Proceedings of the Second International Workshop on the Recent Advances in Intrusion Detection (RAID'99)*, West Lafayette, Indiana, September 1999. 47, 48

A Data Mining and CIDF Based Approach for Detecting Novel and Distributed Intrusions

Wenke Lee[1], Rahul A. Nimbalkar[1], Kam K. Yee[1], Sunil B. Patil[1],
Pragneshkumar H. Desai[1], Thuan T. Tran[1], and Salvatore J. Stolfo[2]

[1] Department of Computer Science, North Carolina State University,
Raleigh, NC 27695, USA
wenke@csc.ncsu.edu
http://www.csc.ncsu.edu/faculty/lee
[2] Department of Computer Science, Columbia University,
New York, NY 10027, USA
sal@cs.columbia.edu

Abstract. As the recent distributed Denial-of-Service (DDOS) attacks on several major Internet sites have shown us, no open computer network is immune from intrusions. Furthermore, intrusion detection systems (IDSs) need to be updated timely whenever a novel intrusion surfaces; and geographically distributed IDSs need to cooperate to detect distributed and coordinated intrusions. In this paper, we describe an experimental system, based on the Common Intrusion Detection Framework (CIDF), where multiple IDSs can exchange attack information to detect distributed intrusions. The system also includes an ID model builder, where a data mining engine can receive audit data of a novel attack from an IDS, compute a new detection model, and then distribute it to other IDSs. We describe our experiences in implementing such system and the preliminary results of deploying the system in an experimental network.

1 Introduction

As network-based computer systems play increasingly vital roles in modern society, they have become the targets of our enemies and criminals. The security of a computer system is compromised when an intrusion takes place. An intrusion can be defined as "any set of actions that attempt to compromise the integrity, confidentiality, or availability of a resource" [3]. Intrusion prevention techniques, such as encryption, authentication (e.g., using passwords or biometrics), and defensive programming, have been used to protect computer systems as the first line of defense. However, intrusion prevention alone is not sufficient because as systems become ever more complex yet security is still often the after-thought, there are always exploitable weakness in the systems due to design and programming errors, or various "socially engineered" penetration techniques. For example, after it was first reported many years ago, exploitable "buffer overflow" security holes, which can lead to an unauthorized root shell, still exist in some recent system software. Furthermore, as illustrated by recent Distributed

H. Debar, L. Mé, and F. Wu (Eds.): RAID 2000, LNCS 1907, pp. 49–65, 2000.

Denial-of-Service (DDOS) attacks launched against several major Internet sites where security measures are in place, the protocols and systems that are designed to provide services (to the public) are inherently vulnerable to attacks such as DOS. Intrusion detection can be used as another wall to protect network systems because once an intrusion is detected, e.g., in the early stage of a DOS attack, response can be put into place to minimize damages, gather evidence for prosecution, and even launch counter attacks.

Intrusion detection techniques can be categorized into misuse detection and anomaly detection. Misuse detection systems, e.g., IDIOT [7] and STAT [4], use patterns of well-known attacks or weak spots of the system to match and identify known intrusions. For example, a signature rule for the "guessing password attack" can be "there are more than 4 failed login attempts within 2 minutes". The main advantage of misuse detection is that it can accurately and efficiently detect instances of known attacks. The main disadvantage is that it lacks the ability to detect the truly innovative (i.e., newly invented) attacks. Anomaly detection systems, e.g., IDES [12], flag observed activities that deviate significantly from the established normal usage profiles as anomalies, i.e., possible intrusions. For example, the normal profile of a user may contain the averaged frequencies of some system commands used in his or her login sessions. If for a session that is being monitored, the frequencies are significantly lower or higher, then an anomaly alarm will be raised. The main advantage of anomaly detection is that it does not require prior knowledge of intrusion and can thus detect new intrusions. The main disadvantage is that it may not be able to describe what the attack is and may have high false positive rate.

In 1998, the Defense Advanced Research Project Agency (DARPA) sponsored the first Intrusion Detection Evaluation [11] to survey the state-of-the-art of research in intrusion detection. The results indicated that the research systems were much more effective than the leading commercial systems. However, even the best research systems failed to detect a large number of new attacks, including those that can lead to unauthorized user or root access. It is very obvious that the enemies, knowing that intrusion prevention and detection systems are installed in our networks, will attempt to develop and launch new attacks. By definition, misuse detection techniques are ineffective against new intrusions. While it is critical that we develop effective anomaly detection algorithms to detect novel attacks, it is also very important that we develop a mechanism where once a novel attack is detected (necessarily as an anomaly at first) its behavior is analyzed and a specific detection model is built and widely distributed. That is, we need to turn a novel attack into a "known" one as quickly as possible so that appropriate detection and response mechanisms are in place in a timely manner.

The recent DDOS attacks pose a serious challenge to the current de facto practice where an IDS is only concerned with its local network environment, without communication with other IDSs in the Internet. As described by Dittrich [2], a DDOS attack is normally accomplished by first breaking into hundreds (and even thousands) of poorly secured machines around the Internet and installing packet generation "slave" programs on these compromised systems. Remote "master" programs (or the attacker) control these slave programs to send packets of various types to a target host on the network. Even though each slave can just send malicious packets in an amount small enough to be considered "acceptable", the resulting flood, due to a huge number of such slaves getting involved simultaneously, can effectively shut the target system out of normal operation for periods ranging up to several hours. Although an IDS on a target system may detect a DOS, it alone cannot determine that there are many compromised systems in the Internet and that they are used to launch the attack. In other words, the localized approach can only detect a small part of the large-scale distributed attack, and can thus suggest only limited (and often useless) response. On the other hand, if IDSs in the Internet have a communication framework where they can exchange attack information, then upon detecting a DOS, an IDS can broadcast the attack instance to other IDSs, which can in turn activate specific modules (if they are not already running) to look for and kill the slave programs (if there are any in their local environments) responsible for the DDOS attack.

Our research aims to develop techniques for detecting novel and distributed intrusions. In this paper, we describe an experimental system, based on the Common Intrusion Detection Framework (CIDF) [17], where geographically distributed IDSs can communicate with each other by following the protocols defined in CIDF. For example, the IDSs can exchange attack information that includes attack source, method, behavior, and response, etc. Moreover, upon detecting a novel attack, an IDS can send the relevant audit data to a "model builder", which in turn automatically analyzes the data and computes a new detection model specifically for the attack, and distributes the model to other IDSs for local customization/translation and installation.

The rest of the paper is organized as follows. We first briefly describe the data mining technologies that enable the model builder. We then give an overview of the specifications of CIDF. We next describe the design and implementation of our experimental system. We then describe the experiments of using our system to detect (new) DDOS attacks. We compare our research with related work, and conclude the paper with a discussion of future research directions.

2   MADAM ID: A Data Mining Approach for Building ID Models

Currently, building an IDS is a labor-intensive knowledge engineering task where "expert knowledge" is codified as the detection models, i.e., the misuse detection rules or the measures on system features for normal profiles. Given the complexities of today's network systems, expert knowledge is often incomplete and imprecise; as a result, IDSs have limited effectiveness (i.e., accuracy). Further, since the development process is purely manual, updates to IDSs, due to new attacks or changed network configurations, are also slow and expensive.

We have been researching and developing a more systematic and automated approach for building IDSs. We have developed a set of tools that can be applied to a variety of audit data sources to generate intrusion detection models. We call the collection of these tools MADAM ID (Mining Audit Data for Automated Models for Intrusion Detection) [8,10]. The central theme of our approach is to apply data mining programs to the extensively gathered audit data to compute models that accurately capture the actual behavior (i.e., patterns) of intrusions and normal activities. This approach significantly reduces the need to manually analyze and encode intrusion patterns, as well as the guesswork in selecting statistical measures for normal usage profiles. The resultant models can be more effective because they are computed and validated using large amount of audit data. Results from the 1998 DARPA Intrusion Detection Evaluation [11] showed that the detection models produced by MADAM ID had one of the best performances (i.e., with the highest true positive rates while keeping the false alarm rates within the "tolerable" ranges) among the participating systems, most of which were knowledge engineered.

The main elements of MADAM ID include the programs for computing activity patterns from audit data, constructing features from the patterns, and learning classifiers for intrusion detection from audit records processed according to the feature definitions. The process of using MADAM ID is shown in Figure 1.

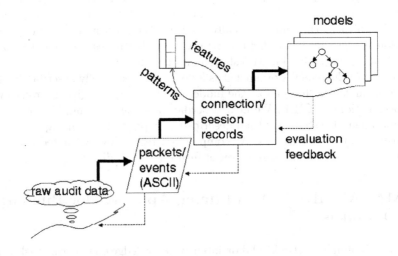

Fig. 1. The data mining process of building ID models

The end product of MADAM ID is a set of classification rules that can be used as intrusion detection models. We consider intrusion detection as a classification problem because ideally we want to classify each audit record into one of a discrete set of possible categories, i.e., normal, a particular kind of intrusion, or anomaly. Given a set of records, where one of the features is the class label (i.e., the concept), classification algorithms can compute a model that uses the most discriminating feature values to describe each concept. An example rule output from RIPPER [1], a classification rule learner, is the following:

```
pod :- wrong_fragment >= 1, protocol_type = icmp.
```

This "ping of death" rule uses a conjunction of two conditional tests, that each checks the value of a feature, e.g., "wrong_fragment". Before we can apply classification algorithms, we need to first select and construct the right set of system features that may contain evidence (indicators) of normal or intrusions. In fact, feature selection/construction is the most challenging problem in building IDSs, regardless the development approach in use.

We exploit the temporal and statistical nature of network traffic and apply data mining programs to compute patterns for feature constructions. As shown in Figure 1, raw audit data, e.g., tcpdump [5] data of network traffic, is first processed into packet/event level ASCII data, which is further summarized into connection/session level records. Each record is defined by a set of basic and general-purpose features, e.g., start time, duration, source and destination hosts and ports, number of bytes transferred, and a flag that indicates the protocol-level behavior of the connection (e.g., SF for normal SYN and FIN), etc. Data mining algorithms that are optimized for audit data are then applied to compute various activity patterns from the audit records, in the forms of per-host and per-service frequent sequential patterns [9]. Given a set of extensively gathered normal audit data and another audit data set that includes an intrusion instance, we can compare the patterns from the normal data and the "intrusion" data to identify the "intrusion-only" patterns, i.e., those that exhibit only in the "intrusion" data. These patterns are then parsed to construct appropriate features that are predictive to the intrusion. For example, a pattern of "SYN flood" is shown in Table 1. Accordingly, the following features are constructed for "SYN flood": a count of the connections to the same destination host in the past 2 seconds, and among these connections, the percentage that are to the same service, and the percentage that have the S0 flag. In prior work [8], we showed that these constructed features have high information gain, and can therefore improve the accuracy of the classification rules.

The process of applying MADAM ID to build intrusion models, as shown in Figure 1, involves multiple steps and iterations. For example, poor performance of a model often suggests that additional features need to be constructed, and/or additional kinds of patterns need to be computed, etc. We have developed a process-centered approach to automate this process: the completion of one step automatically triggers the next step in the process; and heuristics are used to automatically tune the programs of each step, via parameter selection, to achieve performance improvement over the previous iteration. The resulting "process-centered" system can service real-time "model building" request by accepting audit data from an IDS and iterating through the process to compute a desired detection model.

Table 1. An example of intrusion patterns

Frequent episode	Meaning
(flag=S0, service=http, dst_host=victim), (flag=S0, service=http, dst_host=victim) → (flag=S0, service=http, dst_host=victim) [0.93, 0.03, 2]	93% of the time, after two *http* connections with S0 flag (i.e., only one SYN packet is sent) are made to host *victim*, within 2 seconds from the first of these two, the third similar connection is made, and this pattern occurs in 3% of the data

3   An Overview of CIDF

In 1997, a group of research projects funded by DARPA began a collaborative effort called the Common Intrusion Detection Framework (CIDF). The motivation of CIDF was to provide an infrastructure that allows intrusion detection, analysis, and response (IDAR) systems and components to share information about distributed and coordinated attacks.

A major design goal of CIDF is that IDAR systems can be treated as "black boxes" that produce and consume intrusion-related information. According to the roles the IDAR components play in CIDF, they can be categorized as the event generators (E-boxes), analysis engine (A-boxes), response engines (R-boxes), and databases (D-boxes). All four kinds of CIDF components exchange data in the form of Generalized Intrusion Detection Objects (GIDOs), which are represented via a standard common format, defined using the Common Intrusion Specification Language (CISL) [18]. A GIDO encodes the fact that some particular events happened at some particular time, or some analytical conclusion about a set of events, or an instruction to carry out an action.

Given that there is a wide variety of intrusion-related information, CISL needs to be flexible and extensible. The main language construct of CISL is the general-purpose S-expression [16]. S-expressions are simply recursive groupings of tags and data. An example S-expression is:

```
(FileName '/etc/passwd')
```

This S-expression simply groups two terms FileName and '/etc/passwd' together. The advantage of S-expressions is that they provide an explicit association between terms, without limiting what those terms and their groupings might express. In CISL, intrusion-related data is expressed as a sequence of S-expressions with two or more elements. The first element always indicates how to interpret the data that follows, i.e., it is a tag that provides semantic "clue" to the interpretation of the rest of the S-expression. For this reason, these tags are called Semantic IDentifiers, or SIDs for short. As an example, the report of an event "user Joe deleted /etc/passwd" can be expressed as:

```
(Delete
     (Initiator
          (UserName 'Joe')
     )
     (FileSource
          (FileName '/etc/passwd')
     )
)
```

A set of CIDF APIs is provided for encoding and decoding GIDOs. Encoding a GIDO involves first translating the S-expression into a corresponding tree-like structure, then encode the structure into a sequence of bytes. Decoding the byte sequence back into a tree structure simply reverses the above procedure. Each SID code indicates, in a bit of the first byte, the type of argument that the SID takes: an elementary data, an array, or a sequence of S-expressions. The parser then interprets the succeeding bytes accordingly. The tree can be printed in S-expression format for further processing, i.e., extracting the intrusion-related data, by the CIDF component.

CIDF also provides a matchmaking service, i.e., a matchmaker, through which CIDF components can make themselves known to other components, and to locate communication "partners" with which they can share information, and request or provide services. The matchmaker supports feature-based lookup by grouping the CIDF components based on their capabilities. Communications in CIDF need to be as secured as possible because the intrusion-related data being transmitted is obviously critical to the well beings of the IDAR systems. The matchmaker thus provides authenticated and secured communications between CIDF components by acting also as a Certificate Authority (CA). The CIDF messages, i.e., GIDO packets, can include authentication headers and can be encrypted.

4   MADAM ID as a Modeling Engine in CIDF

Researchers have laid a lot of groundwork in defining CISL, GIDO encoding and decoding APIs, and the communication protocols, including matchmaking and authentication, between CIDF components. Research projects or experiments related to CIDF tend to focus on how two IDSs communicate, e.g., by exchanging attack and response data. In addition to studying how IDSs can cooperatively detect distributed attacks in real-time, we are interested in using CIDF to facilitate the distribution of new intrusion detection models so that "novel" attacks will have a very short "life span". That is, we study how a model builder, e.g., MADAM ID, can receive attack data, then rapidly and automatically produce appropriate models, and distribute them to IDSs for installations.

4.1   Design Considerations

When an IDS detects an attack, it can broadcast the instance report to other IDSs, which in turn can check whether the same attack is launched against their local environments or that some local suspicious activities may have caused the attack to other environment(s). Such cooperation among IDSs is well supported by CIDF. The challenge is to build up and maintain a set of SIDs and a dictionary on their possible values that can be used to accurately describe attack scenarios.

Introducing modeling service into CIDF is not as straightforward as it may seem. Note that an "analysis engine" of CIDF has limited capabilities in that it draws a conclusion from event data (i.e., whether and what kind of intrusion has occurred) and can even suggest a response, but it does not provide a detection method. When modeling service is available, upon detecting a new intrusion (as an anomaly), an IDS encodes the relevant audit data (e.g., network traffic within a time window) into GIDOs and transmits the GIDOs to the "modeling engine", i.e., the process-centered MADAM ID system. MADAM ID then performs pattern mining, feature construction, and rule learning using the audit data extracted from the GIDOs. MADAM ID keeps a large store of "baseline" normal patterns so that "intrusion patterns" can be easily identified for the reported attack/anomaly. It also keeps a large amount of "historical" attack data and patterns so that if the reported attack is old attack or a slight variant, an "updated" rule can be produced by training on the combination of "historical" and "new" data. We see here that a modeling engine includes the functionalities of an analysis engine and database.

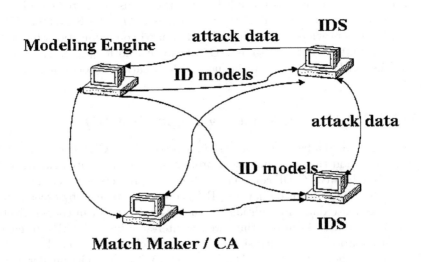

Fig. 2. A CIDF architecture

The most challenging issue in adding a modeling engine into CIDF is the encoding of features and rules into GIDOs. A set of SIDs need to be defined to express the computational instructions for each feature and rule so that an IDS receiving a "ID model GIDO" can automatically parse the instructions and generate local execution modules. Each rule can also include the "accuracy" (i.e. confidence) measurement so that an IDS can decide whether to accept or reject the rule. An updated rule will also have the special tag "updated" so that old rule can be replaced. Figure 2 shows the architecture of CIDF where IDSs can share attack information with each other, and send attack data to the modeling engine, which in turn computes and distributes new detection models. A matchmaker is responsible for hooking up the IDSs with each other and with the modeling engine, and for facilitating authenticated and secured communications between CIDF components.

4.2   Implementation of an Experimental System

We implemented an experimental system, based on CIDF, where MADAM ID is the modeling engine, and Bro [14] and NFR [13] are the two real-time IDSs. We also implemented a system that acts as both a matchmaker and a CA. We described our experiences here.

The Modeling Engine As shown in Figure 1, MADAM ID normally starts the model building process from raw audit data, but can also directly use the processed connection/session records. In either case, an IDS needs to supply audit data to MADAM ID. We used a new SID AuditData that at the encoding end specifies a (local) file that contains the audit data, and another tag AuditData-Size that specifies the size of the audit data. When encoding an S-expression that contains these two tags, the audit data size is recorded in the GIDO object, followed by the content of the audit data file, so that the receiving end has sufficient information to accurately extract the audit data.

To encode features and rules in GIDOs, we first enumerated a set of "essential" (i.e., boot trap) features that all IDSs must know how to compute. These features include: source host, source port, destination host, protocol type, service, duration, flag, etc. We assigned each feature a unique id, and introduced a number of new SIDs for specifying features and their values. For example, the feature condition "flag has value S0" is represented as the following S-expression:

```
(FeatureCond
   (FeatureID 'flag')
   (Cond
        (CondOperator 'equal')
        (CondValue 'S0')
   )
)
```

MADAM ID constructs new features as functions (i.e., some operations or computations) of some (existing) feature conditions for the connections that satisfy certain constraints. The feature construction operators include count, percent, average, etc. The data constraints include same (e.g., same destination host or same-service), different, time window (e.g., 2 seconds), etc. We used a number of new SIDs to define new features. As an example, one of the "SYN flood" features, "for the connections to the same destination host in the past 2 seconds, the percentage that have the S0 flag", is expressed as the following S-expression:

```
(FeatureDef
   (FeatureID 'S0_rate')
   (Constraint
       (ConstraintType 'same')
       (ConstraintValue 'destination host')
   )
   (Constraint
       (ConstraintType 'time')
       (ConstraintValue '2 seconds')
   )
   (Operation
       (Operator 'percent')
       (FeatureCond
           (FeatureID 'flag')
           (Cond
               (CondOperator 'equal')
               (CondValue 'S0')
           )
       )
   )
)
```

An intrusion detection rule, which is simply a sequence of conjuncts on feature conditions, can then be specified using the following form:

```
(DetectionRule
   (AttackType ...)
   (FeatureDef ...) [optional]
   (FeatureCond ...)
)
```

That is, the expression first specifies the type of attack (i.e., an intrusion name) that can be detected by this rule. It then describes the definitions of any new features used in the rule, followed by a sequence of feature conditions.

We can see that as long as the IDSs and the modeling engine understand the same vocabulary, i.e., the set of SIDs and the specific values (i.e., the features, operators, constraints, etc.), new intrusion detection models can be expressed and parsed unambiguously. When an IDS rejoins CIDF after a period of absent, its vocabulary needs to be updated, by exchanging GIDOs with the modeling engine.

In our experimental system, MADAM ID listens to a socket for incoming audit data, and sends new intrusion detection models to all IDSs. A "wrapper", which consists of function calls to CIDF APIs, along with data dictionaries of the features, operators, constraints, etc., is added to MADAM ID so that audit data can be extracted and detection models can be encoded.

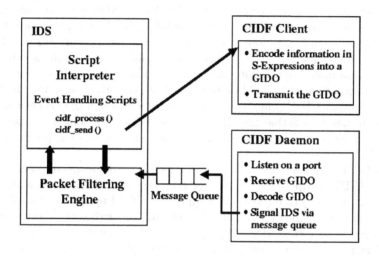

Fig. 3. The CIDF interfaces of IDS

The IDSs We used Bro and NFR in our experimental system for two reasons. First, they are "programmable" IDSs because both filter network traffic streams into a series of events, and execute scripts, e.g., Bro policy scripts or NFR N-codes, which contain site-specific event handlers, i.e., intrusion detection and handling rules. Since the event handling scripts are interpreted by the IDSs, adding new detection rules does not require re-building the IDSs. Such feature facilitates the fast updates of IDSs when new detections models are distributed. The second consideration is a practical one: we have been using these two real-time IDSs for various experiments in the past couple of years, and have the source codes of both systems.

As illustrated in Figure 3, for each IDS, we implemented a CIDF daemon, which is responsible for receiving and decoding GIDOs, and a CIDF client, which is responsible for encoding and sending GIDOs. Upon execution, the CIDF Daemon creates a Shared Message Queue that allows it to communicate with the IDS whenever new messages arrive. This queue will be constantly monitored by the IDS (more details to follow). The CIDF Daemon will be listening on a port, e.g., 3295 (0x0CDF), for incoming GIDOs. Upon connection from a client (i.e., a CIDF Client), the daemon verifies that the received message is a valid GIDO, decodes it to S-expressions. The decoded data is then queued into the Shared Message Queue to signal the IDS for further processing.

The packet filtering engine of the each IDS was modified in order to support communication with the CIDF Daemon. Since "connection-finished" is a condition checked by a packet filtering engine, the probing of the Shared Message Queue is scheduled to occur whenever the engine processes a connection-finished event. Upon receiving the message (i.e., the S-expressions), the packet engine queues an event along with the S-expressions into the Event Queue that it shares with the script interpreter. CIDF-related events e.g., interpreting the S-expressions to take appropriate actions, are handled by the cidf_process script function. A "model interpreter" is implemented as a separate process, invoked by the cidf_process function, to parse the S-expressions that describe a new intrusion detection rule. The generated local intrusion handlers can then be inspected by human experts and loaded into the IDS. Note that the reason that incoming data, from other CIDF components, have to come through the packet engine to reach event handlers is that not all IDSs supports the functionality by which the interpreted script can load data from local file system into the program space (of an IDS).

The CIDF Client provides the means for an IDS to encode and send GIDOs to other CIDF components. Whenever there is information (e.g., audit data, intrusion alerts, etc) to be sent, the request is serviced by the "cidf_send" script function. cidf_send firsts construct S-expressions and writes the data to a local file. It then invokes the CIDF Client process and passes the filename to it. The CIDF Client parses the S-expressions in the file and encodes them into a GIDO. The GIDO is in turn sent to the modeling engine or other IDSs. An example S-expression on a "SYN flood" attack instance is the following:

```
(Attack
          (AttackSpecifics
               (AttackID 0x00000004 0x00000000)
          )
          (When
               (Time 953076974.391314)
          )
          (Message
               (Comment 'SYN flood')
               (SourceIPV4Address 181.162.15.74)
               (TCPSourcePort 1551/tcp)
               (DestinationIPV4Address 152.1.205.85)
               (TCPDestinationPort 80/tcp)
               (TCPConnectionStatus 1)
          )
)
```

The Matchmaker and CA The CIDF matchmaker is used by the components to locate "partners" with whom they can communicate with. For our implementation, the matchmaker is integrated with the CA server, i.e. they are the same process. The matchmaker maintains a list of all CIDF components and their roles (i.e. modeling engine, event engine, etc). New components and roles can be added as desired. When a component needs to communicate with another component, it can do so in either of two ways. If it knows the IP address or hostname of the other component, then it can contact that component directly for communication. In this case, our matchmaker does not play any active role. However, if the component only knows that it wants to communicate with a CIDF component with certain capability, it sends this request to the matchmaker along with any other criteria. The matchmaker then looks up the list of IDSs that satisfy the criteria specified and returns the "matched" list to the component. If no suitable match is found, then a "matchmaking failure" message is returned.

The CA provides authentication of components and enable their secured communications using RSA public key encryption technology. When components A and B need to establish a secured communication, they need to first authenticate each other: A first uses its private RSA key to sign a random nonce generated and given to it by B; it then returns this singed nonce along with its own random nonce to B, who verifies the signature on it using A's public RSA key, signs the A's nonce using its own private RSA key and sends the signed nonce back to A; A then verifies the signature using B's public RSA key. Once the components authenticate each other, they can use their RSA keys to establish a per-session secret key. DES (Data Encryption Standard) secret key algorithm is then used to encrypt the data transmission between the components. Before encrypting any data to be sent to its peer, a component compresses it using the lossless data compression algorithm. Similarly the peer must uncompress the data after decrypting it. Compression not only reduces the size of the data being transmitted, but also provides an added layer of data confidentiality.

Certificates signed by CA are used by the components to exchange their public RSA keys in the first place. A certificate contains the following fields: the ID of the CIDF component (i.e. the IP of the host it is running on); the component's public RSA key; the current time stored as a timestamp. A certificate is considered as valid (i.e. not yet expired) if its timestamp is within the past 90 minutes. We assume that all components know the public RSA key of the CA in advance. This is needed to authenticate the CA and also verify the signature on certificates signed by the CA. This public RSA key must be distributed to the components by some other means such as manual entry.

5 Experiments

We deployed our experimental system in our campus network where Bro, NFR, and MADAM ID are in separate subnets. We conducted a series of experiments to test the limits and strength of this system. We describe some of the findings here.

Our first set of experiments was designed to test the interoperability of the CIDF components. The results were then used to fine-tune the implementation of our system. For example, we simulated "SYN flood" attack against the subnet that Bro was monitoring. Bro detected the attack and sent a GIDO describing the instance to NFR. We compared the S-expressions on both sending (i.e. Bro) and receiving (i.e. NFR) ends to verify that they matched. In another experiment, we took out the "SYN flood" from Bro so that it could not detect the attack as a specific intrusion, but rather an anomaly based on the unusual traffic statistics caused by the attack. Bro then sent then tcpdump data to MADAM ID for a new intrusion detection model. We verified that a new rule was computed and distributed to both Bro and NFR. Both IDSs were able to translate the rule into their local script functions.

Our second set of experiments was designed to test the limit of the modeling engine. In a set of "timing" experiments, we measured how long it took for MADAM ID to compute a detection model after it received the audit data. We found that the results had a wide range, from mere seconds to a few hours. Upon detailed analysis, we discovered that the automated iterative process of mining data, constructing features, computing classifiers, and evaluating performances requires more guidance in its heuristic settings of parameters for the programs. Otherwise, the exhaustive search can be very slow. For example, detecting "SYN flood" may require patterns of "same destination host and same service" be computed and compared (with normal patterns), while "Port-scan" requires "same destination host and different service" patterns. We are studying whether it is feasible for an IDS to include a "high-level" description of the attack behavior in the GIDO so that the modeling engine can have a better chance of setting the correct parameters for the data mining algorithms. In a set of "modeling" experiments, we tried to discover whether some new models could not be expressed as S-expressions because of our current assumptions that every IDS "understands" the same boot-trap set of features and that new features can be expressed using the existing features. We indeed found that for intrusions that require new pre-processing from raw audit data (hence new boot-trap features), it is virtually impossible to express the complex and delicate data pre-processing logic in S-expressions. For example, "teardrop" attacks require special processing of IP fragments, which can only be expressed in high-level programming language such as C/C++. In fact, human experts must get involve in the modeling process when such new data pre-processing is required (since without these new features defined by human experts, the automatic data mining process will not be able to produce a good model and will terminate when it uses up the allotted CPU time in the model building process). We are studying how to distribute new data pre-processing codes in CIDF.

Our third set of experiments was intended to verify that the IDSs could work together to detect distributed attack. We used the Tribal Flood Network (TFN) DDOS attack tool for our experiment. Bro monitored the subnet of the target host and detected the attack, which was launched by several slave programs, each running in a separate host, in the subnet monitored by NFR. When NFR received the attack instance report from Bro, it parsed the GIDO and recognized that a SYN flood seemed to have originated from its subnet (by checking the SourceIPV4Address SID). It then activated a N-code that detects and blocks the "control message" (ICMP echo reply packets) sent by the attack "masters" to the "slaves". It also launched a search for the slave programs, by informing a special daemon on each system in its subnet to look for and kill any running process with a name that matches any in the list of known attack programs. Our results showed that within a few seconds after Bro detected the attack, NFR was able to kill all attacking programs.

6   Related Work

EMERALD [15] provides architecture to facilitate enterprise-wide deployment and configuration of intrusion detectors. A "resolver" is used to combine the alarms from the distributed detectors to make a determination of the state of the (entire) network. This is certainly a right direction for detecting coordinated attack against the enterprise. The resolver technology can also be utilized for event analysis in a CIDF environment. This scope of the system is limited to an enterprise. We are more interested in the problem of how IDSs can collaborate over the Internet, and more importantly, how to automatically produce and distribute new intrusion detection models for "novel" attacks.

Kephart et al. [6] outlined a system architecture where anti-virus systems across the Internet can subscribe to a centralized virus modeling server to receive fast updates whenever a new virus is discovered and a new anti-virus module is produced. This is very similar to our idea of adding the modeling engine to CIDF. Our system has the additional capability of facilitating the IDSs to exchange attack information to detect distributed intrusions.

7   Conclusion and Future Work

In this paper, we discussed the need for new techniques to detect novel intrusions as well as distributed attacks. We proposed to add a modeling service to CIDF so that IDSs can not only exchange attack data to detect distributed intrusions, but also receive detection models once a new attack method surfaces. We described the underlining technologies of our approach, namely, MADAM ID, a data mining framework for automatically building intrusion detection models, and CIDF, a framework for IDAR components to collaborate. We discussed the design and implementation of an experimental system, which uses MADAM ID as the modeling engine, and Bro and NFR as the real-time IDSs. Although our experiments are still preliminary, the promising results showed that these components can interoperate to detect distributed attacks, and can produce and distribute new intrusion detection models.

As for future work, we plan to first conduct more extensive and robust experiments. We will install the components of our experimental system to separate domains over the Internet for a new set of "timing" experiments. We will also run an extensive set of attacks, for example, those that are generated by DARPA "red team", to test whether our system can indeed achieve a better detection performance over a single system.

We will continue to develop the underlying technologies of our system. In particular, we will investigate how to improve the automated process of building intrusion models, and how to encode and distribute features and rules that require detailed system knowledge and are beyond the scope of current CISL.

8   Acknowledgments

This research is supported in part by grants from DARPA (F30602-96-1-0311). Our work has benefited from in-depth discussions with Matt Miller and Dave Fan of Columbia University, and Jim Yuill, Felix Wu, and Doug Reeves of North Carolina State University.

References

1. W. W. Cohen. Fast effective rule induction. In *Machine Learning: the 12th International Conference*, Lake Taho, CA, 1995. Morgan Kaufmann. 53
2. D. Dittrich. Distributed denial of service (ddos) attacks and tools. http://staff.washington.edu/dittrich/misc/ddos/. 50
3. R. Heady, G. Luger, A. Maccabe, and M. Servilla. The architecture of a network level intrusion detection system. Technical report, Computer Science Department, University of New Mexico, August 1990. 49
4. K. Ilgun, R. A. Kemmerer, and P. A. Porras. State transition analysis: A rule-based intrusion detection approach. *IEEE Transactions on Software Engineering*, 21(3):181–199, March 1995. 50
5. V. Jacobson, C. Leres, and S. McCanne. *tcpdump*. available via anonymous ftp to ftp.ee.lbl.gov, June 1989. 53
6. J. O. Kephart, G. B. Sorkin, M. Swimmer, and S. R. White. Blueprint for a computer immune system. Technical report, IBM T. J. Watson Research Center, Yorktown Heights, New York, 1997. 63
7. S. Kumar and E. H. Spafford. A software architecture to support misuse intrusion detection. In *Proceedings of the 18th National Information Security Conference*, pages 194–204, 1995. 50
8. W. Lee. *A Data Mining Framework for Constructing Features and Models for Intrusion Detection Systems*. PhD thesis, Columbia University, June 1999. 52, 53
9. W. Lee, S. J. Stolfo, and K. W. Mok. Mining audit data to build intrusion detection models. In *Proceedings of the 4th International Conference on Knowledge Discovery and Data Mining*, New York, NY, August 1998. AAAI Press. 53
10. W. Lee, S. J. Stolfo, and K. W. Mok. A data mining framework for building intrusion detection models. In *Proceedings of the 1999 IEEE Symposium on Security and Privacy*, May 1999. 52
11. R. Lippmann, D. Fried, I. Graf, J. Haines, K. Kendall, D. McClung, D. Weber, S. Webster, D. Wyschogrod, R. Cunninghan, and M. Zissman. Evaluating intrusion detection systems: The 1998 darpa off-line intrusion detection evaluation. In *Proceedings of the 2000 DARPA Information Survivability Conference and Exposition*, January 2000. 50, 52

12. T. Lunt, A. Tamaru, F. Gilham, R. Jagannathan, P. Neumann, H. Javitz, A. Valdes, and T. Garvey. A real-time intrusion detection expert system (IDES) - final technical report. Technical report, Computer Science Laboratory, SRI International, Menlo Park, California, February 1992. 50

13. Network Flight Recorder Inc. Network flight recorder. http://www.nfr.com, 1997. 57

14. V. Paxson. Bro: A system for detecting network intruders in real-time. In *Proceedings of the 7th USENIX Security Symposium*, San Antonio, TX, 1998. 57

15. P. A. Porras and P. G. Neumann. EMERALD: Event monitoring enabling responses to anomalous live disturbances. In *National Information Systems Security Conference*, Baltimore MD, October 1997. 63

16. R. Rivest. S-expressions. Internet-Draft draft-rivest-sexp-00.txt, expired 1997. 54

17. S. Stainford-Chen. Common intrusion detection framework. http://seclab.cs.ucdavis.edu/cidf. 51

18. B. Tung. The common intrusion specification language: A retrospective. In *Proceedings of the 2000 DARPA Information Survivability Conference and Exposition*, January 2000. 54

Using Finite Automata to Mine Execution Data for Intrusion Detection: A Preliminary Report⋆

Christoph Michael and Anup Ghosh

RST Research Labs

Abstract. The use of program execution traces to detect intrusions has proven to be a successful strategy. Existing systems that employ this approach are *anomaly detectors*, meaning that they model a program's normal behavior and signal deviations from that behavior. Unfortunately, many program-based exploits of NT systems use specialized *malicious executables*. Anomaly detection systems cannot deal with such programs because there is no standard of "normalcy" that they deviate from.

This paper is a preliminary report on an attempt to remedy that situation. We report on a prototype system that learns to identify specific program behaviors. Though the goal is to identify *malicious* behavior, in this paper we report on experiments seeking to identify the behavior of the web-browser, since we did not have enough exemplars of malicious behavior to use as training data.

Using automatically generated finite automata, we search for features in execution traces that allow us to distinguish browsers from other programs. In our experiments, we find that this technique does, in fact, allow us to distinguish traces Internet Explorer from traces of programs that are not web browsers, after training with Netscape and a different set of non-browsers.

Keywords: machine learning, finite automata, feature detection, data mining

1   Introduction

Many kinds of malicious activity in information systems can be detected by monitoring *execution traces*. Broadly speaking, these are just compact synopses of what a program does as it executes. The idea of using execution traces for intrusion detection was pioneered by [2], where the execution traces record what system calls a program makes, and the intrusion detector tries to decide whether a given execution trace reflects normal behavior for that program.

The idea of looking for *features* that identify malicious execution traces brings to mind the idea of signature detection. Many signature detection systems [5,7] do exactly that: look for features that might be used to identify malicious programs. Unfortunately, the signatures in question are usually created by hand,

---

⋆ This work was sponsored under DARPA contract DAAH01-99-C-R205

H. Debar, L. Mé, and F. Wu (Eds.): RAID 2000, LNCS 1907, pp. 66–79, 2000.

and this is time-consuming. It is also hard to determine how well a signature-based system generalizes. Finally, existing signature detection systems do not use execution traces, and we would like to investigate the possibility of doing so, due to the success of execution-trace-based systems in detecting other intrusions that employ executable programs.

It would therefore be appealing to acquire signatures automatically — based on execution traces — with machine learning algorithms. Not only does this lead to an automated process, but the generalization ability of machine-learning algorithms is much better understood than the generalization ability of human-generated rules (see [1,10]). This is because the machine learning algorithm can be scrutinized while the human's thought-processes cannot.

This paper presents the basis of a technique for identifying malicious execution traces with automatically-learned finite automata. What we address is the process of finding *features* that distinguish malicious execution traces from benign ones. In other words, we discuss a data-mining technique for program execution traces.

We use training data that contains exemplars of malicious execution traces as well as benign ones (how we obtain these traces is described in Section 2.1). All traces are thrown together and used to construct a finite state machine using a process we describe in Section 2.2. Once the FSM has been built, we identify the transitions that appear *only* in the malicious traces (Section 3). When a novel execution trace exercises such a transition, this is taken as evidence that the new trace is also malicious.

In Section 4, we present the results of an experiment that suggests this technique can, in fact lead to generalization; we were able to identify specific behavior in programs whose execution traces were not used during training.

Unfortunately, our corpus of execution traces from real malicious executables was not diverse enough for machine learning at the time of these experiments, so we used an artificial definition of "malicious" behavior; we attempted to identify Web browsers based on their execution traces. We trained our FSMs using Netscape as the "malicious" program, and attempted to identify not only novel execution traces from Netscape, but also traces from Internet Explorer, which was not used for training. We also used traces from a number of haphazardly selected programs as exemplars of "benign," e.g., non-browsing behavior. In this particular case, we found that we could, indeed, find features that distinguish execution traces of Internet Explorer from traces of other programs not used during training.

The process we used has human intervention: the choice of benign programs used for training was modified twice before we achieved the desired results. In a full-fledged machine learning system, this would be done automatically, and the system we will describe here would be regarded as a mechanism for feature selection. At the end of the paper, we briefly discuss some ways in which the entire process might be automated.

2   Constructing Finite Automata from Audit Information

Our approach to learning intrusion signatures has two steps: first, we distill the audit information down to a series of symbolic *audit events*, and then we use these audit traces to construct a finite automaton with certain transitions, labelled as "bad," that are believed to be exercised only by malicious programs.

The next two subsections outline our construction of the audit traces and the construction of finite automata from the audit traces.

2.1   Preprocessing of Audit Data

Currently, our behavior data is obtained from NT security logs, making this an off-line prototype. The NT auditing system captures various actions performed by executing programs, such the invocation of a new program by an existing program, the termination of a program, and access to resources. For each program whose invocation is recorded in the audit log, we distill an execution trace by recording these basic events. That is, each event is associated with a unique number, and that number is recorded in the execution trace whenever the event occurs.

When a resource is accessed, an annotation in the audit log describes the way in which it was accessed. For example, a log entry might record that a file was accessed for reading and writing. We treat each such access as an execution event. For example, an audit log entry describing a file access for read and write would results in two entries, a read and a write, being recorded in our execution trace, associating it with a number in the execution trace.

This means that the execution trace may not faithfully record the order of the operations performed on an object in a single access. For example, if a single object access is an access for reading *and* an access for writing, then the audit log does not record whether the read ultimately takes place before the write or vice versa. Therefore, our execution traces also have the read and the write in a standard, canonical order (the read first and the write second) regardless of the order in which they actually took place.

However, the order of accesses may not be critical, since the execution traces are used to identify programs, not to determine their exact semantics. Indeed, the results of our experiments suggest that the execution traces do contain enough information, at least for this particular application.

2.2   State-Merging Algorithms for Learning FSMs

State merging algorithms start with a prefix tree (also called an acceptor tree) describing the training data. The edges of an acceptor tree are labeled with the events that can occur in the training data; in this case it is the set of events that might be extracted from an NT security audit log. Each sequence of events in the training data corresponds to the edge labels on a path through the acceptor tree, starting at the root, and, if there is a unique end symbol, ending in a leaf. (This construct is a prefix tree because each *prefix* of each sequence is also represented by a path starting starting at the root.) Figure 1A shows an acceptor tree for the sequences baadb, baadc, babb, and babc.

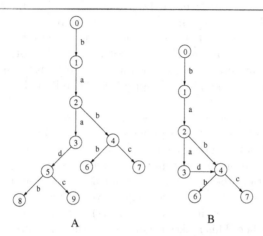

A   B

Fig. 1. Illustration of the state-merging approach to learning finite automata. (A) shows the tree constructed from the four strings baadb, baadc, babb, and babc. Note that each path from the root to a lead has labels corresponding to one of the strings. (B) shows the result of merging states 4 and 5 in the previous figure. These states were merged because the subtrees rooted at states 4 and 5 in (A) are the same. The decision of what states to merge can be made in other ways as well

Learning takes place by selectively merging states in the acceptor tree; this is illustrated in Figure 1B. State merging algorithms differ in their choices of which states will be merged (and this can include a decision not to merge certain states with any others).

At one extreme, one can simply traverse the tree and treat the nodes one at a time, deciding whether to merge the node, and what node to merge it with. At the other extreme, one could devise an optimality condition for the entire tree and then treat the whole learning problem as a global optimization problem (with any merger or separation of nodes being permissible at any time).

Blue-fringe algorithms (see [4]), are a class of algorithms that are at a midpoint between these extremes. A blue-fringe algorithm partitions the set of nodes into three sets: the red nodes, which can no longer be merged with one another; the blue nodes, which may only be merged with red nodes, and the white nodes, which have never been merged and are not yet candidates for merging. Initially, the root node is red and its children are blue, and a blue-fringe algorithm preserves the following invariants:

1. The red nodes form an arbitrary graph but cannot be merged with one another;

2. Each child of a red node is either red or blue;
3. Each blue node is the root of a tree.

Merging a red and blue node results in a red node, meaning that the children of the blue node must, themselves, be promoted to blue, in order to preserve the invariants. The algorithm may also decide to promote a blue node to red without a merge, meaning that there is no red node suitable for merging; here, too, white nodes must be promoted. Finally, the merger of a red and a blue node may cause the automaton to become nondeterministic, and this problem is solved by recursively merging the appropriate children. This can also lead to promotions.

The decision of whether or not to merge two states is often based on the structure of their offspring. For example, the traditional algorithm of [8] merges two nodes if the children of the blue node, which form a tree due to the invariants, can be superimposed on the offspring of the red node without any mismatches.

In our application, the acceptor tree is much more sparse than in many other FSM-learning problems. Each node could have as many children as there are possible audit events (106 in our experiments), but in general, the number of children is far smaller. This makes it hard to use the structure of the offspring as a guide to merging nodes; the graph or tree formed by these offspring is generally incomplete (as compared to a hypothetical acceptor tree where every possible execution path was represented).

Therefore, our algorithm only checks the subtrees to a certain depth. This idea was used in [3] to improve performance, but here, we use it because it reduces the amount of information used in deciding when to merge, and thus reduces the likelihood of a bad merged caused by missing information. (Adopting the terminology of [3], we refer to the bounded-depth subtree of a node as the *signature* of that node.)

The signature is thus simply a smaller acceptor tree, and each string accepted by the signature tree of node k consists of the ℓth through $\ell + D$th symbols of some execution trace in the training data, where ℓ is the depth of node k, and D is the signature depth. For example, the depth-2 signature of node 2 in Figure 1A accepts the strings ad, bb, and bc. We will call these strings — the ones accepted by the signature tree of node k — the *signature strings* of node k.

We use the signature strings to implement the following heuristic: we compare the estimated *probability densities* of the signature strings of two nodes, in order to guess whether the two nodes should be merged. (That is, we merge the nodes if the probability densities appear to be similar). To understand this approach, notice that some nodes in an acceptor tree, such as node two in Figure 1A, are reached by more than one training example. In fact, all four training examples reach node two in Figure 1A, since all four start with the symbols b a. In Figure 1B, after a merge has taken place, all the examples also reach node 4, since all examples start with either b a a d or b a b c. The probability of a signature string s, given that we reach node k, can thus be defined as the probability seeing s after reaching node k. Formally, it is the probability of seeing an execution trace whose ℓth through $\ell + D$th symbols the string s, given that the 1st through $\ell - 1$st symbols in the trace correspond to the edge-labels on the path starting at the root of the tree and ending at node k. ℓ is the depth of node k, as above. (Note that the heuristic is implicitly based on assumption that the nodes act like states in a Markov process, which need not be true of all programs.)

Let $\nu_k(s)$ denote the number of times we see the signature string s after we reach state k, and let n_k denote the number of training examples that reach state k in the first place. Then, the probability estimate for the string s, given that we are at node k, is just ν_k/n_k. We will use $\hat{p}(s|k)$ to denote this estimate.

To score the quality of a merge between two states j and k, we use the L_d metric, which is defined as

$$L_d(j, k) \stackrel{\text{def}}{=} \left(\sum_{i=1}^{m} | \, \hat{p}(s_i|j) - \hat{p}(s_i|k) \, | \right)^{1/d} ,$$

where m is the total number of possible signature strings, and $\hat{p}(s_i|k)$ is taken as zero if the string s_i never reaches state k. Here, d may be any positive number and its actual value is a parameter of the training algorithm.

In summary, when we consider merging two nodes j and k, we judge the quality of the merge by looking at $L_d(j, k)$ for some d; a smaller value indicates a better merge because it indicates that the (estimated) probabilities of all the strings are closer together. If there are several pairs of nodes that we are thinking about merging, we will only merge the one pair that has the lowest L_d score.

It may be that all the merges we are considering are so poor that no merge should take place at all. This happens when each merge has an L_d measure greater than some threshold set by the user. When this happens, we perform a promotion (as described above) instead of a merge.

3   Data-Mining Using Learned FSMs

Our goal is to discover features that can be used to distinguish malicious executables from non-malicious ones. Therefore, our approach uses labeled training data; a given sequence of audit events can be labelled **good**, meaning that the executable is not malicious, or **bad**, meaning that the executable is malicious. The approach works as follows:

1. Build a FSM from the combined **good** and **bad** execution traces.
2. If any transition in the FSM is only exercised by **bad** traces, then label that transition as **bad**. All other transitions are labelled as **good**.

During testing, we follow the trace of a new program through the FSM to determine if the executable should be considered malicious. We can either keep score of the number of **bad** transitions that the trace exercises, or else we can raise an alarm right away when a **bad** transition is exercised.

Note that, in our approach, a transition is **good** if it is exercised by both **good** and **bad** traces from the training data. This isolates that transitions that are *only* exercised by malicious executables; by looking for behavior that is exclusive to malicious executables, we try to find the features that can be used to identify them. We could also have taken the opposite approach, calling any transition bad in case of doubt and thus isolating the features that can be used to identify non-malicious executables. The advantage of our approach is that it still works if some non-malicious traces are accidentally included with the malicious ones. This is meant to simplify the collection of training data; if we know that an intrusion occurred near a certain time, but we are unsure about which executables were involved in carrying out the attack, we can simply throw all execution traces occurring around that time into the bad category.

The overall state-merging algorithm we used was described in Section 2. Some specific details are that we used signatures of depth 2 when comparing to nodes to see if they could be merged, and that we used the L_1 distance for comparison (that is, we used the L_d distance described in Section 2, with $d = 1$). The red-blue pair with the lowest L_1 score was merged, unless the lowest score was greater than 1, in which case the shallowest blue node was promoted to red.

4   Experiments

In this section, we describe several experiments that we used to evaluate our approach. In Section 4.1, we describe the experimental setup, and in Sections 4.2, 4.3, and 4.4 we describe a series of experimental runs in which we zero in on so-called malicious behavior (which, for us, is the behavior of a browser).

4.1   Obtaining Behavior Data for NT Executables

The security logs used in our experiments came from two sources. One was the data for the 1999 Lincoln Labs intrusion detection evaluation, where 5 weeks of data was generated for traffic simulating that of an Air Force base. The second source was one of our own systems, which we used to capture additional traces for Internet Explorer, since the Lincoln data provided only one such trace. In both cases, the security logs were created with base-object auditing enabled. User-level auditing was set to collect the largest possible amount of information, but file and directory auditing were turned off.

For these preliminary results, we did not have a great enough variety of malicious executables to get useful results. The problem with having too few executables is that, with so little data, there is little difference between training and memorization. Execution traces used to test our technique would, with high likelihood, also have appeared verbatim in the training data. Thus, we would only be testing the system's ability to memorize training sequences, not its ability to generalize. Lack of variety in the training data also hurts the generalization ability of the trained system.

Therefore, we used the web-browsers Netscape and Internet Explorer to stand in for malicious executables. The goal in these tests is to train the system with a number of programs, including Netscape or Internet Explorer, with the browser program tagged as being as malicious. The hope is that, due to the functional similarities between the two browsers, we can train a system that recognizes either browser as bad, while recognizing other programs as good. This establishes the ability of finite automata trained on execution traces to find features that identify a program's functionality.

In particular, if we can identify execution traces from one browser after training only on execution traces from the other browser, we will have evidence that this technique can, in fact, isolate features useful for generalization in execution traces. To a lesser extent, it would also be useful to train in execution traces from one browser and then recognize *different* execution traces from the same browser, since this also indicates that we can generalize from one execution-trace to a second, non-identical trace that still performs the same essential functions.

4.2   Experiment 1

In our first experiment, the bad program was Netscape, and the good programs were FINDFAST, LS, SPOOLSS, and advanced. Weeks 2 through 5 of the Lincoln data were used for training (that is, occurrences of the above programs were filtered from Weeks 2-5 of the Lincoln data and used for training).

Testing was done using Week 1 of the Lincoln data. The classifier was first tested on the programs used for training, but the execution traces were taken from Week 1, and were thus generally different than the traces used during training. In addition, the classifier was tested on dotlnetd, explorer, iexplore, nsbind, perl, posix, and rpcss, which were not used during training. For this experiment, an alert was raised whenever a bad transition occurred.

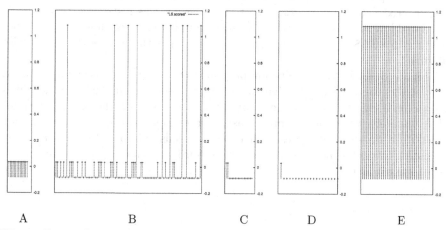

Fig. 2. Scores for programs used for training in experiment 1. (A) FINDFAST; (B) LS; (C) SPOOLSS; (D) advanced; (E) netscape

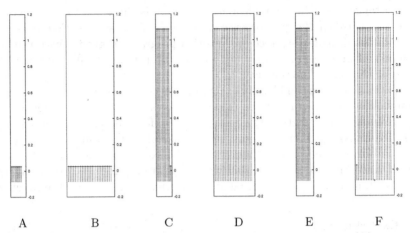

Fig. 3. Scores for programs not used for training in experiment 1. (A) `perl`; (B) `posix`; (C) `iexplore`; (D) `inetinfo`; (E) `nsbind`; (F) `rpcss`

The results for the training programs are shown in Figure 2. Each program was executed several times during Week 1, and the different execution traces are plotted along the horizontal axis. The vertical axis shows the score for each trace, and the scores take on one of three values: 0, meaning that the execution trace was accepted by the automaton and not tagged as being **bad**, 0.1, meaning that the trace was rejected before traversing an edge that would cause it to be tagged as **bad**, and 1, meaning that the execution was tagged as **bad**. (To make all points visible, the vertical range of the plots goes from -0.2 to 1.2.)

For the programs used to train the automaton, the results were more or less as expected. The four programs that the classifier was instructed to regard as good had low scores overall, while Netscape had high scores. However, a number of traces from **LS** had high scores; we might say that those traces triggered false alarms.

Figure 3 shows the results for programs that were not used for training. Our goal is to identify the behavior of web browsers, so the goal is to get high scores for Internet Explorer (`iexplore`) and low scores for the other programs. Unfortunately, three of the programs generate high scores even though they should not do so; again, these can be seen as false alarms. Ten of the eleven execution traces for Internet Explorer were identified, but one was rejected before being tagged as **bad**.

4.3   Experiment 2

To improve this situation — that is, eliminate the false positives caused by `nsbind`, `inetinfo`, and `rpcss`, and prevent `iexplore` from falling off of the FSM, we need more training data. To provide paths for `rpcss`, `nsbind` and `inetinfo` that do not involve **bad** transitions, it may be enough to add more good programs, and since we only want to make the FSM accept `iexplore`, more good training data might suffice for it as well. To this end, we add `dotlnetd` to the training data. (We are concerned with examining the behavior of the learning algorithm; if we were trying to reduce the number of false positives as quickly as possible we would retrain the FSM with one or more of `nsbind`, `inetinfo`, of `rpcss` labelled as good instead of using those programs only during testing.)

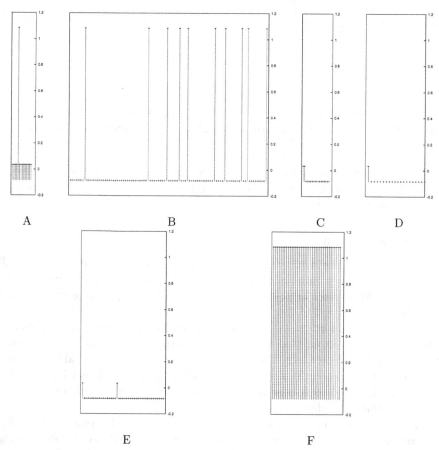

Fig. 4. Scores for programs used for training in experiment 2. (A) `FINDFAST`; (B) `LS`; (C) `SPOOLSS`; (D) `advanced`; (E) `dotlnetd`; (F) `netscape`

Figure 4 shows the results of testing the programs that were also used during training, while Figure 5 shows the results for the programs not used during training.

The results of the second experiment are encouraging. All execution of `iexplore` now trigger an alert, while `nsbind` fails to trigger any alarms before falling off of the FSM.

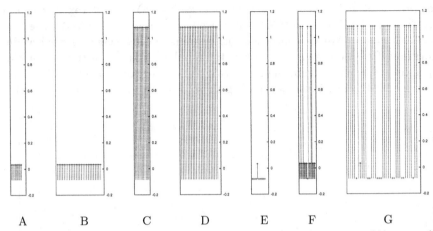

A   B   C   D   E   F   G

Fig. 5. Scores for programs not used for training in experiment 2. (A) `perl`; (B) `posix`; (C) `iexplore`; (D) `inetinfo`; (E) `nsbind`; (F) `rpcss`; (G) `explorer`

Unfortunately, `inetinfo` and `explorer` continue to generate high scores. Additionally, `rpcss` and LS generate many false positives, in spite of the fact that LS was used for training.

4.4   Experiment 3

One way to make `inetinfo` stop generating false positives would be to add still more training data, continuing the process we began above. Unfortunately, we found that adding `perl` or `posix` to the training data as **good** programs did not have the desired affect.

Note that the addition of more training data does not simply add states and transitions to the automaton, but changes its structure, because there are more states available for merging. Therefore, each program we might add as a **good** program to the training data would potentially lead to a different FSM, and it is likely that we would sooner or later stumble across an automaton that met our needs simply by chance.

However, it does not seem worthwhile to demonstrate this point empirically. Therefore, we simply added some execution traces from `inetinfo` to the training data, labelled as **good**. (Recall that the exact execution traces used for training are always distinct from the ones used for testing, though the traces may be generated by different executions of the same program.)

This has the desired affect. Figure 6 shows the results for the programs tagged as **good** during training and Figure 7 shows the results for the programs not used during training.

The programs used for training now behave as they should, with Netscape alone generating high scores. LS no longer generates false alarms.

Among the programs not used during training, the results were also satisfying; the score for the non-browser programs was low (except for an `rpcss` trace

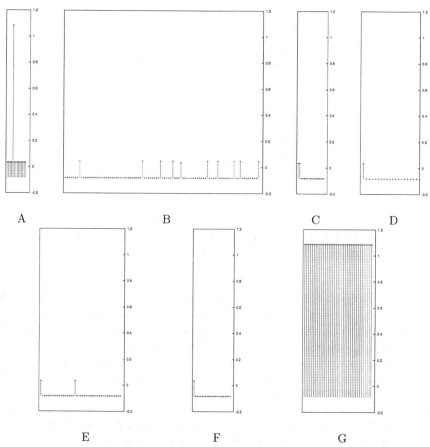

Fig. 6. Scores for programs used for training in experiment 3. (A) FINDFAST; (B) LS; (C) SPOOLSS; (D) advanced; (E) dotlnetd; (F) inetinfo; (G) netscape

that lead to a false alarm), and iexplore's scores were all high. This is shown on Figure 7.

5   Conclusion and Future Work

The experiments reported above are promising. It appears relatively straight-forward to isolate those features of an execution trace that identify particular aspects of program behavior.

We tried to identify web browsers by their execution traces, but the ultimate goal is to identify programs with certain types of malicious behavior. Of course, it is necessary for the programs in question to carry out their malicious activities in similar ways; for example, we would not expect to identify back-door server if the programs labelled as **bad** during training were exploits of race conditions

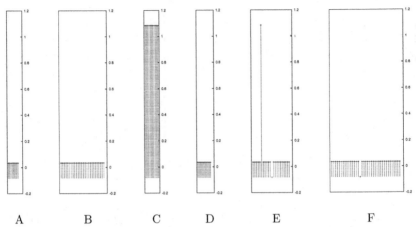

A   B   C   D   E   F

Fig. 7. Scores for programs not used for training in experiment 3. (A) `perl`; (B) `posix`; (C) `iexplore`; (D) `nsbind`; (E) `rpcss`; (F) `explorer`

being used to gain privileged access. In a sense, this approach automates the creation of signatures to identify particular *classes* of malicious executables.

It is worth noting that some of the programs that were initially hard to distinguish from browsers, *inetinfo*, `nsbind` and `rpcss`, have a more browser-like behavior than the others because they access the network while the others do not. `explorer`, which was also harder to distinguish from browsers, could also be said to have behavior similar to that of a browser, though in a different sense since it accesses local files. This suggests that the system is creating meaningful measures of semantic similarity, and not being driven by features that result from statistical flukes. On the other hand, it would be interesting to see whether a totally unique browser implementation, say, a browser implemented as a `perl` script, would be detected.

However, there is an unsatisfying aspect in the experiments just reported. We tweaked the training data until we got satisfactory performance. The actions we took were relatively intuitive, and they led to the desired result fairly quickly; in fact, all traces for `rpcss`, and ten of the eleven traces for `iexplore`, were really added after training was complete, i.e., the system did not require additional training to classify these traces correctly. Nonetheless, it can still be argued that we were certain to achieve our aims eventually in any case, if only we had tried sufficiently many different combinations of training data. We could also have varied the parameters of the training algorithm, such as the depth of the signatures used when comparing two nodes to score a potential merge. We might even have tried completely different merging strategies. Therefore, the question is whether our results reflect the usefulness of the technique we have been discussing, or whether they simply reflect our own skill at homing in on a good training setup.

At the moment, we cannot provide a rigorous answer to this question. We can only say that the comparative ease with which we achieved success *suggests* that our approach is well suited to the task. However, techniques such as structural risk minimization [9] or using a mixture of experts [6] allow the trial-and-error of techniques like ours to be automated in reasoned way. That is, a machine learning algorithm can empirically examine a number alternative automata trained by a number of alternative learning techniques; it can choose the best automaton (or best combination of automata) based on their performance on a test sample, and still have some confidence of obtaining a result that works well on new data. This is the next step in our work.

References

1. L. Devroye, L. Györfi, and G. Girosi. *A Probabalistic Theory of Pattern Recognition*, volume 31 of *Applications of Mathematics*. Springer-Verlag, New York, 1996. 67

2. Stephanie Forrest, Steven A. Hofmeyr, Anil Somayaji, and Thomas A. Longstaff. A sense of self for unix processes. In *Proceedinges of the 1996 IEEE Symposium on Research in Security and Privacy*, pages 120–128. IEEE Computer Society, IEEE Computer Society Press, May 1996. 66

3. Yoav Freund, Michael Kearns, Dana Ron, Ronitt Rubinfeld, Robert E. Schapire, and Linda Sellie. Efficient learning of typical finite automata from random walks. *Information and Computation*, 138(1):23–48, 10 October 1997. 70

4. R. Price K. Lang, B. Pearlmutter. Results of the abbadingo one dfa learning competition and a new evidence driven state merging algorithm. In *Proceedings of the International Colloquium on Grammatical Inference (ICGA-98)*, volume 1433 of *Lecture Notes in Artificial Intelligence*, pages 1–12. Springer-Verlag, 1998. 69

5. Sandeep Kumar and Eugene Spafford. A pattern matching model for misuse intrusion detection. In *Proceedings of the 17th National Computer Security Conference*, pages 11–21, October 1994. 66

6. N. Littlestone and M. K. Warmuth. The weighted majority algorithm. *Information and Computation*, 108(2):212–261, 1994. 79

7. S. Staniford-Chen, S. Cheung, R. Crawford, M. Dilger, J. Frank, J. Hoagland, K. Levitt, C. Wee, R. Yip, and D. Zerkle. GrIDS – A Graph Based Intrusion Detection System for Large Networks. In *Proceedings of the 19th National Information Systems Security Conference*, 1996. 66

8. B. A. Trakhtenbrot and Ya. A. Barzdin. *Finite Automata: Behavior and Synthesis*. North-Holland, 1973. 70

9. V. Vapnik. *Estimating Dependancies Based on Empirical Data*. Springer Series in Statistics. Springer-Verlag, New York, 1982. 79

10. T. L. H. Watkin, A. Rau, and M. Biehl. The stastical mechanics of learning a rule. *Rev. Mod. Phys.*, 65:499–556, 1993. 67

Adaptive, Model-Based Monitoring for Cyber Attack Detection

Alfonso Valdes and Keith Skinner

SRI International
{valdes,skinner}@sdl.sri.com

Abstract. Inference methods for detecting attacks on information resources typically use signature analysis or statistical anomaly detection methods. The former have the advantage of attack specificity, but may not be able to generalize. The latter detect attacks probabilistically, allowing for generalization potential. However, they lack attack models and can potentially "learn" to consider an attack normal.
Herein, we present a high-performance, adaptive, model-based technique for attack detection, using Bayes net technology to analyze bursts of traffic. Attack classes are embodied as model hypotheses, which are adaptively reinforced. This approach has the attractive features of both signature based and statistical techniques: model specificity, adaptability, and generalization potential. Our initial prototype sensor examines TCP headers and communicates in IDIP, delivering a complementary inference technique to an IDS sensor suite. The inference technique is itself suitable for sensor correlation.

Keywords: Intrusion detection, Innovative approaches, IDS cooperation, Bayes nets.

1 Introduction

To date, two principal classes of inference techniques have been used in intrusion detection systems (IDS). In signature analysis [1], descriptions of known attacks are encoded in the form of rules. Statistical systems [2,3,6] intend to "learn" normal behavior from data, and then issue alerts for suspected anomalies. Whatever inference techniques are used in IDS, they must typically meet stringent requirements of extremely high throughput and extremely low false alarm rate. In this paper we describe eBayes TCP, which applies Bayesian methods [4,5] as an IDS inference technique.

We have developed eBayes TCP as a component of the broad EMERALD system, which permits us to leverage from a substantial component infrastructure. Specifically, eBayes TCP is an analytical component that interfaces to the EMERALD ETCPGEN and EMONTCP components [6]. ETCPGEN can process either live TCP traffic or TCPDUMP data in batch mode. EMONTCP extracts the TCP state for a number of generally simultaneous TCP connections. When we refer to "events", we mean events from EMONTCP, which already represents a considerable reduction from the raw TCP data.

H. Debar, L. Mé, and F. Wu (Eds.): RAID 2000, LNCS 1907, pp. 80–93, 2000.

The innovation provided by eBayes TCP is that it captures the best features of signature-based intrusion detection as well as anomaly detection (as in EMERALD ESTAT). Like signature engines, it can embody attack models, but has the capability to adapt as systems evolve. Like probabilistic components, it has the potential to generalize to previously unseen classes of attacks. In addition, the system includes an adaptive capability, which can "grow" quite reasonable models from a random start.

EBayes TCP analyzes TCP sessions, which are temporally contiguous bursts of traffic from a given client IP. It is not very important for the system to demarcate sessions exactly. The analysis is done by Bayesian inference at periodic intervals in a session, where the interval is measured in number of events or elapsed time (inference is always done when the system believes that the session has ended). Between inference intervals, the system state is propagated according to a Markov model. After each inference, the system writes text and Intrusion Detection Internet Protocol (IDIP) alerts for sufficiently suspicious sessions.

EBayes TCP consists of two components: a TCP-specific module that interfaces to appropriate EMERALD components and manages TCP sessions, as well as a high-performance Bayesian inference class library. The latter has potential not simply to analyze a specific data stream, but also as a fusion engine considering heterogeneous sensors.

The remainder of this paper is organized as follows. We give a brief discussion of Bayesian inference in trees, although the reader should refer to the bibliography for a more in-depth treatment. This is followed by a description of eBayes TCP itself, including the session concept, the TCP Bayes model structure, and the important nodes (measures) considered. After the eBayes definition, we present our innovative approaches to model adaptation and state transition. We follow this with results from using simulated data from the Lincoln Laboratory 1999 Intrusion Detection Evaluation study [7], as well as live data monitored in real time from our LAN.

2   Bayesian Inference

Mathematically, we have adapted the framework for belief propagation in causal trees from Pearl [4]. Knowledge is represented as nodes in a tree, where each node is considered to be in one of several discrete states. A node receives π (prior, or causal support) messages from its parent, and λ (likelihood, or diagnostic support) messages from its children as events are observed. We think of priors as propagating downward through the tree, and likelihood as propagating upward. These are discrete distributions, that is, they are positive valued and sum to unity. The prior message incorporates all information not observed at the node. The likelihood at terminal or "leaf" nodes corresponds to the directly observable evidence. A conditional probability table (CPT) links a child to a parent. Its elements are given by

$$CPT_{ij} = P(state = j | parent\_state = i)$$

As a consequence of this definition, each row of a CPT is a discrete distribution over the node states for a particular parent node state, that is,

$$CPT_{ij} \geq 0, \forall i, j$$

$$\sum_j CPT_{ij} = 1, \forall j$$

The basic operations of message propagation in the tree are most succinctly expressed in terms of vector/matrix algebra. We will adopt the convention that prior messages are represented as row vectors. Downward propagation of the prior messages is achieved by left multiplication of the parent's prior by the CPT, that is,

$$\pi(node) = \alpha \pi(parent\_node) \bullet CPT$$

where a is a normalizing constant to ensure that the result sums to unity. Note that since CPT is not required to be square, the number of elements in $\pi(node)$ and $\pi(parent\_node)$ may be different. Since we limit ourselves to trees, there is at most one parent per node. However, there may be multiple children, so upward propagation of the likelihood messages requires a fusion step. For each node, the λ message, represented as a column vector, is propagated upward via the following matrix computation:

$$\lambda\_to\_parent(node) = CPT \bullet \lambda(node)$$

Note that $\lambda(node)$ has number of elements equal to the number of states in the node, while $\lambda\_to\_parent(node)$ has number of elements equal to the number of states in the parent node. These messages are fused at the parent via elementwise multiplication:

$$L_i(parent) = \prod_{c \in children(parent)} \lambda\_to\_parent_i(c)$$

$$\lambda_i(parent) = L_i(parent) / \sum_j L_j(parent)$$

Here, L represents the raw elementwise product, and λ is obtained by normalizing this to unit sum. Finally, the belief over the states at a node is obtained as follows:

$$BEL_i = \beta \pi_i \lambda_i$$

where β is a normalizing constant so that BEL has unit sum. Figure 1 illustrates propagation in a fragment of a tree.

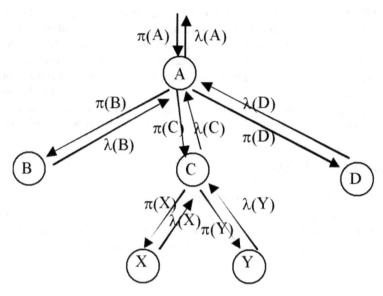

Fig. 1. Message Propagation in a Tree Fragment

3   Session Model

We evaluate bursts of traffic as a means of integrating the signal (observable evidence of an attack or anomaly). Our simplest model considers temporally contiguous traffic from a particular IP address as a session. To detect distributed attacks, we also consider traffic to a protected resource, such as a server in the protected LAN. When we see an event, we examine our list of active sessions and see if we have a match. If we do, we update the matching session with the new event. Otherwise, we allocate a new session structure and initialize its observables with the event data. We manage the growth of the session list in two ways. First, we have a regularly scheduled "housecleaning" operation. All sessions are allowed to remain active for some time interval after the last event seen for the session. This interval is longer if the system believes the session has open (active) connections, but exists even if all connections are believed to be closed. The timeout intervals for sessions with and without open connections are configuration parameters. When housecleaning is invoked, all sessions for which the timeout is before the time of the housecleaning operation are deallocated. If the session table is at a maximum size set via system configuration and an event for a new session is observed, we invoke a "hindmost" operation, which deallocates the session with the most distant last event time. The inference engine is invoked periodically throughout each session, and always when a session is deallocated.

Identification of when a burst begins or ends is itself not an assertion that can be made with certainty. Even in the case that all connections are closed, we must be careful not to deallocate immediately, as some attacks (such as

MAILBOMB) consist of a large number of successful open/close events, any one of which looks normal. Conversely, we must not wait indefinitely (or for the timeout interval) for all open connections to close, as many attacks work by opening connections which the attacker has no intention of completing. Again, a statistical determination of return to the idle state is appropriate, from the point of view of sensitivity as well as response time. The potential downside of deallocating a session prematurely is slight. At worst, we potentially report multiple events for the same attack (although in practice this is rarely seen).

4   eBayes TCP Structure

Our TCP model represents the (unobservable) session class at the root node, and several observed and derived variables from the TCPDUMP data as children. All child nodes are also leaf nodes (that is, considered observable). This structure is represented Figure 2, and is assumed to hold at each inference interval (or time slice).

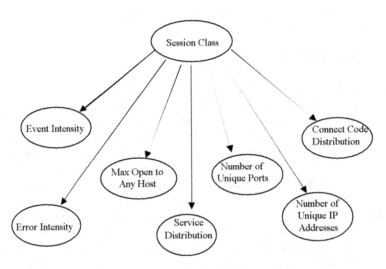

Fig. 2. eBayes TCP

This structure is sometimes referred to as the naïve Bayes model, and tacitly assumes conditional independence of the child nodes given the parent.

In this model, we apply Bayesian inference to obtain a belief over states of interest (hypotheses) for the session under consideration (or more generally, a burst of traffic from a given IP address). In our TCP model, the session class hypotheses at the root node are MAIL, HTTP, FTP, TELNET/REMOTE USAGE, OTHER NORMAL, HTTP_F, DICTIONARY, PROCESSTABLE, MAILBOMB, PORTSWEEP, IPSWEEP, SYNFLOOD, and OTHER ATTACK. The first five represent normal usage modes, while the rest are attack modes. HTTP_F describes a pattern of long http sessions with abnormal terminations that is frequently seen in real-world traffic. At this point, we do not consider these sessions to represent attacks.

EBayes-TCP is coupled with the eBayes service availability monitor, which learns valid hosts and services in the protected network via a process of unsupervised discovery. This enables detection of "stealth" port sweeps (scanning for a small, sensitive set of ports) without a predefined model of which sets of services are to e considered sensitive.

For each session (as determined by the session model above) we accumulate a number of observables. Inference is done periodically for each session, where the period is a configurable number of events or elapsed time, and always when the system believes the session has ended. The model has three types of measures: intensity, high water marks, and distribution.

Intensity measures are similar to the intensity measures we employed in EMERALD ESTAT. Specifically, an intensity measure is an exponentially decayed count. The intensity measures in eBayes TCP are defined as:

$$Event\_Intensity_{event} = e^{k\Delta t}Event\_Intensity_{event-1} + 1.0$$
$$Error\_Intensity_{event} = e^{k\Delta t}Error\_Intensity_{event-1} +$$
$$(\text{event has error return})?1.0:0.0$$
$$\Delta t = \text{Time between the present and the immediately}$$
$$\text{preceding event}$$
$$k = \text{Decay constant}(\le 0)$$

Intensity measures have the property that as long as behavior is normal and the decay constant is appropriately chosen, they do not grow without bound. The range of these measures is categorized to obtain the observed state values for the respective nodes.

High-water-mark measures track a maximum count of an underlying observable. Our system maintains a list of ports and unique hosts accessed by this session. From these, we derive the maximum number of open connections to any unique host. As a configuration option, this maximum may or may not be reset at each inference interval. The total number of unique ports and hosts accessed by the session is also recorded. As with intensity measures, the range is categorized to obtain the respective node states.

Distribution measures track the distribution of the categories over an underlying discrete-valued measure. For example, for each event, we classify the service into one of MAIL, HTTP, FTP, or OTHER. Over an inference interval, we maintain a count of the number of times each was observed. The service distribution is then obtained as

$$svc\_dist=\{count(MAIL)\ count(HTTP)\ count(FTP)\ count(REMOTE)\ count(OTHER)\}$$

Strictly, we should divide by the total count to obtain a true distribution, but the normalization in the internals of the Bayes inference handle this for us.

Setting the observables means setting the λ messages at the child nodes. We have overloaded the set_state function to accept either an observed integer state value (in which case we set $\lambda_{obs} = 1, \lambda_i = 0$ for $i \neq obs$) or a distribution (in which case we set, for example, $\lambda = svc\_dist$).

5   Adaptive Capability

Our system can potentially adapt by reinforcing its built-in models for the current observation (adjusting rows in the CPTs corresponding to the observed state at the parent) or by adding a new state (hypothesis) at the parent if the current observation is not in good agreement with any of the currently modeled hypotheses.

5.1   Adaptive CPT Adjustment

Adaptation via reinforcement proceeds as follows. We recall that the CPT relates a child node to its parent. In our representation, the rows of the CPT correspond to parent states, while the columns correspond to child states. If a single hypothesis is dominant at the root node, we adapt the corresponding row of the CPT matrix at each child slightly in the direction of the λ message at the child node for the present observation. Specifically, if hypothesis i "wins" at the root node, we adjust CPT as follows. First, we decay the internal effective counts via a decay function:

$$counts_i^{decay} = \gamma counts_i + (1 - \gamma)$$

The decayed count is used as a "past weight" for the adjustment, and is the effective number of times this hypothesis has been recently observed. The CPT row is first converted to effective counts for each child state, and the present observation is added as an additional count distributed over the same states. Then the row elements are divided by the row sum so that the adjusted row has unit sum. This is accomplished by the following equation:

$$CPT_{ij}^{adj} = \frac{counts_i \times CPT_{ij} + \lambda_j}{\sum_j counts_i \times CPT_{ij} + \lambda_j}$$

Finally, the internal counts are recomputed for all parent states:

$$counts_i = counts_i^{decay} + \begin{cases} \gamma, & \text{hypothesis } i \text{ is the winner} \\ 0, & \text{otherwise} \end{cases}$$

By this procedure, the effective count never decays below 1.0 (if the hypothesis is never observed) and never grows beyond $\frac{1}{(1-\gamma)}$ if the hypothesis is always observed. We typically choose the decay factor so that the effective count grows to between 200 and 1000 observations. Observations for frequently seen hypotheses have a smaller CPT adjustment than do observations for rare hypotheses. In addition, since only "winning" hypotheses cause a potential CPT adjustment, our system has one key advantage over other statistical ID systems. A large number of observations for a hypothesis corresponding to an attack will not be considered "normal" no matter how frequently it is observed, as its adjustment only reinforces the corresponding internal attack hypothesis model in the system.

5.2   Dynamic Hypothesis Generation

Another form of adaptation is the potential ability to add a state. Naïve Bayes models such as the one described above work well in practice as classifiers, and are typically trained with observations for which the true class is known. Dynamic hypothesis generation as described here takes on a more difficult problem, namely, the situation where the data cases are unlabeled and even the underlying number of hypothesis states is unknown. In this situation, it is legitimate to ask if a system can self-organize to a number of hypotheses that adequately separate the important data classes. In this respect, the ability to separate attack classes A and B from each other is less important than the ability to separate both A and B from the set of nonattack classes.

To build this capability, we need to enable the system to add hypotheses at the root node (the reader will recall that the root node state value is not directly observable). As a configuration option, the system will create a "dummy state" at the root node (or more generally, at any node that is not directly observable), with an effective count of 1. If this node has children, a new CPT row is added at each child. We use a uniform distribution over the child state (each element has value $\frac{1}{nstate_{child}}$) for this CPT at present.

Adding a state then proceeds as follows. The inference mechanism is applied to an observation, and a posterior belief is obtained for the dummy state as if it were a normal state. If this state "wins", it is promoted to the valid state class and the CPT rows for all children are modified via the CPT adjustment procedure described above. Note that since the effective count of the dummy state is 1, the adjustment makes the CPT rows look 50observation. Then a new dummy state is added, allowing the system to grow to the number of root node states that adequately describe the data. This dummy state is not to be confused with the OTHER ATTACK hypothesis, for which there is an initial model of nonspecific anomalous behavior (e.g., moderate error intensity).

There are two ways to exploit the hypothesis generation capability. In the first, we initialize the system with the normal and attack hypotheses described above, using CPTs derived from our own domain expertise. We observe that the system does adjust the CPTs somewhat, but does not choose to add more hypotheses when running in this fashion. From this, we tentatively conclude that no more than 12 hypotheses are needed to classify these data.

Our next experiment examined the other extreme. We initialized the system with a single valid hypothesis and a dummy hypothesis at the root node. We then presented a week of normal (attack-free) data, and the system generated two valid states. As these states were generated, the CPTs were adjusted according to the procedure previously outlined. We then arbitrarily decided that any new states learned would be reported as potential attacks, and presented data known to contain attacks. The system added 2 new states, which captured the attacks seen previously by the 11-state expert-specified model. There were a few false alarms, but well under the Lincoln Laboratory guideline of 10 per day for operational usefulness. Therefore, with the capabilities of adaptation via reinforcement as well as state space expansion described above, it is in fact possible to start the system with essentially no initial knowledge. It then organizes to an appropriate number of hypotheses and CPT values. Interestingly, this system does nearly as well at separating the important classes (here, attack versus nonattack) as the expert-specified model with only 4 root node hypothesis states. Normal data is adequately represented by two states, and the variety of attack data by two abnormal states. While this does tend to separate important normal and attack classes into separate hypotheses, explaining the result is more difficult. Nonetheless, this minimal knowledge approach does remarkably well, and is a very favorable indicator of the generalization potential of our methodology.

In between inference steps, the belief state over session class passes through a Markov transition model, so as to yield a pre-observation belief state immediately before the next inference step. The following sections provide more detailed discussion of the observables used, the state transition, and the Bayes update mechanism.

6   State Transition

As a simplifying assumption, the states observed for the respective variables are considered to be independent of what was observed for these variables in past inference intervals, given the session class. In addition, given the value of the session class in the current interval, X is independent of any other observable variable Y. In other words, for all observable variables X, Y and inference intervals 0 to k, we have

$$P(X_k = x | Sess\_class_k = s, X_{k-1}...X_0, Y_{k-1}...Y_0) = P(X_k = x | Sess\_class_k = s)$$

The evolution of session class over inference intervals is modeled as a discrete time-and-state Markov process. The transition matrix is a convex combination of an identity matrix (to express state persistence) and a matrix whose rows are all equal to some prior distribution over the possible values of session class (to express the tendency of the process to decay to some prior state). In other words, for some $0 \leq \gamma \leq 1$, the transition matrix M is given by

$$M = \gamma I + (1 - \gamma)P$$

where I is an identity matrix and each row of P is given by

$$P_{i,.} = \text{PRIOR}$$

and PRIOR is a prior distribution over possible values j for session class, that is,

$$\text{PRIOR}_j = \text{Prior probability}(Sess\_class = j)$$

M_{ij} is the probability that if the process is currently in state i it will be in state j at the next event. More generally, if POST_BEL is our current belief state (a distribution over the possible state values, given the evidence up to and including this time interval), left multiplication with M redistributes our belief to obtain the prior belief before the next observation:

$$\text{PRE\_BEL}_k = \text{POST\_BEL}_{k-1}M$$

We manipulate the parameter γ to capture, albeit imperfectly, the continuous nature of the underlying process. We typically invoke the inference function every 100 events within a session, and always when the session enters the idle state. Some sessions are less than 100 events in total, while others (particularly many denial-of-service attacks) consist of tens of thousands of events in a very short time interval. In the latter case, even though many inference steps are invoked, we prefer to have a moderately high persistence parameter (about 0.75) because very little time has elapsed. If the parameter is 0, the belief reverts to the prior at each event.

It can be shown that, unless γ is unity, iteratively multiplying M by itself results in a matrix that approaches P, that is,

$$lim_{n\to\infty}M^n = P$$

In practice, this limit is nearly reached for fairly small values of n. The result of this observation is attractive from the intuitive standpoint: in the absence of reinforcing evidence from subsequent events, the belief distribution tends to revert to the prior.

The inference operation at interval k begins by setting the Bayes π message to PRE_BEL$_k$. Then the observables over the interval are presented to the leaf nodes, and the belief state at the root node is extracted. If this is deemed sufficiently suspicious, alert messages are written both to an alert log and in IDIP format.

7   Results

7.1   Lincoln Laboratory 1999 Evaluation Study

We have run our model against the TCP dump data from the 1999 Lincoln Laboratory IDEVAL data sets [7]. It is highly effective against floods and nonstealthy probe attacks, and moderately effective against stealthy probe attacks.

This data simulates activity at a medium-size LAN with typical firewalls and gateways. Traffic generators simulate typical volume and variety of background traffic, both intra-LAN and across the gateway. Attack scripts of known types are executed at known times, and the traffic (a mix of normal background as well as attack) is collected by standard utilities, such as TCPDUMP.

For this prototype we examined external to internal traffic using the TCP/IP protocol. This means that console attacks, insider attacks, and attacks exploiting other protocols such as IDP and UDP are invisible. These are not theoretical limitations of eBayes, and we intend to include the UDP protocol in the near future. However, this did limit attacks that were visible to the system. The fourth week of the data set was considered the most difficult, as it contained the most stealthy attacks. We detected three visible portsweeps and missed one that accessed 3 ports over 4 minutes with no errors. All of the portsweeps in this data set are stealthy by the standards of the Lincoln training data and the week 5 data (we detect 100nonstealthy sweeps). A Satan attack and a TCPRESET attack are also detected as portsweeps. This particular Satan attack was run in a mode where it in fact is characteristic of a portsweep. For the TCPRESET, the portsweep hypothesis slightly edges out the OTHER hypothesis. Other detected attacks in this data include MAILBOMB and PROCESS TABLE (both 100as three password-guessing attacks (one detected as OTHER, two as DICTIONARY). The latter three detections demonstrate the power of the approach. They were not in the set of attacks that Lincoln thought should be detected by this sensor, so we initially considered them false alarms. Further review of the full attack list indicated that they were in fact good detections, even though at that time we had no DICTIONARY hypothesis and they were called OTHER. By elucidating characteristics of these attacks, we added the DICTIONARY hypothesis (indicative of password guessing), which now captures two of these attacks and is a close second to OTHER as a classification for the third. Also, one of these attacks was detected first by probabilistic methods (eStat and later eBayes) because the eXpert sensors had no signature for it. This signature has now been added, but the generalization potential of probabilistic detection is nonetheless clear.

7.2   Real-World Experience

We have eBayes-TCP active on our own TCP gateway, and it has proved to be stable for indefinite periods of time. The TCP event generator, EMONTCP, and Bayes inference components require about 15M on a Free BSD platform, and never use more than a few percent of the CPU. For real-world traffic, we of course have no ground truth, but the results have nonetheless proved interesting to us in the sense of scientific experimentation, as well as being of practical interest to our system administrators.

Our initial observation was that, not surprisingly, real-world data contains many failure modes not seen in a set such as the IDEVAL data described above. For example, we regularly observe a pattern of http sessions of moderate or long duration in which a significant number of connections terminate abnormally, but on such a time scale and in such modes that we are fairly certain they are not malicious. To capture these sessions, we decided to add the HTTP_F hypothesis (for failed http). This reduced the alert volume to a manageable

15 or so per day. A representative two-week period comprised about 470,000 connection events, grouped by the session model into about 60,000 sessions of which 222 produced alerts. It is important to point out that many of these are almost certainly attacks, consisting of IP and probe sweeps and some attempted denials of service. Some of the false alert mechanisms are understood and we are actively working to improve system response to these without being too specific (for example, ignoring alerts involving port 113 requests, which are screened in our environment but will be seen from normal mail clients).

7.3   The Utility of Learning

The learning procedures described above have proven useful in our experimentation, guiding us both in refinement of existing hypotheses as well as developing new hypotheses for both normal and attack modalities. However, we have observed better operation if the adaptive capability is disabled, for several reasons. First, attacks and alert-worthy events are a very small fraction of total traffic in a real-world setting, so that learning an attack modality that may only be seen once is problematic. Second, we found that the normal hypotheses become "hardened" so as to be relatively intolerant of erroneous outcomes. The fraction of such outcomes for non-malicious reasons is too high to be tolerable from an alert standpoint, but is too low to permit sufficient "breathing room" if adaptation is permitted indefinitely. For the present, therefore, we run the system in adaptive mode to identify un-anticipated modalities and large CPT deviations from what is observed in true traffic. We then take the results of this phase and moderate it with our judgement (sanding the corners off very hardened hypotheses, so to speak) and arrive at a batch specification of the CPT. We then verify that this new encoding remains sensitive against simulated datasets (such as the Lincoln data). At present, we detect the most attacks we have ever detected in the Lincoln data, and detect alert-worthy events in our real-world data with an acceptable level of apparent false alerts.

8   Summary

We have described the eBayes monitoring capability, which employs Bayesian inference steps with transition models between inference to assess whether a particular burst of traffic contains an attack. A coupled component monitors availability of valid services, which are themselves learned via unsupervised discovery.

The efficacy of this system was demonstrated by results from the Lincoln Laboratory Intrusion Detection Evaluation data, and also by a live operation on a real-world site for weeks at a time.

This provides us with several important new capabilities:

- Probabilistic encoding of attack models provides a complementary capability to anomaly detection and signature analysis, retaining the generalization potential of the former and the sensitivity and specificity of the latter.

- We now potentially detect distributed attacks in which none of the attack sessions are individually suspicious enough to generate an alert. This comprises correlation by aggregation.
- Once a successful denial of service has taken place, we are much less likely to generate false alerts for nonmalicious clients requesting the service during the attack (we refer to these clients as "collateral damage"). This form of correlation fuses the belief that an attack is in progress with the symptom of the attack (the service is disabled when the attack achieves its objectives) to explain away subsequent alerts from "collateral damage" sessions. As such, the system correlating symptoms and attacks provides effective false alarm reduction, while still providing the administrator with an alert for the original attack as well as an indication of the status of the victim host/port.

We continuously run this system along with our TCP session monitor on our own TCP gateway. While we do not have ground truth for this traffic, we regularly identify probe attacks and "spidering" activity, as well as the occasional DOS attempt. We also detect service outages and recovery for what appear to be nonmalicious faults.

Acknowledgements

This research was sponsored by DARPA under contract number F30602-99-C-1049. The views herein are those of the author(s) and do not necessarily reflect the views of the supporting agency.

References

1. Porras, P. and Neumann, P. "EMERALD: Event Monitoring Enabling Responses to Anomalous Live Distrurbances", National Information Security Conference, 1997. http://www.sdl.sri.com/emerald/emerald-niss97.html 80
2. Valdes, A. and Anderson, D. "Statistical Methods for Computer Usage Anomaly Detection", Third International Workshop on Rough Sets and Soft Computing, San Jose, CA, 1995. 80
3. P. A. Porras and A. Valdes. Live traffic analysis of TCP/IP gateways. In Proceedings of the Symposium on Network and Distributed System Security. Internet Society, March 1998. 80
4. Pearl, J. "Probabilistic Reasoning in Intelligent Systems", Morgan-Kaufman (1988). 80, 81
5. Boyen, X. and Koller, D. "Tractable Inference for Complex Stochastic Processes", Proceedings of the 14th Annual Conference on Uncertainty in Artificial Intelligence (UAI-98), Madison, WI, July 1998. http://robotics.Stanford.EDU/ xb/uai98/index.html 80
6. Skinner, K. and Valdes, A. "EMERALD™ TCP Statistical Analyzer 1998 Evaluation Results", http://www.sdl.sri.com/emerald/98-eval-estat/index.html 80
7. Lippmann, Richard P, et al. "Evaluating Intrusion Detection Systems: The 1998 DARPA Off-Line Intrusion Detection Evaluation," Proceedings of DARPA Information Survivability Conference and Exposition, DISCEX'00, Jan 25-27, Hilton Head, SC, 2000, http://www.ll.mit.edu/IST/ideval/index.html 81, 89

A Real-Time Intrusion Detection System Based on Learning Program Behavior

Anup K. Ghosh, Christoph Michael, and Michael Schatz

Reliable Software Technologies
21351 Ridgetop Circle, #400, Dulles, VA 20166 USA
{aghosh,ccmich,mschatz}@rstcorp.com
http://www.rstcorp.com

Abstract. In practice, most computer intrusions begin by misusing programs in clever ways to obtain unauthorized higher levels of privilege. One effective way to detect intrusive activity before system damage is perpetrated is to detect misuse of privileged programs in real-time. In this paper, we describe three machine learning algorithms that learn the normal behavior of programs running on the Solaris platform in order to detect unusual uses or misuses of these programs. The performance of the three algorithms has been evaluated by an independent laboratory in an off-line controlled evaluation against a set of computer intrusions and normal usage to determine rates of correct detection and false alarms. A real-time system has since been developed that will enable deployment of a program-based intrusion detection system in a real installation.

1   Introduction

Today, most commercial intrusion detection systems monitor network packets for unusual patterns, or patterns of known suspicious actions. Recent advances in high bandwidth local area networks have presented significant challenges to performing network monitoring in real-time. In addition, as end-to-end encryption protocols are adopted enterprise wide, many of today's network-based intrusion detection systems will be rendered obsolete.

Host-based intrusion detection systems attempt to detect computer intrusions by monitoring audit trails created on host computer systems. Many modern day operating systems provide audit trails for processes that run on the machine. On the Solaris platform, the Basic Security Module (BSM) provides a configurable audit manager that facilitates recording system events requested by executing processes.

We leverage this audit reporting mechanism in this research. The motivation for our work is that a large class of computer intrusions involves program misuse. Most program misuse attacks exploit privileged programs in clever ways in order to gain unauthorized privileges that are subsequently used to commit malicious acts of sabotage or data theft. Buffer overrun attacks are the most frequent form of program misuse attacks. Other types of program misuse attacks include using

H. Debar, L. Mé, and F. Wu (Eds.): RAID 2000, LNCS 1907, pp. 93–109, 2000.

rarely used features (such as debug features), exploiting race conditions, and triggering Trojan horse functionality in order to gain higher privileges.

When a program is misused, its behavior will differ from its normal usage. Therefore, if the normal range of program behavior can be adequately and compactly represented, then behavioral features captured by audit mechanisms can be used for intrusion detection.

A well-recognized failing of today's commercial intrusion detection systems is that they cannot detect novel attacks against systems, and they often fail to detect variations of known attacks. The reason is that most commercial intrusion detection systems detect attacks by matching audit events against well-known patterns of attacks. This approach is known as signature-based detection. The problem with a signature-based detection approach is that it is reactive by nature. Once a new form of intrusion is developed, it is often perpetrated against many systems before its signature is captured, codified, and disseminated to individual detection sensors. In a worm-type of infection, millions of machines can potentially be compromised before a signature-based system can be upgraded with the appropriate signature.

To detect novel attacks against systems, we develop anomaly-based systems that report any unusual use of system programs as potential intrusions. The advantage of this approach is that both known attacks and novel attacks are detected. The disadvantage is that if the training mechanism for the detection sensor is not robust, a large number of false alarms may be reported. In other words, perfectly legitimate behavior may be reported as intrusions.

Another large challenge in intrusion detection is to generalize from previously observed behavior (normal or malicious) to recognize similar future behavior. This problem is acute for signature-based misuse detection approaches, but also plagues anomaly detection approaches that must be able to recognize future normal behavior that is not identical to past observed behavior, in order to reduce false positive rates.

In the research reported here, we address both challenges: detecting novel attacks as well as generalizing from previously observed behavior in order to reduce the false positive rate to acceptable levels from an administration standpoint.

We develop an anomaly detection system that uses machine learning automata to learn the normal behavior for programs. The trained automata are then used to detect possibly intrusive behavior by identifying significant anomalies in program behavior. The goal of these approaches is to be able to detect not only known attacks and but also detect future novel attacks using off-the-shelf auditing mechanisms provided by the operating system vendor.

We develop three algorithms for learning program behavior profiles and detecting significant deviations from these profiles. The algorithms were evaluated by an independent laboratory in a controlled off-line experiment to determine their effectiveness against program misuse attacks. The performance of the algorithms is presented as a measure of the probability of correct detection against the probability of false alarm.

Finally, in Section 5, we describe a real-time system that implements one of the learning algorithms to detect intrusions in real-time.

2 Related Work

Analyzing program behavior profiles for intrusion detection has recently emerged as a viable alternative to user-based approaches to intrusion detection (see [11, 18, 14, 6, 4, 7, 16, 2] for other program-based approaches). Program behavior profiles are typically built by capturing system calls made by the program under analysis under normal operational conditions. If the captured behavior represents a compact and adequate signature of normal behavior, then the profile can be used to detect deviations from normal behavior such as those that occur when a program is being misused for intrusion.

For a detailed comparison of our general approach to program-based intrusion detection with those of others in this area, please see [10].

3 Three Machine Learning Algorithms for Anomaly Detection

As described in the introduction, we are interested in detecting novel attacks against systems by detecting deviations from normal program behavior. To this end, we have developed three machine learning algorithms to train automata to learn a programs' normal behavior. The trained program automata are subsequently used to detect program misuse. The three algorithms are: an Elman recurrent artificial neural network, a string transducer, and a finite state tester. Each algorithm is described next.

3.1 Elman Recurrent Neural Network

The goal in using artificial neural networks (ANNs) for anomaly detection is to be able to generalize from incomplete data and to be able to classify online data as being normal or intrusive. An artificial neural network is composed of simple processing units, or *nodes*, and connections between them. The connection between any two units has some *weight*, which is used to determine how much one unit will affect the other. A subset of the units of the network acts as *input nodes*, and another subset acts as *output nodes*. By assigning a value, or *activation*, to each input node, and allowing the activations to propagate through the network, a neural network performs a functional mapping from one set of values (assigned to the input nodes) to another set of values (retrieved from the output nodes). The mapping itself is stored in the weights of the network.

We originally employed ANNs because of their ability to *learn* and *generalize*. Through the learning process, ANNs develop the ability to classify inputs from exposure to a set of *training inputs* and application of well defined *learning rules*, rather than through an explicit human-supplied enumeration of classification rules. Because of their ability to generalize, ANNs can produce reasonable

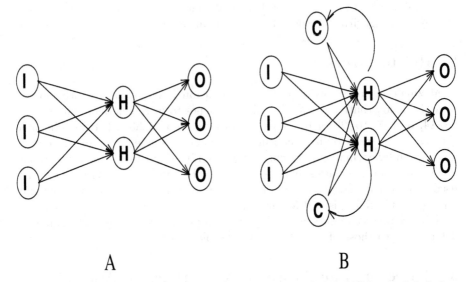

A   B

Fig. 1. In each of the examples above, the nodes of the ANNs are labeled as input nodes (*I*), hidden nodes (*H*), output nodes (*O*), or context nodes (*C*). Each arc is unidirectional, with direction indicated by the arrow at the end of the arc. A) A standard feed-forward topology. B) An Elman network

classifications for novel inputs (assuming the network has been trained well). Further, since the inputs to any node of the ANN used for this work could be any real-valued number, no sequence of BSM events could produce an encoding that would fall outside of the domain representable by the ANN.

In order to maintain state information between inputs, we require a recurrent ANN topology. A recurrent topology (as opposed to a purely feed-forward topology) is one in which cycles are formed by the connections. The cycles act as delay loops—causing information to be retained indefinitely. New input interacts with the cycles, affecting both the activations propagating through the network and the activations in the cycle. Thus, the input can affect the state, and the state can affect the classification of any input.

One well known recurrent topology is that of an Elman network, developed by Jeffrey Elman [5]. An Elman network is illustrated in Figure 1. The Elman topology is based on a feed-forward topology—it has an *input layer*, an *output layer*, and one or more *hidden layers*. Additionally, an Elman network has a set of *context nodes*. Each context node receives input from a single hidden node and sends its output to each node in the layer of its corresponding hidden node. Since the context nodes depend only on the activations of the hidden nodes from the previous input, the context nodes retain state information between inputs.

We employ Elman nets to perform classification of short sequences of events as they occur in a larger stream of events. Therefore, we train our Elman networks to *predict* the next sequence that will occur at any point in time. The *n*th input, I_n, is presented to the network to produce some output, O_n. The output O_n is then compared to I_{n+1}. The difference between O_n and I_{n+1} (that is, the sum of the absolute values of the differences of the corresponding elements of O_n and I_{n+1}) is the measure of anomaly of each sequence of events. Or, in other words, the anomaly measure is the error in predicting the next input in sequence. The classification of a sequence of events will now be affected by events prior to the earliest event occurring within the sequence.

3.2   String Transducer

A string transducer is an algorithm that associates a sequence of input symbols with a series of output symbols. String transducers are most often used in computational biology and computational linguistics, where they are usually implemented using finite automata whose transitions or states are associated with output symbols. In the current context, we use automata as well, but the input sequence is a string of BSM events, and the output sequence is a prediction for the next several events.

Our use of string transducers as intrusion detectors is based on an examination of the *probabilities* of the output symbols at each state. During training, we estimate the probability distribution of the symbols at each state, and during testing, deviations from this probability distribution are taken as evidence of anomalous behavior.

Our implementation of this idea is relatively simple. We use a finite automaton whose states correspond to n-grams in the BSM data, and the output symbols associated with each state are also BSM ℓ-grams (for $\ell < n$). More specifically, the output symbol represents sets of ℓ BSM events that may be seen when the automaton is in a given state. During training, our goal is to gather statistics about these successor ℓ-grams; we estimate the probability of each ℓ-gram by counting.

During actual intrusion detection, the deviation of the successor ℓ-grams from their expected values are used for anomaly scores. Of course, the anomaly scores are usually non-zero, but if the program is behaving normally these deviations should average out over time.

In the ideal case, it can be shown that the anomaly scores are uncorrelated if the probability distributions have, in fact, been correctly estimated (this is due to the fact that the deviations are then an innovations process; see [1]). That means that if we subtract the mean anomaly score for each state from the actual anomaly scores generated there, the result is zero-mean white noise.

If these values are integrated over a sufficiently long period, the result should be close to zero if the program is behaving normally. However, if abnormal program behavior results in a significant deviation of the successor ℓ-grams from their expected values, then the resulting scores will not integrate to zero, and this fact can be used to detect anomalous behavior.

In practice, there are obviously a number of factors preventing the realization of this ideal case:

1. If the probabilities of the successor ℓ-grams have not been correctly estimated, then the deviations may not be uncorrelated.
2. During detection, n-grams may be encountered that do not correspond to any known state because they were not seen during training.
3. An intrusion may not result in a systematic deviation from the expected ℓ-gram values; in other words, the intrusion may look normal. Although this seems unlikely, we cannot prove that all intrusions really cause the necessary deviations.
4. The window of integration needed to get sufficiently low anomaly scores during normal behavior may be large. This delays the detection of anomalies (though if it prevented them from being detected we would arguably be in case 3).

The fourth is an intrinsic problem of change detection [15]; there is an inevitable tradeoff between the time to detection and the susceptibility to false positives. The third problem is also, in some sense, unavoidable; it seems unlikely that we could guarantee the detection of all intrusions without assuming something about the nature of those intrusions, which is contrary to our assumptions. (We may, of course, be able to make guarantees for certain classes of intrusions).

The second problem cited above is more directly related to our specific application. It results from having too little training data to characterize all states. It dictates that states should not be too highly specialized, since such specialization makes it less likely for all states to be seen during training.

The first problem dictates a wise choice of states. For example, it has been observed that programs go through different phases of behavior [3], so the probability of a given ℓ-gram may depend on how far along the program is in its execution. Thus, states should reflect the state of the program itself. Even if the distribution of ℓ-grams varies over time, the distribution *from a given state* should be constant. Unfortunately, this condition can be best achieved by using highly specialized states to avoid having two or more states of the underlying program represented by a single state of the automaton. Thus, the solutions to the first and second problems are in some sense at odds. This tradeoff between expressiveness and ease of training is also well-known in machine learning [19].

As we have said, the probability densities of the successor ℓ-grams in a given state are estimated by counting (that is, we simply count the number of occurrences of each ℓ-gram in the training data). This approach is feasible with BSM data because it tends to be fairly regular; the number of BSM ℓ-grams is much smaller than, say, the number of possible BSM events raised to the ℓth power.

We measure deviations from expected behavior by treating the estimated probability distribution as a vector, which we first normalize with respect to the L_k metric,

$$\left| \sum_i x_i^k \right|^{1/k},$$

for some k. When a given ℓ-gram occurs during detection, we treat it as a vector with a 1 in the position corresponding to the actual ℓ-grams that were seen, and a 0 in the other positions. The deviation is proportional to the L_k distance between this vector and the normalized density vector. In other words, if $\hat{p}_i$ is the estimated probability of the ith ℓ-gram, according to some arbitrary ordering, then the elements of the normalized probability vector are given by

$$h_i = \frac{\hat{p}_i}{\left| \sum_j \hat{p}_j^k \right|^{1/k}},$$

and the deviation d_i, reported when the ith ℓ-gram is seen during detection, is given by

$$d_i = 2^{-1/k} \left(\sum_j c_{i,j}^k \right)^{1/k}$$

where

$$c_{i,j} = \begin{cases} 1 - h_j, & \text{if } i = j; \\ h_j, & \text{otherwise.} \end{cases}$$

We treat these as summations over all possible ℓ-grams, though the actual implementation only has to sum over those that were seen during training since p_j is zero for the others. But if a novel ℓ-gram is seen during testing, this convention assures that d_i is still defined, and, in fact, its value is just 1.

3.3 State Tester

The goal of the third algorithm, we call simply a state tester, is to automatically create finite automata to represent program behavior. Since data representing intrusive behavior is not used during training, the first goal is simply to build a finite automaton that accepts all audit sequences in the training data, but without being so generous that it accepts *all* data, or being so rigid that it rejects every novel audit sequence after training.

In [13], finite automata (FA) of this kind were generated largely by hand. First, the BSM data was pre-processed so that commonly occurring sequences of events could be combined into a single meta-event. Then, the meta-events were encoded as an FA. The combination of events into meta-events, called *macros* in that paper, was done manually, and though the paper does not say whether the FAs were then also created by hand, it is implied that they were.

Our approach is to automate the process of inferring finite automata. Something along these lines is done in [3], where training data is used to learn hidden Markov models of normal program behavior. This technique proved effective at the task of intrusion detection, but training (using the Baum-Welch algorithm, see [17]) was found to be expensive. This raises the question of whether simpler algorithms that only infer an FA, and not the transition probabilities associated with a Markov model, might also be effective without requiring as much training.

Below, we present an algorithm for automatically constructing finite automata from training data. In this context, it should be noted that the inference of finite automata is not intractable, although the automatic inference of finite automata *is* intractable in a number of other settings (C.f., [12, 9]). What makes the problem tractable in the case of anomaly detection is that the requirements are simple. The finite automaton merely has to accept any training sequence that is not abnormal. Of course, it should also reject abnormal BSM sequences, but since there are no abnormal BSM sequences in the training data this requirement cannot be formalized within the learning algorithm itself. Rather, we will evaluate the performance of the FAs empirically.

By way of example, we could create an FA with a single state, where every BSM event results in a transition from that state back to itself. We could also create an FA with no cycles that accepts exactly the BSM sequences occurring in the training data.

The first approach is too weak because it tends to accept *any* sequence of BSM events, and thus fails to notice abnormal BSM sequences. The second approach is probably too strong, because it rejects any sequence as being abnormal unless exactly the same sequence was seen during training. Our goal is to create a reasonably expressive FA, but one that can still generalize. Of course, this is a qualitative requirement.

The first issue is how to define the states of the automaton. The technique reported in this paper associates each state with one or more n-grams of BSM data, where n is a parameter of the learning algorithm. For example, the FA might have a state corresponding to the event sequence lstat, open, ioctl, and enter that state whenever the sequence lstat, open, ioctl is seen. The idea, however, is to be parsimonious in the creation of new states, and not simply have one state in the FA for every n-gram of BSM events. Instead, we will have more than one n-gram assigned to most of the states.

During training, separate automata are created for the different programs whose audit data are available for training. As with the intrusion detection systems of [8], the training algorithm is presented with a series of n-grams taken from non-intrusive BSM data for a given program. Conceptually, the goal of the automaton is to predict the entire n-gram based on the automaton's current state and on the first ℓ audit events in the n-gram, $\ell < n$.

The FA's transitions correspond to specific sequences of ℓ audit events, and each state corresponds to one or more n-grams. We say that the FA predicts an n-gram G if there is a transition from the current state to the state corresponding to G, and if that transition is labeled with the first ℓ elements of G. Thus, the automaton predicts a set of states, and these states are simply the ones reachable by transitions labeled with the first ℓ elements of G. If this set is empty (*e.g.*, there is no transition labeled with the first ℓ elements of G) then we say that the FA makes no prediction at all. Otherwise, a *prediction error* occurs if the predicted set of states does not contain the one associated with G.

During training, an incorrect prediction results in the creation of a new transition and possibly a new state. The training algorithm starts with an FA having a single state and no transitions. We say that the FA is initially in this state. Whenever a new training n-gram is seen, there are three possibilities:

1. The current state has an outgoing edge that corresponds to the first ℓ events in the n-gram, and that edge leads to the correct state (the correct state is the state that is assigned to the newly obtained n-gram). In this case, the FA needs no modifications.
2. The current state has outgoing edges that correspond to the first ℓ events in the n-gram, but none of the edges lead to the correct state. In this case, the FA may contain a correct state (but no edge from the current state to the desired state), or else the FA may not even have any state assigned to the new n-gram.

   We simply create a state for the new n-gram if one doesn't already exist. In either case, we create a transition from the current state to the new state, and label that transition with the first ℓ events of the new n-gram (recall that we will use these ℓ events when trying to make future predictions).
3. The current state has no outgoing edges that correspond to the first ℓ events in the newly obtained n-gram. If there is already a state assigned to the newly obtained n-gram, then we simply create a transition to that state, and label it with the ℓ events as in the previous case.

   However, if the new n-gram doesn't have any state assigned to it, we can assign any one of the already existing states, or create a new state, without introducing any prediction errors. Currently, the algorithm just creates a transition back to the current state, and assigns the new n-gram to the current state (where it joins whatever n-grams were assigned to that state previously).

In all three cases, the FA transitions to the state assigned to the new n-gram.

4   Performance of Algorithms

The three algorithms described in the preceding section were implemented and evaluated by an independent laboratory, Lincoln Laboratory of the Massachusetts Institute of Technology, in the 1999 U.S. Defense Advanced Research Projects Agency (DARPA) Intrusion Detection Evaluation. The full extent of the experimental setup, the data, the participants, system descriptions, full attack descriptions, raw scores, and results are available online at the Lincoln Laboratory's Intrusion Detection Evaluation page (http://ideval.ll.mit.edu). In this section, we summarize the results of our systems.

Lincoln established four categories of attacks: Denial of Service (DoS), probe, remote-to-local (R2L), and user-to-root (U2R). Within these categories they ran several select instances of attacks. Lincoln does not claim these attacks are comprehensive of the category of attacks. Rather, the attacks can be considered as samples from the attack space within a category. DoS and probe attacks were network-based attacks that leave traces in network packet data. Remote-to-local attacks involved network-based attacks again, but also included some attacks that attempted to misuse host-based programs. User-to-root attacks attempt to gain super user privileges on the host machine either by misusing programs or by running malicious software.

While our approach is not exclusive to any single category of attacks as partitioned by Lincoln, our approach is best suited to detect user-to-root attacks according to the Lincoln partitions. Our approach will detect program misuse attacks regardless of which of the four Lincoln categories the attacks falls in, as long as the attack leaves some trace in the audit data we use. In addition to the user-to-root attacks, a few instances of the remote-to-local attacks involved program misuse. So, we also include results from detecting remote-to-local attacks in this section.

Table 1. List of programs monitored by intrusion detection automata

admintool	dhcpcd	kswapd	ping	sperl5.00404	wu.ftpd
allocate	dos	list_devices	procmail	ssh1	xlock
aspppd	eject	lockd	ps	sshd	xscreensaver
at	exrecover	login	pt_chmod	su	xterm
atd	fdformat	lpd	pwdb_chkpwd	suidperl	Xwrapper
atq	ff.core	lpq	rcp	syslogd	ypbind
atrm	ffbconfig	lpr	rdist	tcpd	yppasswd
auditd	fsflush	lprm	rdistd	timed	zgv
automountd	gpasswd	m64config	rlogin	traceroute	
cardctl	gpm	mingetty	routed	umount	
chage	hpnpd	mkdevalloc	rpcbind	uptime	
chfn	untd	mkdevmaps	rpciod	userhelper	
chkey	in.*	mount	rpld	usernetctl	
chsh	inetd	newgrp	rsh	utmp_update	
cron	kcms_calibrate	nispasswd	rusersd	utmpd	
crond	kcms_configure	nmbd	rwhod	uu.*	
crontab	kerbd	nscd	sacadm	volcheck	
ct	kerneld	nxterm	sadmind	vold	
cu	kflushd	pageout	sendmail	w	
deallocate	klogd	passwd	smbd	whodo	

Since our approach involves training program monitors, we must first choose which programs to monitor. Most attacks, in practice, are launched against privileged programs on network servers. So, our rule was to train program monitors on SUID root programs that run on Unix servers. Table 1 lists the programs we monitor for intrusions and also represents a superset of program monitors run against the Lincoln Laboratory data because not all programs in Table 1 are exercised by the Lincoln data.

4.1   Performance of Elman Networks

Figure 2 shows the performance of the Elman networks on the BSM data against both U2R (Figure 2(a)) and R2L (Figure 2(b)) attacks. The plots are called Detection/False Alarm plots by Lincoln Laboratory. The plot shows the probability

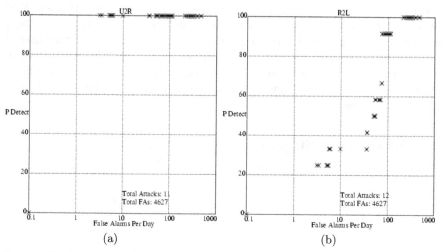

Fig. 2. Performance of Elman networks on BSM data against User-to-Root (U2R) and remote-to-local (R2L) attacks

of correct detection versus the false alarm rate per day. Examining the user-to-root attacks first, it becomes clear that the Elman networks performed very well against this class of attacks. The Elman networks achieved 100% detection of attacks very quickly at a false alarm rate of close to 3 per day. This false alarm rate is considered acceptable in an operational environment and is vastly superior to current commercial tools.

A closer examination of the attacks showed that the vast majority of them involved program misuse types of attacks such as buffer overrun attacks. However, our technique is not limited to buffer overrun attacks. Rather the approach is designed detect any program misuse attack. It turns out that the sample U2R attacks chosen by Lincoln were all buffer overrun attacks. As more different types of program misuse attacks are captured in evaluation sets, we will be able to verify this claim in the future.

The performance of the Elman networks against Lincoln's remote-to-local attacks was not nearly as good, as shown in Figure 2(b). At a rate of approximately 10 false alarms per day, we detected roughly 30 percent of R2L attacks. If you are willing to accept a false alarm rate of up to 100 per day, the correct detection rate goes over 90 percent. However, operationally speaking, that false alarm rate is not acceptable.

In the 1999 evaluation, the R2L attacks run by Lincoln by-and-large did not involve program misuse. Thus, most of these attacks fall outside the scope of our approach. For example, the `guessftp`, `ftpwrite`, and `guest` R2L attacks all involve using the legitimate protocol to either guess passwords or write files (when the program was configured to do so).

Other remote-to-local attacks involved malicious clients acting on behalf of an outside perpetrator. Since we only monitor programs we know about, we do not detect malicious programs. However, our technique can detect intrusions that may have been precursors to installing malicious clients. In summary, attacks that involve programs we do not monitor or attacks that involve normal uses of programs fall outside the scope of our detection mechanism. The reason we did end up detecting them at all (even at a high false alarm rate) is that side effects from the intrusion tend to show up in other programs we monitor, albeit at a high false alarm rate.

4.2   Performance of String Transducer

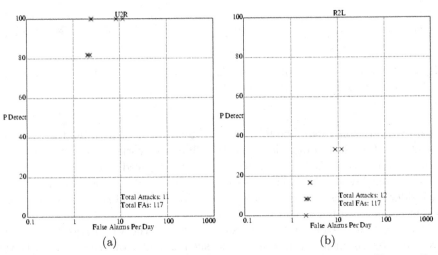

Fig. 3. Performance of string transducer on BSM data against User-to-Root (U2R) and remote-to-local (R2L) attacks

Figure 3 shows the performance of the string transducer against U2R and R2L attacks. The performance of the string transducer is very close to that of the Elman network. At a rate of about 3 false positives a day we detected 100% of the user-to-root attacks. What is most significant about this result, however, is that since the training time for the string transducer is orders of magnitude less than that of the Elman neural network, we can achieve comparable detection performance with significantly less training time. Where training the Elman nets takes on the order of thousands of minutes for all the programs monitored, training the string transducer and the state tester takes on the order of tens of minutes.

Again, the performance against the R2L attacks was not very good for the same reasons. At the same false positive rate we detected about 15% of the remote-to-local attacks. If you raise the false positive rate to about 9 false positives a day we detected about 35% of the remote-to-local attacks. The reasons

why our string transducer failed to detect many R2L attacks is the same as in
the Elman network: most of the R2L attacks launched by Lincoln Laboratory
did not misuse programs, or they involved malicious clients.

4.3 Performance of State Tester

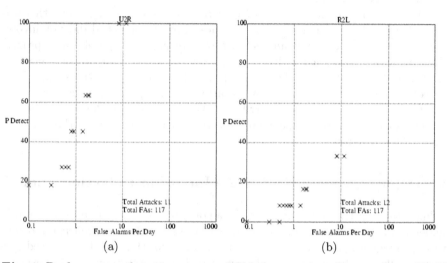

(a)

(b)

Fig. 4. Performance of state tester on BSM data against User-to-Root (U2R)
and remote-to-local (R2L) attacks

   The performance of the state tester is shown in Figure 4. At a rate of about
9 false positives a day we detected 100% of the user-to-root attacks. Figure 4a
shows a more gradual progression towards 100 percent detection, compared to
Figure 2a, whose progression looks more like a unit step function. The upshot
is that with the state tester, one can tune the performance of the system more
easily to meet the acceptable detection requirements within the organization's
tolerance to false alarms. On the other hand, the performance of the Elman
network indicates, more or less, all-or-nothing detection, which does not leave
much to tune. However, it is important not to over generalize, as the results may
vary from experiment to experiment depending on the attacks launched and the
training data.
   At a false alarm rate of about 9 per day, we detected about 35% of the remote-
to-local attacks. While the state tester did not perform as well as the Elman
networks or the string transducer, its performance is still good, nonetheless, by
existing commercial standards. The reason we believe the state tester had a
higher false alarm rate is because the likelihood of falling off the deterministic
automata is greater than for the string transducer or the Elman neural network.
We believe, though, that its performance can be improved with more robust
training data.

Overall, the performance of our systems on user-to-root attacks is good, roughly 100 percent detection at a rate of less than 10 false positives per day. Two of our systems, the Elman neural network and the string transducer, were able to detect all user-to-root attacks with fewer than four false alarms per day. This, combined with the fact that our systems can be trained in much less time than it takes to configure a rule-based intrusion detection system, makes our approach very promising.

Our systems did not fare as well on remote-to-local attacks, but this was because many of the remote-to-local attacks Lincoln launched did not involve program misuse. Thus, not all such attacks are in the scope of our approach. Conversely, our approach will be able to detect attacks that fall in other categories, so long as the attacks involve program misuse. Thus, the scope of our detection has more to do with how an attack affects program behavior then it has to do with other types of attributes. While we do not claim to detect all attacks, we do claim the scope of our detection mechanism to cover those attacks that misuse programs.

5   Implementing a Real-Time Intrusion Detection Tool

While, studying the performance of the algorithms off-line is a necessary step to understand the strengths and limitations of the algorithms, we felt it important to implement a real-time intrusion detection system that can be deployed in a real installation. In order to implement a real-time prototype, we performed a feasibility study, determined how to collect audit data in a real-time, modified our algorithms to work in a real-time environment, then designed and implemented a working prototype. These are described briefly in this section.

The first task in creating a real-time intrusion detection tool was to make sure that our approach was actually feasible in a real-time environment. In order to work in real-time, the intrusion detection prototype should be able to process audit data that is generated by a computer under normal use, as fast, or faster than the data is being generated. We measured this by collecting a set of audit data, and then measuring how long it took us to process that data off-line.

Our first approach was to use `praudit`, the built-in Solaris utility for translating binary BSM files to a text format, to translate the collected BSM files, and perform simple processing on the result. We did this because our off-line evaluation techniques processed `praudit` format data, and not BSM files directly. Next, an example of the results from real-time processing of BSM files is presented.

Amount of data processed:

- amount of BSM data: 8,195,371 bytes
- number of events: 48,871
- time frame that BSM data was collected over: 5 minutes 3 seconds

Amount of CPU time required:

- clock time: 14 minutes 57.79 seconds
- user cpu time: 5 minutes 20.98 seconds
- system cpu time: 6 minutes 38.27 seconds

As can be seen, processing this data took longer than it took the system to create the data. The solution to this problem was to not use `praudit`, but rather to process the binary BSM data directly. When we did this, processing the above data set gave us better timing results as shown below.

Amount of data processed:

- amount of BSM data: 8,195,371 bytes
- number of events: 48,871
- time frame that BSM data was collected over: 5 minutes 3 seconds

Amount of CPU time required:

- clock time: 1 minutes 48.12 seconds
- user cpu time: 0 minutes 10.99 seconds
- system cpu time: 1 minute 36.96 seconds

These results show that our approach is feasible to be implemented in real-time.

We had to make sure our intrusion detection algorithms were amenable to a real-time domain. This meant three things. First, the algorithms had to run fast enough. Second, they had to be able to process data as it is generated, and not require all of the audit data at the same time. Third, the algorithm had to be reentrant, meaning that it had to process multiple data streams simultaneously.

We chose the Elman networks as the first intrusion detection algorithm to implement in a real-time prototype. Neural networks perform recall quickly, so the first real-time requirement was already satisfied. The way that we use the Elman nets in the off-line evaluations was to process the data in order, so it already met the second real-time requirement as well. The third requirement was not met, because our implementations of the Elman Nets were in C, which meant that only one instance would exist at a time. This was not satisfactory because in a real-time environment it is possible to have multiple copies of the same program being run at the same time, and it is important that each execution is evaluated by its own neural net. To solve this problem, we modified the Elman networks so that they were implemented as C++ objects, allowing multiple instantiations to exist simultaneously. This satisfied our third real-time requirement.

Our last step was to actually design and implement a real-time prototype. This was a straight forward software engineering task. We designed the prototype such that it is modular enough to incorporate the other intrusion detection algorithms in a plug-and-play manner. We reviewed it to make sure that it would achieve our immediate goals of having something to use for internal testing and for ease of modification.

The initial prototype has now been implemented and is in testing. A demonstration of the real-time prototype has been created as well. In the process of creating the real-time prototype, we created a library called BSMart ("be smart") to parse BSM data directly from the operating system in binary form in any number of configurable ways. Because we deem this library to be a valuable contribution to the ID community wishing to perform host-based intrusion detection on the Solaris platform, we are releasing the library in source code form to the research community. The goal is to foster research in host-based intrusion detection by eliminating obstacles (such as engineering a prototype to read BSM data directly from the platform) for other researchers. Please contact the authors for more information on how to download the library.

6   Conclusions

Most of today's commercial intrusion detection systems are designed only to detect known attacks. Because new attacks are discovered on a weekly and sometimes daily basis, we feel it is imperative that approaches to detecting novel attacks be developed. To this end, we have developed an anomaly detection approach that learns normal program behavior.

We implemented three different machine learning algorithms for the purpose of program-based intrusion detection: Elman artificial neural networks, a string transducer, and a state tester. The results from evaluating these algorithms in the 1999 Lincoln Laboratory/DARPA Intrusion Detection evaluation are summarized here. The results demonstrate that these techniques are very good at detecting user-to-root types of attacks, and program misuse attacks in general, with low false alarm rates.

We have implemented a real-time prototype that implements the Elman network. The robust real-time prototype allows for swapping in and out different ID algorithms, including the three described in this paper. We have currently released the real-time BSM parser, BSMart, for other researchers in the community. In the future, we intend to release our robust real-time prototype as well.

Acknowledgment

This work was sponsored under the Defense Advanced Research Projects Agency (DARPA) Contract DAAH01-98-C-R145. The views and conclusions contained in this document are those of the authors and should not be interpreted as representing the official policies, either expressed or implied, of the defense advanced research projects agency or the U.S. Government. We also acknowledge Aaron Schwartzbard for his contributions to this paper.

References

[1] Michèle Basseville and Igor V. Nikiforov. *Detection of Abrupt Changes - Theory and Application.* Prentice-Hall, Inc., Englewood Cliffs, NJ, 1993. 97

[2] B. Pearlmutter C. Warrender, S. Forrest. Detecting intrusions using system calls: Alternative data models. In *1999 IEEE Symposium on Security and Privacy*, pages 133–145, 1999. 95

[3] B. Pearlmutter C. Warrender, S. Forrest. Detecting intrusions using system calls: Alternative data models. In *1999 IEEE Symposium on Security and Privacy*, pages 133–145, 1999. 98, 99

[4] P. D'haeseleer, S. Forrest, and P. Helman. An immunological approach to change detection: Algorithms, analysis and implications. In *IEEE Symposium on Security and Privacy*, 1996. 95

[5] J. L. Elman Finding structure in time. *Cognitive Science*, 14:179–211, 1990. 96

[6] S. Forrest, S. A. Hofmeyr, and A. Somayaji. Computer immunology. *Communications of the ACM*, 40(10):88–96, October 1997. 95

[7] S. Forrest, S. A. Hofmeyr, A. Somayaji, and T. A. Longstaff. A sense of self for unix processes. In *Proceedings of the 1996 IEEE Symposium on Security and Privacy*, pages 120–128. IEEE, May 1996. 95

[8] Stephanie Forrest, Steven A. Hofmeyr, Anil Somayaji, and Thomas A. Longstaff. A sense of self for unix processes. In *Proceedinges of the 1996 IEEE Symposium on Research in Security and Privacy*, pages 120–128. IEEE Computer Society, IEEE Computer Society Press, May 1996. 100

[9] Yoav Freund, Michael Kearns, Dana Ron, Ronitt Rubinfeld, Robert E. Schapire, and Linda Sellie. Efficient learning of typical finite automata from random walks. *Information and Computation*, 138(1):23–48, 10 October 1997. 100

[10] A. K. Ghosh, A. Schwartzbard, and M. Schatz. Learning program behavior profiles for intrusion detection. In *Proceedings of the 1st USENIX Workshop on Intrusion Detection and Network Monitoring*. USENIX Association, April 11-12 1999. To appear. 95

[11] A. K. Ghosh, J. Wanken, and F. Charron. Detecting anomalous and unknown intrusions against programs. In *Proceedings of the 1998 Annual Computer Security Applications Conference (ACSAC'98)*, December 1998. 95

[12] M. Kearns and L. G. Valiant. Cryptographic limitations on learning boolean formulae and finite automata. In *Proceedings of the Twenty First Annual ACM Symposium on Theory of Computing*, pages 433–444, New York, NY, 1989. ACM. 100

[13] Andrew P. Kosoresow and Steven A. Hofmeyr. Intrusion detection via system call traces. *IEEE Software*, 14(5):24–42, September/October 1997. 99

[14] A. P. Kosoresow and S. A. Hofmeyr. Intrusion detection via system call traces. *Software*, 14(5):35–42, September-October 1997. IEEE Computer Society. 95

[15] T. L. Lai. Information bounds and quick detection of parameter changes in stochastic systems. *IEEE Transactions on Information Theory*, 44(7):2917–2929, 1998. 98

[16] W. Lee, S. Stolfo, and P. K. Chan. Learning patterns from unix process execution traces for intrusion detection. In *Proceedings of AAAI97 Workshop on AI Methods in Fraud and Risk Management*, 1997. 95

[17] L. Rabiner and B.-H. Juang. *Fundamentals of Speech Recognition*. Prentice Hall (Signal Processing Series), Englewood Cliffs, NJ, 1993. 99

[18] R. Sekar, Y. Cai, and M. Segal. A specification-based approach for building survivable systems. In *Proceedings of the 1998 National Information Systems Security Conference (NISSC'98)*, pages 338–347, October 1998. 95

[19] V. N. Vapnik. *The Nature of Statistical Learning Theory*. Springer, New York, 1995. 98

Intrusion Detection Using Variable-Length Audit Trail Patterns

Andreas Wespi, Marc Dacier, and Hervé Debar

IBM Research, Zurich Research Laboratory,
Säumerstrasse 4, CH-8803 Rüschlikon, Switzerland
{anw,dac,deb}@zurich.ibm.com

Abstract. Audit trail patterns generated on behalf of a Unix process can be used to model the process behavior. Most of the approaches proposed so far use a table of fixed-length patterns to represent the process model. However, variable-length patterns seem to be more naturally suited to model the process behavior, but they are also more difficult to construct. In this paper, we present a novel technique to build a table of variable-length patterns. This technique is based on Teiresias, an algorithm initially developed for discovering rigid patterns in unaligned biological sequences. We evaluate the quality of our technique in a testbed environment, and compare it with the intrusion-detection system proposed by Forrest *et al.* [8], which is based on fixed-length patterns. The results achieved with our novel method are significantly better than those obtained with the original method based on fixed-length patterns.

Keywords: Intrusion detection, Teiresias, pattern discovery, pattern matching, variable-length patterns, C2 audit trail, functionality verification tests.

1 Introduction

In [9], Forrest *et al.* introduced a new approach to the problem of protecting computer systems. The problem is viewed as an instance of the more general problem of distinguishing *self* (i.e. normal process execution) from *other* (i.e. anomalous process execution). Based on the way natural immune systems distinguish *self* from *other*, Forrest *et al.* have developed a change-detection method that can be applied to virus detection [9] and intrusion detection [8]. The method models the way an application or service running on a machine normally behaves by registering characteristic subsequences, i.e. patterns, of system calls invoked. An intrusion is assumed to pursue abnormal paths in the executable code, and is detected when new sequences are observed that cannot be matched with registered patterns (see also [6, 7]).

Forrest *et al.* use fixed-length patterns to represent the process model. However, a main limitation of this approach is that there is no rationale for selecting the optimal pattern length. As shown in [10], the pattern length has an influence on the detection capabilities of the intrusion-detection system. Therefore, in [2]

H. Debar, L. Mé, and F. Wu (Eds.): RAID 2000, LNCS 1907, pp. 110–129, 2000.

the concept of using variable-length patterns to model the process behavior was introduced. However, preliminary results obtained with variable-length patterns revealed no clear advantage of that method. In this paper, we present a novel method to generate variable-length patterns. We can show that the results obtained with variable-length patterns clearly outperform those achieved with the original method, which is based on fixed-length patterns.

The structure of the paper is as follows. Section 2 describes the basic principles of detecting suspicious process behavior by analyzing the sequences of system calls a process can generate. Readers familiar with the previous work on this topic [2, 3, 8, 10, 11, 13, 14, 15] can skip this section and go directly to Section 3 where our novel intrusion-detection method, which uses variable-length patterns, is presented. Section 4 compares our novel method with the one proposed by Forrest *et al.* [8, 10] based on experiments performed in a testbed [5] environment. Section 5 concludes the paper by summarizing the results obtained and offering ideas for future work. In the Appendix, formal descriptions of the variable-length pattern-extraction and the variable-length pattern-matching algorithm are given.

2   Background

We describe the basic principles of intrusion-detection systems that use characteristic subsequences of system call traces to model the process behavior and to detect intrusions by looking for deviations from the process model. First, we show the generic architecture of such intrusion-detection systems. Then we describe in more detail the intrusion-detection system proposed by Forrest *et al.* [8, 10], which will be used as the reference system to evaluate the quality of our novel approach.

2.1   Architecture

The intrusion-detection system proposed by Forrest *et al.* [8, 10] is a behavior-based [4] intrusion-detection system. In a training phase, normal process behavior is defined. During real-time operation, it is decided whether the observed process behavior corresponds to the learned normal behavior, or whether significant deviations are observed, which may be an indication of an intrusion.

There are different interpretations of what the expression *"normal" behavior* means. In [10] the authors differentiate between *synthetic* normal and *real* normal behavior. Synthetic normal behavior is created by exercising a program in an isolated environment in as many modes as possible and recording its behavior. Real normal behavior is observed by tracing the behavior of a program in a live user environment. For a discussion of the advantages and disadvantages of each approach see [2].

Forrest *et al.* [8, 10] are mainly interested in real normal behavior because this allows them to detect abnormal but legitimate behavior, i.e., behavior that is valid according to the process specification but has not been seen during the training phase. In our work, we concentrate on synthetic normal behavior and furthermore try to learn the normal process behavior exhaustively. We achieve this by using functionality verification test suites (FVT) that systematically exercise all valid process invocations. Our objective is to detect attacks against the process itself, i.e. attacks that succeed in exercising process execution paths that were hitherto unknown and do not correspond to the process specification. However, it is important to note that the intrusion-detection technique itself, specifically whether to use fixed- or variable-length patterns, does not depend on the method used to learn normal behavior.

The architecture of our intrusion-detection system is depicted in Figure 1. The system comprises two main parts: an off-line part, which corresponds to the training system, and an on-line part, which corresponds to the detection system. The main components of each part are described in the next two subsections.

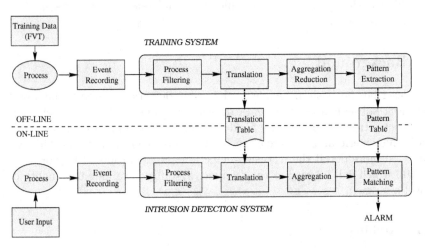

Fig. 1. Intrusion-detection system

Training System The behavior of the process under study is traced by recording either the system calls or the audit events generated on behalf of the process. In [8], system calls are used. Although on most operating systems not every system call is represented as an audit event, it has been shown in [2] that audit events are a viable alternative offering the same detection capabilities. For our work we use audit events because, as our experiments have shown, collecting audit events is a less intrusive technique than recording system calls.

The audit events generated on behalf of different process executions are sent to a *filtering module*. Its task is to sort the events by process id while keeping the chronological event order. The events are given as tuples comprising the process and event name. For easier processing, the *translation module* translates the events into an internal format. We use characters to represent this internal format. The translation rules are generated on the fly and stored in a *translation table*. Figure 2 shows the translation steps from the stream of audit events to the sequences of characters.

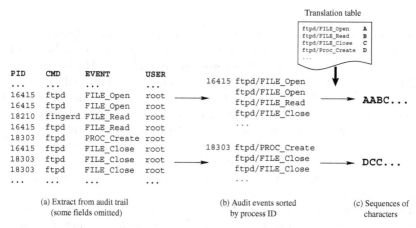

Fig. 2. Translation of audit events to characters

The translated sequences are forwarded to the *aggregation and reduction module*. The purpose of this module is twofold:

- It aggregates consecutive occurrences of the same character, i.e., of the same event.
- It removes duplicate sequences.

The following example shows the usefulness of the aggregation of consecutive identical characters. When a new instance of the *ftpd* process is invoked, it inherits several file handles from *inetd*, its parent process. As one of its first tasks, the ftp daemon closes the file handles, resulting in consecutive FILE_close events. The number of inherited file handles may vary because the inetd process is not always in the same state. Closing all unneeded file handles will therefore result in a varying number of FILE_close events. As a consequence, the resulting sequence of system calls is dependent on the environment in which the process runs. Because we would like to have a process description that is independent of the environment, we aggregate consecutive occurrences of the same character.

There are different ways to do the aggregation. We follow the approach proposed in [2] and aggregate identical consecutive characters in a single character, i.e., $A = A+$ in regular expression formalism. We make no claim of equivalence between the simplified event sequence and the original one. The aggregation is an experimental choice and would be removed if any negative impact on the detection capabilities of the intrusion-detection system were observed.

During the training phase, duplicate event sequences may occur. Because they contain no new patterns, duplicate event sequences do not have to be considered and are hence removed.

After all process executions have taken place, the preprocessed sequences are forwarded to the *pattern-extraction module* where the *pattern table* is generated.

Detection System The structure of the detection system is similar to that of the training system. In the detection system, events generated on behalf of the process under study are collected and processed in real time. The *filtering module* is identical to that of the training system. The *translation module* is slightly different from its counterpart in that audit events are translated based on the entries already contained in the *translation table*. Events without a corresponding entry in the translation table constitute quite an unusual event because they have not been seen in the training phase of the process. They are translated into a dummy character, and one may consider issuing an alarm whenever such a character is observed. In the current implementation of our intrusion-detection system, they are treated the same way as unmatched characters.

The reduction component of the *reduction and aggregation module* is no longer needed. Pattern matching is done in real time, and initiated as soon as possible for each sequence. This means we do not wait until the complete sequence has been received before the pattern matching is started, and therefore the reduction of entire sequences is not applicable.

The task of the *pattern-matching module* is to match the arriving event sequences with the entries in the *pattern table*. Based on how well the pattern matching can be done, it is decided whether anomalous behavior is observed and thus an *alarm* has to be raised.

2.2   A Review of Forrest *et al.*'s Approach

This description of Forrest *et al.*'s work is based on the original paper [8] as well as a more recent publication [10] in which some modifications of the original concepts are described. We show the techniques applied for pattern extraction and pattern matching as well as the metrics used to differentiate between normal and abnormal behavior.

Pattern Extraction The algorithm to build the table of fixed-length patterns is very simple. From the sequences sent to the pattern-extraction module, all unique subsequences, i.e. patterns, of a given length k are extracted. This is achieved by sliding a window of length k across all input sequences and recording the encountered subsequences. Duplicates are not considered.

The construction of the pattern table is best illustrated with an example. For $k = 3$ and the sample training sequence ABCCABC, we obtain the following pattern table:

$$\{ \text{ABC, BCC, CCA, CAB} \}.$$

Note that the pattern ABC shows up only once in the pattern table although it is encountered at two window positions, namely the first and the last position.

Pattern Matching The pattern-matching technique is similar to the pattern-generation technique. We move a window of length k across the sequence that is recorded during real operation. Each window position is checked for a *match*, i.e., whether there is a pattern that matches the subsequence in the window. If no matching pattern exists, we speak of a *mismatch*.

Given the pattern table of the previous example and the sample sequence ABCCACC, we observe three matches, namely {ABC, BCC, CCA}, and two mismatches, namely {CAC, ACC}.

Metric Note that the measure for raising an alarm must not depend on the sequence length. Arriving events have to be processed in real time, and we do not want to wait until all events of a process have arrived before we check them for possible signs of intrusions. This would be problematic, for example, in cases of continuously running processes. In [10], three measures are given to differentiate between normal and abnormal behavior. However, only the measure we are going to describe in this section is independent of the sequence length.

Let a and b be two sequences of length k. The expression a_i designates the character at position i. The difference $d(a, b)$ between a and b is defined as

$$d(a,b) = \sum_{i=1}^{k} f_i(a,b) \qquad \text{where } f_i(a,b) = \begin{cases} 0 \text{ if } a_i = b_i \\ 1 \text{ otherwise.} \end{cases}$$

During pattern-matching, we determine for each subsequence u of the translated event sequence the *minimum* distance $d_{\min}(u)$ between u and the entries in the pattern table:

$$d_{\min}(u) = \min \{d(u, p) \ \forall \text{ patterns } p\}.$$

To detect an attack, at least one of the subsequences generated by the attack must be classified as anomalous. In terms of the above measure, there is at least one subsequence u for which

$$d_{\min}(u) > 0.$$

It is assumed that the higher the $d_{\min}$ value, the more likely it is that the subsequence was actually generated by an intrusion. In practice, the maximum $d_{\min}$ value observed is used as the measure for an intrusion because it represents the strongest anomalous signal. The signal of anomaly, S_A, is defined as

$$S_A = \max \{d_{\min}(u) \ \forall \text{ subsequences } u\}.$$

In the ideal case, an S_A value that is greater than 0 can be considered a sign of an intrusion. However, as experimental results show, a complete match cannot always be achieved [10]. Therefore, a threshold is defined such that only sequences whose S_A value is above this threshold are considered suspicious.

3   Variable-Length Patterns

Before building a table of fixed-length patterns, one has to decide which pattern length to use. However, selecting the most appropriate pattern length is not straightforward:

- Long patterns are expected to be more process-specific than short patterns. The longer a pattern, the lower the probability that a pattern would match part of an event sequence generated on behalf of an attack.
- It is desirable to have a small pattern table because it reduces the amount of computation needed for the detection process. As experimental results show, increasing the pattern length to a certain length also increases the size of the corresponding pattern table [2].

Using variable-length patterns enables us to cope with these two apparently contradictory constraints. To describe the normal behavior of a process, variable-length patterns appear to be more naturally suitable than fixed-length patterns. A careful look at the sequences of events that can be generated by a process shows that there are many cases in which very long subsequences are repeated frequently. For example, more than 50% of the process images we have obtained for the *ftpd* process start with the same string. After aggregation, this string contains 40 audit events and should be incorporated as a whole in the pattern table. However, approaches based on fixed-length patterns use much shorter pattern lengths and would therefore not detect such a long pattern.

Variable-length patterns are also motivated by the fact that, for example, the ftp daemon answers user commands, and that each such command can probably be represented by its own sequence of audit events.

Variable-length patterns are not as easy to generate as fixed-length patterns. A technique based on building and pruning suffix trees [2] showed that variable-length patterns are an interesting alternative to fixed-length patterns, but it also showed some limitations of the chosen pattern-generation technique.

3.1   Pattern Extraction

We present a novel method to generate the table of variable-length patterns. This method comprises two steps. In the first step, all maximal variable-length patterns contained in the set of training sequences are determined. Because the patterns can share common subsequences, not all patterns may be needed to cover, i.e. fully match, the training sequences. Therefore, in the second step, a reduction algorithm is applied to prune entries in the pattern table. The goal is to obtain the minimum pattern set that still covers all training sequences.

Generating the Pattern Set The input to the pattern-extraction module (see Fig. 1) are sequences of audit events that have been preprocessed as described in Section 2.1. We define a variable-length pattern as a subsequence that has a minimum length of two and occurs at least twice, be it in the same or in different sequences. Furthermore, we consider only maximal variable-length patterns. A pattern p is maximal if there is no other pattern q that contains the pattern p as a subsequence and has the same number of occurrences as pattern p. For example, if there are two patterns DEA and EA, pattern EA is considered maximal only if it occurs more often than pattern DEA.

There are several algorithms to determine variable-length patterns [1]. We use the Teiresias algorithm [12], an algorithm developed initially to discover rigid patterns in unaligned biological sequences. Teiresias has many interesting properties. It is well suited to our problem for the following two main reasons:

- It finds the maximal variable-length patterns by avoiding the generation of non-maximal intermediate patterns during the pattern-extraction process [12].
- Its performance scales quasilinearly with the size of the output [12].

It follows that Teiresias very efficiently finds all the maximal variable-length patterns in the set of training sequences.

Reducing the Pattern Set We want the pattern set to be as process-specific as possible. This means that the pattern set should contain all the patterns needed to cover the training sequences but not more. The set of maximal variable-length patterns usually contains overlapping patterns, i.e. patterns that have common subsequences. Let us have a look at the following sample set of training sequences:

{ ABCDEAFDE, BCFDEABCD, BCEADEFDE }.

Extracting the maximal variable-length patterns results in the following pattern table:

{ ABCD, DEA, FDE, BC, DE, EA }.

The question arises whether all patterns are needed to cover the training sequences. Let us decompose the training sequences such that the resulting subsequences correspond to entries in the pattern table. A possible decomposition of the training sequences is listed below. We use the symbol "–" to mark the decomposition points:

{ ABCD-EA-FDE, BC-FDE-ABCD, BC-EA-DE-FDE }.

As we can see, of the six patterns in the pattern table only five are needed in the above decomposition. The pattern DEA is not used. We conclude that the pattern set determined by Teiresias can be reduced.

There are various ways to construct the reduced pattern set. The rationales for the approach described in the remainder of this section are based on the observation that there are patterns that have a clear semantical representation.

A pattern may, for example, represent a subroutine that is invoked several times or the statements that are executed in a loop. Such patterns can be regarded as building blocks out of which the event sequences of any possible process instantiation can be composed.

In our experiments, we observed that many training sequences have the same beginning and end, i.e., the same initialization and termination routine is executed for different process instantiations. As a first step, we can add the corresponding pattern to the reduced pattern set. Subsequences that match this pattern are removed from the training sequences, and the reduction process continues with the pruned training sequences. This procedure is reiterated until no training sequences are left, i.e., until all training sequences can be covered with the patterns added to the reduced pattern set.

There is a single requirement that must be fulfilled by the reduced pattern set:

- The training sequences must be covered by the patterns in the reduced pattern set.

In addition, as explained at the beginning of Section 3, the following properties are desirable:

- The reduced pattern set should contain long patterns.
- The number of patterns in the reduced pattern set should be small.

The two inputs for the reduction algorithm are the pattern table as produced by the Teiresias algorithm and the set of training sequences. The algorithm itself comprises four steps, which are executed repeatedly until all training sequences have been processed. We outline here only the basic steps of the algorithm. A detailed description can be found in Appendix A.2.

Step 1

The function bCover(p, s) returns the number of characters covered at the beginning and at the end of a sequence s by a pattern p. bCover(p, s) considers the fact that a pattern may match several times at the beginning or end of a sequence, e.g.

$$\mathrm{bCover}(\mathbf{AB}, \mathbf{ABCDEABAB}) = 6.$$

If S designates a set of sequences, bCover(p, S) is the sum of all events matched at the beginning and end of all sequences by the pattern p. We call the returned value the *boundary coverage*.

For each entry in the pattern table, we calculate its boundary coverage of the set of training sequences. The pattern with the highest boundary coverage is added to the reduced pattern set. This pattern is used further in Steps 2 and 3.

Step 2

All the subsequences at the beginning and end of the training sequences that are matched by the pattern determined in Step 1 are removed. For example, if the pattern AB is selected in Step 1, the sequence ABABCDAB will be transformed as follows:

$$\text{ABABCDAB} \rightarrow \text{CD}.$$

Furthermore, we have to avoid training sequences being reduced to sequences that are shorter than the minimal pattern length. By definition, there would be no pattern to match such a short sequence. For example, if the minimal pattern length is two and ABC is an entry in the pattern table, the following transformation of the sequence ABCD is invalid:

$$\text{ABCD} \rightarrow \text{D}.$$

because the remaining sequence D is shorter than the minimum pattern length.

Step 3

After removing the matching subsequences at the boundary of the training sequences, we now also remove matching subsequences p that are not adjacent to the boundary. We call this process nonboundary matching. Removing such subsequences results in splitting the original sequence into two new sequences. As in the case of boundary matching, it has to be ensured that the length of the resulting sequences is equal to or greater than the minimum pattern length. If a sequence has several subsequences that can be matched, the longest subsequence is removed first. Nonboundary matching may again be applied to the resulting sequences. For example, given the pattern AB and a maximal pattern length of two, the following transformation can be applied to the sequence CDABABEFABGH:

$$\text{CDABABEFABGH} \rightarrow \{ \text{ CD}, \text{ EFABGH } \} \rightarrow \{ \text{ CD}, \text{ EF}, \text{ GH } \}.$$

Step 4

No further transformation can be applied to sequences whose length is less than two times the minimal pattern length. Any further transformation would result in a new sequence that is less than the minimal pattern length, which contradicts our requirements. As a result, any sequence that cannot be further reduced will be added to the reduced pattern set. However, they are first moved to the pattern table and treated the same way as the patterns determined by the Teiresias algorithm. Note that, as a consequence, the reduced pattern set may contain entries that were not determined by Teiresias.

If after execution of Step 4 no sequences remain in the training set, the reduction algorithm terminates, otherwise execution continues at Step 1.

Figure 3 illustrates how the algorithm works for a sample training set of three sequences. In this example, five steps are needed to derive the reduced pattern table. For each step, we show the state of the training sequences, the entries in the pattern table, their corresponding bCover values, and the state of the reduced pattern table.

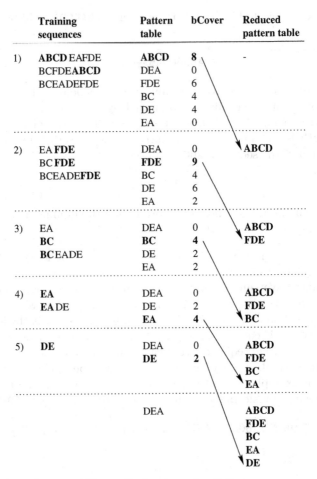

	Training sequences	Pattern table	bCover	Reduced pattern table
1)	**ABCD** EAFDE BCFDE**ABCD** BCEADEFDE	**ABCD** DEA FDE BC DE EA	8 0 6 4 4 0	-
2)	EA **FDE** BC **FDE** BCEADE**FDE**	DEA **FDE** BC DE EA	0 9 4 6 2	**ABCD**
3)	EA **BC** **BC**EADE	DEA **BC** DE EA	0 4 2 2	**ABCD** **FDE**
4)	**EA** **EA**DE	DEA DE **EA**	0 2 4	**ABCD** **FDE** **BC**
5)	**DE**	DEA **DE**	0 2	**ABCD** **FDE** **BC** **EA**
		DEA		**ABCD** **FDE** **BC** **EA** **DE**

Fig. 3. Reduction algorithm

To show the importance of the reduction algorithm, let us take a look at the following numbers. The training sequences of the experiment that we are going to describe in Section 4 contained a total of 167,187 patterns. Of this total, 554 patterns are maximal. These are the patterns that we generate using the Teiresias algorithm. It becomes obvious that generating the maximal patterns directly as Teiresias does offers a significant advantage over other approaches that also generate the intermediate patterns. Of the 554 maximal variable-length patterns, a pattern set of only 71 patterns can be constructed that covers all the training sequences. This shows the usefulness of reducing the pattern sets generated by Teiresias. A pattern-matching process that has to consider only 71 patterns will run faster than one that has to consider 554 entries. The statistics for the variable-length patterns are summarized in Table 1.

Table 1. Example of table sizes of variable-length patterns

Patterns	167,187
Maximal patterns	554
Covering patterns	71

3.2 Pattern Matching

As stated in the previous section, variable-length patterns can be seen as building blocks out of which any valid event sequence can be constructed. This idea is also reflected in the juxtaposed pattern-matching technique we apply for variable-length patterns.

The sequence to be matched is processed starting from the beginning of the sequence to its end. One out of three conditions holds at a given point of the pattern-matching process.

1. Exactly one pattern matches at a given position. The corresponding events are marked as matched and the pattern matching continues right after the last event marked.

2. Several patterns match at a given position. To decide which of the matching patterns to select, a look-ahead algorithm determines for a predefined value of n whether a sequence of up to n patterns can be found that matches the continuation of the sequence. The pattern whose continuation results in the longest match is selected, the corresponding events are marked as matched, and the pattern matching continues right after the last event marked.

3. No matching pattern can be found. The event at the current position of the pattern-matching process is marked as unmatched and skipped. The pattern matching continues right after the skipped event.

A detailed description of the pattern-matching algorithm can be found in Appendix A.3.

3.3 Metric

For each sequence, the pattern-matching algorithm returns the g groups of consecutive uncovered events and the length l_i, $i = 1 \ldots g$, of each of these groups. It is assumed that the greater the length l_i, the more likely it is that an intrusion is observed. Based on the length of the longest group of uncovered events, T, it has to be decided whether an attack is observed. T is defined as follows:

$$T = \max(l_i), i = 1 \ldots g.$$

4   Results

We have set up a test environment [5] to evaluate the quality of Forrest *et al.*'s intrusion-detection method and our novel method, which is based on variable-length patterns. We report the results obtained for the *ftpd* process. We focus on this process because it is widely used and is known to contain many vulnerabilities (either due to software flaws or configuration errors). Furthermore, it provides a host of possibilities for user interaction and is therefore a challenging process from an intrusion-detection point of view. We have also successfully applied our intrusion-detection approach to other network services, e.g. finger and sendmail. For space reasons, only the results obtained for the ftp service are presented in this paper.

To train the system, we use the functionality verification test suites (FVT) running under AIX [3]. The test suite allows us to automatically exercise all ftp subcommands and thus to learn the complete process behavior.

4.1   Problem Size

The FVT for the ftp process consists of 487 individual tests. Because many of these tests do not differ in the subcommands invoked but only in the arguments used, they result in identical sequences of audit events. When running the ftp test suite, 68 unique sequences (after aggregation and reduction) were recorded comprising a total of 23,302 audit events. Table 2 summarizes these numbers.

Table 2. Problem size of the ftp experiment

Tests	487
Training sequences	68
Events	23,302

For the comparison of the fixed- and variable-length approaches, we use two tables of fixed-length patterns and one of variable-length patterns. The pattern sizes of the fixed-length pattern tables are six and ten, respectively. Six was selected because it is stated in [10] that the pattern size makes only little difference for the normalized signal of anomaly, i.e. S_A/k, once we have a length of at least six, and ten because this is the pattern size used in the experiments reported in [10]. It is worth noting that, coincidentally, the mean pattern length of the variable-length pattern table is ten. Table 3 lists the size of the respective pattern tables. We see that the size of the variable-length pattern table is much smaller than that of the fixed-length pattern tables.

4.2   Normal User Sessions

In our testbed [5], we simulated series of user sessions. The simulation resulted in 65 unique sequences comprising a total of 26,025 audit events. We used these sequences to evaluate the quality of the fixed-length and variable-length pattern-matching techniques in combination with the respective pattern tables. As we have used the FVT to learn the complete process behavior and the user sessions contain no attacks, the intrusion-detection system should not generate an alarm.

Table 3. Table sizes of fixed-length patterns

Pattern type	(Mean) pattern size	Table size
Fixed-length	6	396
Fixed-length	10	702
Variable-length	10	71

Table 4 shows the results obtained. The first column lists the number of unique sequences recorded. The second column specifies a value n that is used as a comparison value for columns three to five. Columns three and four give a measure of how well the normal user sessions could be matched with the entries of the respective fixed-length pattern tables, and column five does the same for the variable-length pattern table.

To understand the content of columns three to five, we have to recall the meaning of the two metrics S_A and T. The metric S_A is the signal of anomaly defined in Section 2.2 and is used to differentiate between normal and abnormal behavior when fixed-length patterns are used. The values of S_A lie between 0 and k, where k is the pattern size. The higher the value of S_A, the more likely it is that an intrusion is observed. The metric T is the number of consecutive uncovered characters defined in Section 3.3 and is the metric used in our intrusion-detection system that is based on variable-length patterns.

The entries in columns three to four list the number of sequences for which S_A is equal to the comparison value n of the same row. For example, the row with $n = 4$ indicates that for a window size of six (ten), we have observed a maximum of four uncovered characters in all subsequences of six (ten) characters. This has been seen in five (eight) out of 65 sequences.

The last column lists the results obtained for the variable-length approach. Here, the row with $n = 4$ indicates that there are two sequences out of 65 where the maximum number of consecutive uncovered characters is 4.

Table 4. Experimental results for normal user sessions

Number of sequences	n	Fixed $k = 6$ $S_A = n$	Fixed $k = 10$ $S_A = n$	Variable $T = n$
65	0	11	11	47
	1	19	0	14
	2	19	25	1
	3	11	15	1
	4	5	8	2
	5	0	4	0
	6	0	2	0
	> 6	–	0	0

In the ideal case, we would like to see $S_A = 0$ and $T = 0$, i.e. full coverage of all test sequences. However, Table 4 shows that with the two fixed-length approaches only 17% of the sequences, i.e. 11 out of 65, can be fully matched. With the variable-length pattern approach, 72% of the sequences, i.e. 47 out of 65, can be covered. We see that variable-length patterns result in much a better coverage of the test sequences than fixed-length patterns.

Table 4 also allows us to set thresholds to differentiate between normal and abnormal behavior. Any value of S_A or T that is above the threshold would be considered a sign of an intrusion. If we do not want to issue false alarms, the threshold for S_A has to be set to four (six) in the case of fixed-length patterns. In the case of variable-length patterns, the threshold of T has to be set to four.

4.3 Attacks

We have implemented seven attacks against the ftp service. Some of the attacks exploit server misconfigurations, others take advantage of vulnerabilities in older versions of the ftp daemon.

The *put forward* attack consists of putting a *.forward* file in the home directory of the ftp user, and then sending a mail to the ftp user. This vulnerability results from a misconfiguration of the ftp service because this directory should obviously not be world writable.

The *site exec* suite of attacks exploits a vulnerability that was enabled by wrongly setting the _PATH_EXECPATH variable when compiling the ftpd program. Precompiled binaries containing this vulnerability were shipped with an older release of the Linux Slackware distribution. Two different attack scripts were executed, *ftpbug* and *copy*. To make the two scripts difficult to detect, they were given the names *ftpd* and *ls* (hence the code names of the attacks).

The *tar exec* type of attacks use the option of the GNU *tar* program to specify a compression program in combination with the tar command. The attack becomes possible because some older versions of the ftp daemon do not release their root privileges quickly enough before forking other processes. To exploit this vulnerability, we let the tar program invoke renamed copies of the *ftpbug* and *copy* program as compression programs.

A detailed description of the attacks can be found in [5]. The results we obtained are shown in Table 5.

We see that all three approaches can be used to detect the attacks. For the two fixed-length pattern tables, S_A is equal to the maximum value of six (ten) for all attacks. All the values obtained are above the threshold we have defined for S_A. For the variable-length method, the values for T vary between 13 and 36. These values are significantly higher than the threshold we have set for T, namely four.

4.4 Discussion

The quality of an intrusion-detection method is given by its capability to differentiate between normal and abnormal behavior. For the intrusion-detection

Table 5. Experimental results for attacks

Attack description	Fixed $k = 6$	Fixed $k = 10$	Variable
	S_A	S_A	T
put forward	6	10	36
site copy	6	10	18
site exec copy ftpd	6	10	16
site exec copy ls	6	10	18
site exec ftpbug ftpd	6	10	16
tar exec ftpbug ftpd	6	10	13
tar exec ftpbug ls	6	10	14

methods we investigate, the differentiator is the threshold that has to be set for the measures S_A and T. In the case of fixed-length patterns, the threshold for S_A, i.e. four or six, is relatively high compared to the pattern length of six or ten, and implies an increased risk to miss an attack. In the case of variable-length patterns, we observe quite a difference between the threshold for T, i.e. four, and the minimum value of T obtained for the attack sequences, namely 13. Therefore, the risk of issuing a false alarm is quite low if variable-length patterns are used.

We conclude that intrusion-detection methods based on variable-length patterns can be more reliably used to differentiate between normal and abnormal behavior. This is mainly because variable-length patterns better match normal user sessions.

5 Conclusions

We have presented a host-based intrusion-detection system that can model the normal process behavior based on the audit sequences created on behalf of the process. The process model is a pattern table whose entries are subsequences of the audit event sequences determined during a training phase.

Because the fixed-length pattern approach has certain limitations, including the inability to represent long, meaningful substrings, it appears to be more natural to use variable-length patterns to build the process model. We have developed a novel technique to generate tables of variable-length patterns automatically. To construct the patterns, the Teiresias algorithm, a method initially developed for discovering rigid patterns in unaligned biological sequences, is used in combination with a pattern-reduction algorithm.

We have shown that the variable-length pattern model has several advantages over the fixed-length model. Fewer patterns are needed to describe the normal process behavior, and the quality of the results achieved is significantly better than that of the results obtained with fixed-length patterns. Our results also show that behavior-based intrusion-detection systems can be built that do not suffer from one of the main problems observed in behavior-based intrusion detection, namely generating (too) many false alarms.

Future work will concentrate on validating our approach for other network services and on investigating techniques that would result in 100% coverage of normal user sessions. Furthermore, as our technique to build variable-length pattern tables has some similarities with techniques used for data compression, we plan to investigate the potential of this technology for intrusion-detection purposes.

A   Algorithms

The pattern-reduction and pattern-matching algorithms have been briefly described in Sections 3.1 and 3.2, respectively. Here, we describe them in more detail.

A.1   Terminology and Notation

Consider a finite set of characters $\Sigma = c_1, c_2, \ldots, c_n$. The set Σ is called alphabet. To denote a string of $n, n > 0$, consecutive identical characters $c \in \Sigma$, we write c^n. c^+ denotes a string of identical consecutive characters of arbitrary length l, $l > 0$.
The length of a string s is written as $|s|$. We write $c \in s$ if the character c is contained in the string s.

Given is a set of strings $S = \{s_1, s_2, \ldots, s_n\}$ over the alphabet Σ. A substring p that

- occurs at least twice in the set of strings S, and
- has a length $|p|$ of two or more characters

is called a pattern.

p^n denotes the pattern p repeated $n, n > 0$ times. p^+ denotes the pattern p repeated $l, l > 0$ times.

A pattern p is maximal if there is no pattern q for which holds that

- p is a substring of q with $|p| < |q|$, and
- the number of occurrences of the pattern q in S is equal to or larger than the number of occurrences of the pattern p in S.

A character $c \in s$ is said to be covered by the pattern p if $c \in p$ and p is a substring of s.

A string s is said to be covered by a set of patterns P if for each character c, $c \in s$, there is a pattern $p, p \in P$, such that c is covered by p.

A set of strings S is said to be covered by a set of patterns P if each string $s, s \in S$, is covered by P. Additionally, P is said to cover S.

Given are a pattern p and a string s. Let us decompose the string s as follows:

$$s = p^l s' p^r \quad l, r >= 0, \quad |s'| >= 0$$

It is assumed that the decomposition is maximal, i.e., there is no l' and r' for which holds $l' + r' > l + r$.

The expression $(l+r) \cdot |p|$, i.e. the sum $l+r$ times the pattern length $|p|$, is called boundary coverage of pattern p and string s. It is written as $\mathrm{bCover}(p, s)$.

The boundary coverage of a pattern p and a string set $S = s_1, s_2, \ldots, s_n$, written as $\mathrm{bCover}(p, S)$, is defined as

$$\mathrm{bCover}(p, S) = \sum_{i=1}^{n} \mathrm{bCover}(p, s_i).$$

A.2   Pattern Reduction

Out of the set of patterns P consisting of all the maximal patterns found for the string set S, a subset of patterns $R, R \subset P$, is selected that covers S. μ denotes the minimal pattern length that was used to generate the set of maximal variable-length patterns. The reduced pattern set R is constructed as follows:

1. If $P = \emptyset$, then add all $s \in S$ to the reduced pattern set R and exit.
2. For each $p \in P$ calculate $\mathrm{bCover}(p, S)$.
3. Select a pattern $r \in P$ for which $\mathrm{bCover}(r, S)$ is maximal, i.e., there is no other pattern $p \in P$ for which holds:
   - $\mathrm{bCover}(p, S) > \mathrm{bCover}(r, S)$, or
   - $\mathrm{bCover}(p, S) = \mathrm{bCover}(r, S) \wedge |p| > |r|$.
4. Add r to the reduced pattern set R and remove it from P.
5. Remove all matching substrings adjacent to the beginning or end of a string, i.e., remove strings of the form $s = r^+$, and replace strings of the form $s = r^+ s'$, $|s'| > \mu$, or $s = s'' r^+$, $|s''| > \mu$, with s' or s'', respectively.
6. Remove the matching substrings that are not adjacent to the beginning or end of a string, i.e., as long as there is an $s \in S, s = s' r s''$, $|s'| \geq \mu, |s''| \geq \mu$, replace s with the two strings s' and s''.
7. If there is an $s \in S$ with length $|s| < 2 \cdot \mu$, remove s from the set of strings S and add it to the pattern set P.
8. If $S \neq \emptyset$, go to Step 1, otherwise exit.

A.3 Pattern Matching

At certain points of the pattern-matching process, there may be several patterns that match the input stream. To decide which pattern to select, the algorithm uses a look-ahead approach. A pattern is selected if $\delta, \delta > 0$, patterns can be found that match the continuation of the string. We designate δ as *look-ahead parameter*. An alarm is raised if the number of consecutive uncovered characters exceeds a threshold τ.

The pattern matching is done as follows:

1. Set the look-ahead parameter to a value $\delta > 0$, and set the threshold for the number of consecutive uncovered characters to a value $\tau > 0$.
2. Set the counter of consecutive uncovered characters, κ, to 0.
3. When there is a sufficient number of characters in the input stream I, find a pattern $p \in P$ that covers the beginning of the input stream I. If no pattern can be found, go to Step 6.
4. Find $\delta > 0$ patterns $q_1, q_2, \ldots, q_\delta$, such that the string $t = pq_1q_2...q_d$ covers the beginning of the stream. If there are ϵ patterns $q_1, q_2, ..., q_\epsilon$, $0 < \epsilon < \delta$, that cover the entire input sequence, set $t = pq_1q_2...q_\epsilon$.
    (a) If t matches the entire input sequence, remove it and go to Step 2.
    (b) If δ patterns can be found that cover the beginning of the input stream, remove pattern p from the input stream, and go to Step 2.
5. Determine all pattern combinations that match the beginning of the input stream. If there is a match, select the pattern combination that covers the longest input sequence, remove it from the input stream, and go to Step 2.
6. Skip one character, and increase κ by 1.
7. If $\kappa = \tau + 1$, raise an alarm.
8. Go to Step 2.

References

[1] A. Brazma, I. Jonassen, I. Eidhammer, and D. Gilbert. Approaches to the automatic discovery of patterns in biosequences. Technical report, Department of Informatics, University of Bergen, 1995. 117

[2] Hervé Debar, Marc Dacier, Medhi Nassehi, and Andreas Wespi. Fixed vs. variable-length patterns for detecting suspicious process behavior. In Jean-Jacques Quisquater, Yves Deswarte, Catherine Meadows, and Dieter Gollmann, editors, *Computer Security - ESORICS 98, 5th European Symposium on Research in Computer Security*, LNCS, pages 1–15, Louvain-la-Neuve, Belgium, September 1998. Springer. 110, 111, 112, 113, 116

[3] Hervé Debar, Marc Dacier, and Andreas Wespi. Reference Audit Information Generation for Intrusion Detection Systems. In Reinhard Posch and György Papp, editors, *Information Systems Security, Proceedings of the 14th International Information Security Conference IFIP SEC'98*, pages 405–417, Vienna, Austria and Budapest, Hungaria, August 31–September 4 1998. 111, 122

[4] Hervé Debar, Marc Dacier, and Andreas Wespi. Towards a taxonomy of intrusion detection systems. *Computer Networks*, 31(8):805–822, April 1999. Special issue on Computer Network Security. 111

[5] Hervé Debar, Marc Dacier, Andreas Wespi, and Stefan Lampart. A workbench for intrusion detection systems. Technical Report RZ 6519, IBM Zurich Research Laboratory, Säumerstrasse 4, CH-8803 Rüschlikon, Switzerland, March 1998. 111, 121, 122, 124

[6] Patrick D'haeseleer, Stephanie Forrest, and Paul Helman. An immunological approach to change detection: algorithms, analysis, and implications. In *Proceedings of the 1996 IEEE Symposium on Research in Security and Privacy*, pages 110–119. IEEE Computer Society, IEEE Computer Society Press, May 1996. 110

[7] Stephanie Forrest, Steven A. Hofmeyr, and Anil Somayaji. Computer immunology. *Communications of the ACM*, 40(10):88–96, October 1997. 110

[8] Stephanie Forrest, Steven A. Hofmeyr, Anil Somayaji, and Thomas A. Longstaff. A sense of self for Unix processes. In *Proceedinges of the 1996 IEEE Symposium on Research in Security and Privacy*, pages 120–128. IEEE Computer Society, IEEE Computer Society Press, May 1996. 110, 111, 112, 114

[9] Stephanie Forrest, Alan S. Perelson, Lawrence Allen, and Rajesh Cherukuri. Self-nonself discrimination. In *Proceedings of the 1994 IEEE Symposium on Research in Security and Privacy*, pages 202–212. IEEE Computer Society, IEEE Computer Society Press, May 1994. 110

[10] Steven A. Hofmeyr, Stephanie Forrest, and Anil Somayaji. Intrusion detection using sequences of system calls. *Journal of Computer Security*, 6(3):151–180, 1998. 110, 111, 114, 115, 122

[11] Andrew P. Kosoresow and Steven A. Hofmeyr. Intrusion detection via system call traces. *IEEE Software*, pages 35–42, September/October 1997. 111

[12] Isidore Rigoutsos and Aris Floratos. Combinatorial pattern discovery in biological sequences. *Bioinformatics*, 14(1):55–67, 1998. 117

[13] Andreas Wespi, Marc Dacier, and Hervé Debar. An intrusion-detection system based on the Teiresias pattern-discovery algorithm. In Urs E. Gattiker, Pia Pedersen, and Karsten Petersen, editors, *Proceedings of EICAR '99*, Aalborg, Denmark, February 1999. European Institute for Computer Anti-Virus Research. ISBN 87-987271-0-9. 111

[14] Andreas Wespi, Marc Dacier, Hervé Debar, and Mehdi M. Nassehi. Audit trail pattern analysis for detecting suspicious process behavior. In *Proceedings of RAID 98, Workshop on Recent Advances in Intrusion Detection*, Louvain-la-Neuve, Belgium, September 1998. 111

[15] Andreas Wespi and Hervé Debar. Building an intrusion-detection system to detect suspicious process behavior. In *Proceedings of RAID 99, Workshop on Recent Advances in Intrusion Detection*, West Lafayette, Indiana, USA, September 1999. 111

Flexible Intrusion Detection Using Variable-Length Behavior Modeling in Distributed Environment: Application to CORBA Objects*

Zakia Marrakchi, Ludovic Mé, Bernard Vivinis, and Benjamin Morin

Supélec, France
Surname.Name@supelec.fr

Abstract. This paper presents an approach of the intrusion detection problem applied to CORBA-type distributed environments. The approach is based on the measure of deviation from client reference behaviors towards the CORBA servant objects to be protected. We consider a client behavior as a sequence of invoked requests between each couple of client-server, during each connection of the observed client. We construct, during a training period, a client behavior model based on variable-length branches tree representation. This model both takes into account the series of invoked requests and their parameter values. To make our approach more flexible, we construct, at the end of the training period, a tolerance interval for each numerical parameter. These intervals allow deviation between observed and learned values to be measured. This article presents our preliminary results and introduces our future works.

1 Introduction

CORBA (Common Object Request Broker Architecture) is a distributed architecture which enables heterogeneous objects to freely communicate regardless of the hardware, OS and programming languages of the interacting objects, thanks to a software bus called ORB (Object Request Broker). In spite of the preventive security mechanisms in CORBA (authentification, authorisation, etc), it may be still possible to take advantage of ORB vulnerabilities to perform attacks[1] It is therefore necessary to make use of an intrusion detection mechanism, which implies a permanent surveillance of the exchanges between objects to make sure of their legitimity.

There are two approaches in intrusion detection: misuse detection and anomaly detection. Misuse detection searches for known attacks in the event

---

* This work is partly funded by The France Telecom R&D Center. We would like to thank especially Anne Lille, Eric Malville, and Michel Milhau for many interesting discussions.
[1] With respect to the threats and attacks, we don't know of any published work.

H. Debar, L. Mé, and F. Wu (Eds.): RAID 2000, LNCS 1907, pp. 130–144, 2000.

logs. It implies preliminary knowledge of CORBA attacks which is hard to constitute *a priori*. Then, we decided on the anomaly approach which models the behaviors of CORBA clients involved in a communication, in order to detect further deviation from reference behaviors called "normal" behaviors. To construct our behavior base from the information collected, we need to decide on the data used to characterize a normal behavior. In our approach, invoked requests during each CORBA client connection[2] are considered as the most relevant data for a client behavior definition. We think that the obtained variable-length sequences of invoked requests express accurately the real client behavior towards involved CORBA objects[1]. Currently, we only consider the requests order in a sequence; the frequency of request invocation is not taken into account.

Our work focuses on intrusion detection at the application level. In fact, detection is based on application audit source generated by message interceptors. These interceptors, provided by CORBA environment, are able to spot, modify and redirect every message passing through the ORB. We used these mechanisms to collect information about observed objects in order to construct event logs. The logs analysis allows intrusion detection.

Some works, in the context of intrusion detection in CORBA-type distributed environments, were conducted by Odyssey Research Associates [3]. The approach considers exchanged messages between clients as the discriminant data for the definition of a normal behavior. They only consider the signatures of the intercepted client requests. The parameters are not taken into account. Successive observed signatures allow the construction of behavior patterns (a pattern consists of a series of fixed-length consecutive calls organized into a behavior base). During the real activity of the observed client, the detection algorithm (called *sliding window algorithm*) can determine whether the observed behavior is consistant with the past. Each pattern found in the base is considered as normal, all the rest is not. The number of observed anomalies and the elapsed time between these anomalies are decisive for the computation of an anomaly value. If the computed value exceedes a certain threshold during a certain time, an alert is raised.

We are also interested in CORBA client behavior modeling. We propose a tree representation for the client behavior. Information about for client request messages are collected at server side but the client tree can be hosted elsewhere. The tree root marks a connection, a leaf marks a disconnection. Each node corresponds to an invoked request. Each branch represents a normal behavior observed between a connection and a disconnection. Contrary to [3], we consider in addition to request signatures, their parameter values. Each node contains information about request parameters (see section 3). We construct tolerance

---

[2] If the server is made of one object (which is the case in our current application), the connection and disconnection correspond respectively to *bind* and *unbind* between client and servant objects. If the server is made of several objects (which is the case in real applications), the defintion of connection and disconnection becomes more complicated. We didn't work on this point for the moment.

intervals around these values which will be used by our detection algorithm (see section 4).

In short, we propose to generate, during the training period, a tree representation of a client behavior. At the end of this period, we construct tolerance intervals. During the detection period we navigate through the tree starting from the root and compute a similarity degree. The observed behavior is considered as normal if we find a leaf with an acceptable value of the similarity degree. Otherwise, an alert is raised.

We have developed a testbed which is the platform for testing our ideas. It consists of a simple banking application. This platform doesn't constitute a real application with real CORBA users in interaction, but it allowed us to test the whole proposed approach (interception, training, detection). The results presented in this article are obtained from this platform.

The first part of this article describes how information about CORBA client-server intercations is acquired. The second part details the training period. The third part deals with the detection period. The last part shows the preliminary experimental results. We finally present our conclusions and future works.

2   Acquisition of Information on Client-Server Interactions

This part gives a brief resume of CORBA security services, describes the basic surveillance features and presents a communication architecture based on these features.

The OMG defines CORBA security. First, it offers some security services (cf chapter 15 of [4]). Then, it provides the interceptors which constitute the basic mechanism to implement security or any other service placed between the client-server communication (see chapter 21 of [5]).

Three security service levels are defined:

- first level services: authentification, access control, confidentiality and audit are provided to CORBA applications without any possibility to read related parameters or to have special security knowledge;
- second level services: add a protection against replay and offer access to a security administration interface;
- non repudiation which is an optionnal service.

If security is specified, we are still far from a portable implementation in the commercial ORBs, especially for the audit service. That's why we decided to use the interceptors to acquire information on client-server interactions.

Interceptors can plug specific processing in request paths to CORBA objects, in both client or server side. The OMG presents this extension as the basis for services to allow observation and transformation of requests and responses without any impact on the ORB kernal, it just calls a standard interface.

There are two levels of interceptors: request and message interceptors. Request interceptors receive the request parameters, can modify them, invoke other objects and then redirect the request. We make use of these interceptors because message interceptors access fragments carrying requests and responses, which is not interesting for us. Moreover, Visibroker (the ORB used for our testing model) only offers request level interceptors[3]. The implementation of a client and/or server side interceptor is done at the client-server connection (bind).

The proposed architecture for our platform is shown in Figure 1. The choice of this architecture is based on these important factors:

- The interception process has no impact on the client that can evolve in an unsecure context;
- servant objects can be fit up with interceptors without any code modification;
- there is a clear distinction between a capture agent, which holds the interceptors, and an administrator; they communicate through the ORB and can be hosted in different machines.

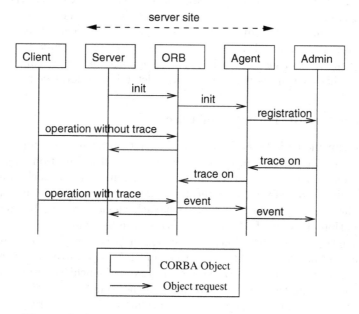

Fig. 1. Architecture and principles of object exchanges

Giving this architecture, the client surveillance follows these steps:

1. start of the administrator which observes the agent registrations;
2. start of the server which initializes the ORB and loads, without its knowledge, the agent thanks to a command line option;

---

[3] Visibroker for Java version 3.3 proposes three classes of request level interceptors [2]: BindInterceptor, ClientInterceptor et ServerInterceptor.

3. the loaded agent initializes the interception mechanism and registrates itself to the administrator;
4. server requests are not captured until the administrator asks explicitly for trail;
5. When the administrator asks for an interception, information is then communicated from the ORB to the agent which carries it to the administrator.

The client surveillance is made during the training period and the resulting audit file constitutes the starting point for both the client behavior modeling and the detection period presented in the next two parts.

3   The Training Period

During each client connection, request messages to CORBA objects are observed in order to construct their behavior model. During this period which is transparent to clients, the learned behaviors are considered as attack-free. In the behavior modeling, we consider a series of requests and their parameter values between each connection and disconnection (see section 3.1). Further, we construct tolerance intervals around observed values (see section 3.2). These intervals offer flexibility in the measure of deviation from learned behavior, called reference behavior. This measure is performed in the detection period (see section 4).

3.1   Structure of the Behavior Base

Our behavior model is based on a variable-length branches tree representation. The tree root marks a connection, a leaf marks a disconnection. A tree node corresponds to a request and its parameters. Then, a tree branch is a normal behavior observed between a connection and a disconnection (see Figure 2). During the training period, we represent each client behavior by such a tree representation. The set of all trees constitutes the behavior base.

The tree construction is done by insertion of branches. We approximate the final state of the tree by adding branches until N successive behaviors are already known. However this approximation can only be achieved practically. The training period and the value of N depend on the complexity of the application: the richer the application, the longer the training period. For a real application, several weeks and even several months are probably required.

In our behavior model, only the order of invoked requests is considered in the definition of normal behavior. No time consideration is taken into account, for the moment. In addition to invoked requests, a behavior is defined by their parameter values. An important gap between learned and observed values of the parameter can reveal an anomaly. Nevertheless, a reasonnable repartition around learned values should be accepted. To allow small variations around normal values, we construct tolerance intervals. These intervals consider arounding values as acceptable even if they have never been observed in the past.

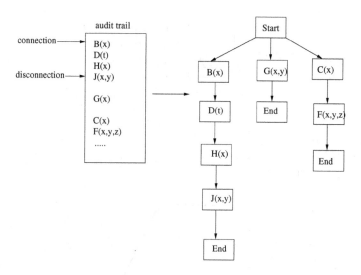

Fig. 2. Construction of the behavior base

3.2   Construction of Tolerance Intervals

The difficulty here is to determine a threshold from which the observed value must be considered too different from those learned. In other words, the problem is to define a measure of the gap between what has been learned and what is observed. An analysis of what is learned is essential to construct the corresponding tolerance intervals. Intervals are defined only for numerical data. For symbolic data, such as the connected client name, only observed values can be accepted.

The first step of data analysis is to represent in clusters (as shown in the first part of Figure 4 for the numerical parameter x) the number of occurences of all observed values for each numerical parameter. The second step consists of isolating clusters of learned values. Eventually, these clusters may be reduced to isolated values.

Further, we associate to each cluster a tolerance interval which width δ depends on the security level associated to the request. For example, for a parameter such as the amount of money taken from a bank account, small variation around learned values is allowed, δ is then small. The analysis may be improved by adapting the degree of deviation δ for each numerical parameter within the same request. In fact, δ can also depend on the width and the density of the associated cluster. We think that for large clusters (values frequently observed) we should allow more deviation than for isolated values. Of course, these assumptions should be tested for real data. Currently, this step is made by hand but we are working on automatizing this process using a distance criteria which is context dependant.

The tolerance interval is represented by a trapezoidal function expressed by the following formula (see Figure 3):

$$va(x) = \begin{cases} 0 & \text{for } x < x_1 \text{ or } x > x_4 \\ 1 & \text{for } x \in [x_2, x_3] \\ \frac{x - x_1}{x_2 - x_1} & \text{for } x \in [x_1, x_2[\\ \frac{x_4 - x}{x_4 - x_3} & \text{for } x \in]x_3, x_4] \end{cases} \tag{1}$$

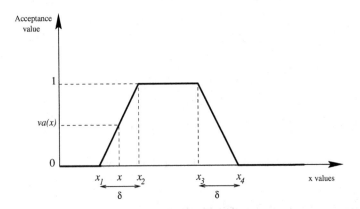

Fig. 3. Trapezoidal representation of an interval. Points x_2 and x_3 delimit the cluster of observed values. Points x_1 and x_4 express the authorized gap δ around x_2 and x_3

The constructed interval allows, as explained previously, the client to deviate from his learned behavior with a certain authorized degree. Moreover, it limits the false alert rate during detection by providing a computed degree of similarity. This notion will be defined in the next part.

4   The Detection Period

During the detection period, the CORBA application client is observed between each connection and disconnection. The objective is no longer to learn his behavior but to decide of its legitimity, by computing a degree of similarity d_i. This degree measures the deviation between learned and observed behaviors.

During each client connection, we navigate through the tree and we adjust the similarity degree at each node until a leaf is reached. The computed degree allows us to decide whether the observed client behavior for the connection i is normal or not. If the degree is less than a first acceptance threshold, called *instantaneous threshold* (s), the client behavior is deemed anomalous and an *instantaneous alert* is raised (see Figure 6).

It is also interesting to observe the client behavior during a longer period covering several connections. In fact, small variations around learned values may reveal, during a certain period, an anomalous behavior. We propose to observe,

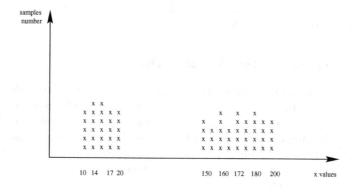

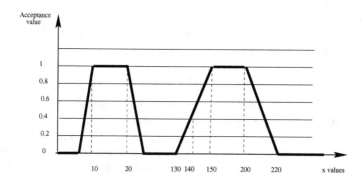

Fig. 4. Flexible representation of the cluster

We consider, for example, the values of the parameter x in the request $F(x)$. The observed values for x during the training period are: 10,12,14,14,17,18,20,20,150,155,160,172,200. We notice that these values are distributed in two intervals [10,20] and [150,200]. During the detection period, an observed value 148 should not be considered as anomalous because it is close to the learned values ([150,200])

during successive connections, the obtained values of the similarity degree d_i. We use a second threshold, called *composed threshold* (s'), to decide on the activation of a second alert, called *composed alert*.

If the degree d_i keeps less than a second threshold (s') for a certain time δt greater than Δt, the client behavior is deemed anomalous and a *composed alert* is raised (see Figure 6). This alert shows possible correlations between several connections that may constitute an attack.

Section 4.1 details the computation of the similarity degree. Section 4.2 shows the two types of generated alerts.

4.1 Computation of the Similarity Degree

The observed behavior is considered as anomalous if its similarity degree is less than a certain instantaneous threshold s (a low threshold implies a low correspondance between observed and learned behavior). The lower the threshold, the higher the number of accepted behaviors. Increasing the threshold limits the number of accepted behaviors, but increases the rate of false alerts. The problem is to find a compromise between detection efficency and an acceptable rate of false alerts. This compromise is currently obtained experimentally (see section 5).

The computation of the similarity degree d_i for the connection i begins at the tree root with $d_i^0 = 1$. Then, this degree is adjusted at each visited node by applying an eventual penalty. This penalty depends on the acceptance values va_i obtained for each numerical parameter of the request (cf. definition in section 3.2). The value of d_i at the current node k (d_i^k) is expressed in terms of its value at the previous node (d_i^{k-1}):

$$d_i^k = d_i^{k-1} - P(va_i..va_n)(k \neq 0) \tag{2}$$

$P(va_i..va_n)$ expresses the global penalty applied to the current request. This penalty is obtained by the conjunction of elementary penalties $p_i(va_i)$ computed for each numerical parameter of the request. This allows all elementary values to contribute to the computation of the penalty P applied to the request. We must choose a conjunction operator from three possible: *min*, *max* and *average*. The *min* operator computes the minimum of the $p_i(va_i)$. The major inconvenient of the *min* is its high sensibility to null values. It implies a null penalty P for the request and then, may accept wrongly some requests. In opposition to the *min*, the *max* operator applies to the request the highest elementary penalty observed in the parameters, by considering the maximum of all the $p_i(va_i)$, which is restrictive. We then decided on the *average* operator. Contrarely to the previous ones, this operator has a compensatory effect that implies a low sensibility to null values. The global penalty is expressed in terms of the elementary penalties p_i as follows:

$$P(va_i..va_n) = \frac{\sum_{i=1}^{n} p_i(va_i)}{n} \tag{3}$$

The elementary penalty p_i of the parameter i is obtained in terms of the acceptance value va_i of this parameter. This penalty decreases when va_i increases, starting from the point $(va_i, p_i) = (0,1)$ up to the point $(1,0)$ as shown in Figure 5. If the observed value of a parameter is not found in the previously defined interval, the acceptance value va_i of this parameter is low. Indeed, the associated elementary penalty p_i is high and the degree d_i decreases. The higher the acceptance value, the lower the penalty and the less the similarity degree will decrease. The elementary penalty is expressed by the following formula:

$$p(va) = (1 - va)^o \tag{4}$$

This function allows the control of the curve slope by varying the degree o. To illustrate this, let's consider the same example as in the training period. Suppose that the first client invoked request is $F(x)$ with $x = 140$. Its acceptance value is then equal to 0.4 (see Figure 4). The table 1 shows the variation of the similarity degree in terms of the penalty. Our preliminary results are based on a quadratic penalty function ($o = 2$) applied to all invoked requests. We propose, in our future works (see section 6), to vary the degree o for each parameter in terms of its sensibility towards the application. A high degre o expresses the acceptance of a larger variation of the associated parameter.

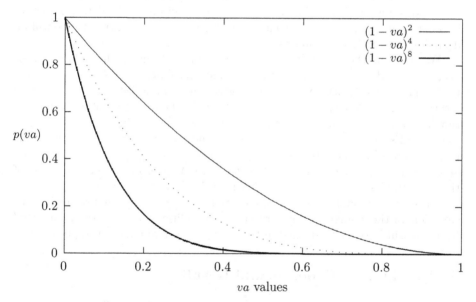

Fig. 5. Penalty function for the acceptance values

4.2 The Detection Results

The detection algorithm provides two types of alerts. First, at each client connection, we perform a test which can activate an *instantaneous alert*. This test consists in verifying whether we reached a tree leaf or not. In the event that we do, if the computed value of d_i during the connection i is higher than the threshold s, no alert is raised. Otherwise, an *instantaneous alert* is raised. When

Table 1. Variation of d_i in terms of $p_i(va_i)$

o	$pi(va_i) = (1 - 0.4)^o$	$d^1 = d^0 - P(va)$
2	0.36	0.64
4	0.1296	0.8704
8	0.0167	0.9832

the client disconnects without reaching a leaf, we consider that this behavior is intrusive and we activate an *instantaneous alert*. During the navigation through the tree branches, the degree d_i may be annuled in two cases: either the client has cumulated several suspect requests which implies a null value of d_i, or he invoked an unexpected request in the path already selected in the tree. In the latter case, we immediatly annul the similarity degree because we consider each unexpected request as intrusive, which can be restrictive. We propose in the future to take into account request insertions and deletions in the detection period in order to authorize certain deviation. In this case, the similarity degree will be decreased but no longer annuled.

We continue the observation of a client behavior during the following connections in order to detect a series of anomalous connections. A *composed alert* is raised if the similarity degree d_i keeps less than a *composed threshold* s' during a certain time δt longer than Δt. Figure 6 shows the evolution of d_i during the time and states the two types of alerts. We note that during δt_1, d_i keeps less than s and s', which activates for each disconnection an *instantaneous alert* but no *composed alert* as δt_1 is less than Δt. During δt_2, d_i keeps less than s' which activates a *composed alert* as δt_2 is longer than Δt. During the same interval of time δt_2, there's no *instantaneous alert* as d_i keeps higher than s.

For want of a real application, no reaction strategy is expected regarding this situation for the moment. Various reaction possibilities against intrusive detected behavior will have to be studied in the future for a real CORBA application.

5   Preliminary Experimental Results

We tested our approach on the developed testbed which exhibits encouraging results.

The learned behavior is made of a series of basic operations on a banking account (account creation, payment, withdrawl, balance consultation, etc.). The IDL specification of these operations is the following :

```
module Bank{
    interface Account{
        float getBalance();
        float deposit (in float sum);
        float withdraw  (in float sum);
    }
```

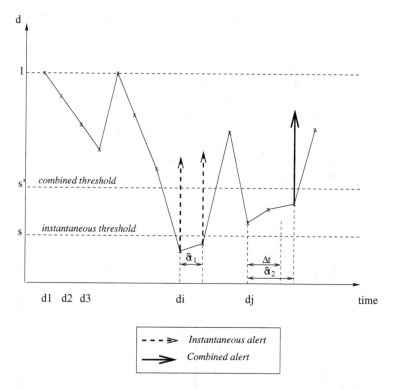

Fig. 6. Generated alerts

```
interface AccountManager{
    void open  (in string clientName);
    void close (in string clientName);
    Account search (in string clientName);
  }
}
```

The collected data is contained in an audit trail file. After filtering, the audit trail file contains information about the object invoked, the request and corresponding parameters, as shown in the following example :

```
connection
Bank::AccountManager::open(string bv)
Bank::AccountManager::search(string bv)
Bank::Account::deposit(float 200.0)
Bank::Account::getBalance()
Bank::Account::withdraw(float 100.0)
Bank::Account::withdraw(float 50.0)
Bank::Account::getBalance()
Bank::Account::withdraw(float 20.0)
```

```
Bank::AccountManager::search(string zm)
Bank::Account::getBalance()
disonnection
connection
Bank::Account::deposit(float 100.0)
Bank::Account::withdraw(float 100.0)
Bank::Account::getBalance()
Bank::AccountManager::open(string lm)
Bank::AccountManager::search(string lm)
Bank::Account::getBalance()
disconnection
```

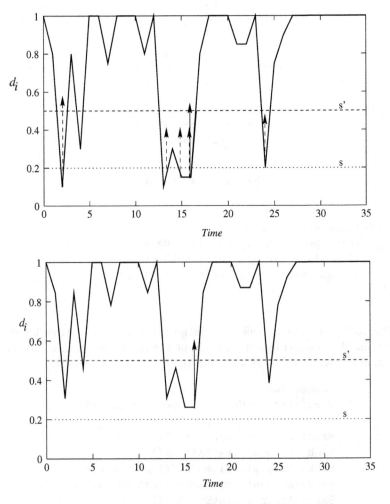

Fig. 7. Variation of the similarity degree

First tests consist in applying small variation of the client behavior to test the pertinence of the tolerance intervals previously defined. Results show that the number of raised alarms depends on the authorized gap δ (see Figure 7). We are working on the automatic adjustment of this gap regarding the associated parameter sensibility. Further studies will focus on the gap δ variation for each clusters of values of a given parameter.

Once the gap δ is fixed, we made a second series of tests aiming at adaptating the threshold s considering what has been learned. The number of raised alarms also depends on this threshold which depends on the context. In fact, this threshold must vary considering both the complexity of the application and the variation of the learned client behavior. To carry on these studies, a real CORBA application should be provided. We are waiting for such application.

Currently, we use previously fixed values of the thresholds s and s' and the gap δ to decide on the activation of alarms. However, these parameters are context dependant. We hope to dispose soon of a real application to test our approach and to conduct further studies on theses parameters.

6   Conclusion

We presented in this article our approach of the intrusion detection problem and a tree representation for the modeling of client behavior. This approach was tested in a CORBA environment. The detection algorithm is based on the measure of deviation between observed and learned behaviors. Giving the authorized degree of deviation for each parameter of the invoked requests, the algorithm computes a similarity degree. This degree is computed during each connection and allows us to decide on the activation of an alarm considering a fixed threshold. The surveillance of the client during many connections can reveal an attack composed of successive suspicious deviations.

The results show a good efficiency of the detection algorithm. A the end of a connection, it provides the corresponding similarity degree showing (or not) an anomalous behavior. Depending on this degree, we should decide on the consistency of the alarm but we are not able to make such a decision as we don't have a real CORBA application. The false alarm rate was not studied for the moment.

We propose to conduct complementary researches to our current work. Further studies concern especially the following points:

- The variation of the penalty function degree o: we used for our preliminary tests a quadratic penalty function but we propose to vary this degree and test other penalty functions.
- The dependance between successive request parameters: in fact, we think that the invocation of a request with certain values has an influence on the values of the following request. We are interested in studying these correlations by expressing them using constraints defined at each node.
- We have also raised in this article the problem of insertion and deletion of requests. We suggest to accept these situations to allow flexibility in the

client behavior. However, we will point out these situations by decreasing the similarity degree.

- We discussed the possibility of reacting after detecting. An intrusion detection system should be able to activate alarms, be sure of their consistency and then react against these intrusions. Currently, we just work on detection mechanisms. We are also thinking about a reactive mechanism for a real CORBA application. One of the reviewers suggest us to propose a virtual environment for a suspected client. One of the possible reactions against an intruder is then to protect the real system from an eventual damage.
- The variation in the time elapsed between successive invocations may reveal an anomalous behavior. Thus, we plan, as suggested by a reviewer, to consider, in addition to the order of invoked requests in a sequence, the time interval between successive requests.

Acknowledgments

We want to thank the reviewers for their helpful remarks and interesting suggestions.

References

1. H. Debar, M. Dacier, M.Nassehi, and A. Wespi. Fixed vs. variable-length patterns for detecting suspicious process. In J. J. Quisquater, Y. Deswarte, C. Meadows, and D. Gollmann, editors, *Proceedings of the 1998 ESORICS Conference*, number 1485 in LNCS, pages 1–16, september 1998. 131
2. Inprise. Programmer's guide, visibroker for java (v3.3). http://www.inprise.com/, 1998. 133
3. M. Stillman M. Stillman, C. Marceau. Intrusion detection for distributed applications. *Communications of the ACM*, 42(7):62–69, July 1999. 131
4. OMG. Corba services : Common object services specification. http://www.omg.org/, december 1998. 132
5. OMG. Corba / iiop specification (v2.3.1). http://www.omg.org/, June 1999. 132

The 1998 Lincoln Laboratory IDS Evaluation
A Critique*

John McHugh

CERT® Coordination Center, Software Engineering Institute
Carnegie Mellon University
jmchugh@cert.org

Abstract. In 1998 (and again in 1999), the Lincoln Laboratory of MIT conducted a comparative evaluation of Intrusion Detection Systems developed under DARPA funding. While this evaluation represents a significant and monumental undertaking, there are a number of unresolved issues associated with its design and execution. Some of methodologies used in the evaluation are questionable and may have biased its results. One of the problems with the evaluation is that the evaluators have published relatively little concerning some of the more critical aspects of their work, such as validation of their test data. The purpose of this paper is to attempt to identify the shortcomings of the Lincoln Lab effort in the hope that future efforts of this kind will be placed on a sounder footing. Some of the problems that the paper points out might well be resolved if the evaluators publish a detailed description of their procedures and the rationale that led to their adoption, but other problems clearly remain.

Keywords: Evaluation, IDS, ROC Analysis

1 Introduction

The most comprehensive evaluation of research Intrusion Detection Systems that has been performed to date is an ongoing effort by MIT's Lincoln Laboratory, performed under DARPA sponsorship. While this work is flawed in many respects, it is the only large scale attempt at an objective evaluation of these systems of which the author is aware. As such, it does provide a basis for making a rough comparison of existing systems under a common set of circumstances and assumptions.

It is important to note that the present paper is a critique of existing work, not a direct technical contribution or a proposal for new efforts, *per se*. Its purpose is to examine the work done by the Lincoln Laboratory group in a critical but scholarly fashion, relying on the public (published) record to the greatest extent possible. The role of the critic is to ask questions and to point out failings and omissions, but not necessarily to provide solutions to all the issues raised. Indeed, the problem is large and complex and one of the likely reasons

---

* This work was sponsored by the U.S. Department of Defense.

H. Debar, L. Mé, and F. Wu (Eds.): RAID 2000, LNCS 1907, pp. 145–161, 2000.
© Springer-Verlag Berlin Heidelberg 2000

for many of Lincoln's failures that its size and complexity clearly outstripped the resources available to apply to it. Many of the issues raised in this paper will require substantial resources and effort to resolve, and, at the time of writing, these resources were not available. Still, it is to be hoped that the community as a whole will be able to address these problems in connection with future efforts.

The analysis given here is presented with the goal of promoting a discussion of the difficulties that are inherent in performing objective evaluations of software. Although the software in question performs security related functions, the questions raised in its evaluation should be of interest to the broader software engineering community, particularly to that portion of the community that deals with software testing or evaluation and reliability estimation. As far as we have been able to determine, no comparable efforts have been reported elsewhere in the software evaluation and testing community. Only the usage modeling and statistical testing used by the Cleanroom methodology [13, Ch. 10] seems to come close.

We concentrate on the 1998 evaluation. The 1999 evaluation was under way when the original version of this paper was written and its results, though presented in a number of meetings (including RAID 2000) have not been published in detail. Many of the changes made during the 1999 evaluation do not affect the observations or conclusions of this paper. The data used in 1999 was similar in form to that of 1998. Sessions were not identified in the training data, making the unit of analysis problem described in section 5.1 more difficult. TCP dump data was sensed both inside and outside the target system and a Windows NT victim was added. A relatively permissive security policy was described for the targets. A wider variety of attacks were represented in the data, including several insider attacks. Initial presentations of the 1999 results relied heavily on ROC analysis (see section 5.2), but more recent presentations have dropped this approach entirely. Missed attacks were analyzed in some detail with investigators being asked to explain why their system did not detect them. In many cases, especially for rule based systems, the misses were due to decisions by the investigators (encouraged by the sponsor) to concentrate on detection technique at the expense of complete rule bases. It would be interesting to rescore the 1999 results, using the optimistic assumption that such misses are correctable in a production version of the system.

The discussion begins with a consideration of the methods used to generate the data used for the evaluation. There are a number of questions that can be raised with respect to the use of synthetic data to estimate real world system performance. We concentrate on two of these; the extent to which the experimental data is appropriate for the task at hand and the possible effects of the architecture of the simulated test environment. This is followed by a discussion of the taxonomy developed to categorize the exploits involved in the evaluation. The taxonomy used was developed solely from the attacker's point of view and may introduce a bias in evaluating manifestations seen by the attacked.

The Lincoln Lab evaluation uses the ROC, variously known as the receiver operating curve or relative operating characteristic as the primary method for presenting the results of the evaluation. This form of analysis has been used in a variety of other fields, but it appears to have some unanticipated problems in its application to the IDS evaluation. These involve problems in determining appropriate units of analysis, bias towards possibly unrealistic detection approaches, and questionable presentations of false alarm data.

2   Evaluation Overview

The descriptions of the evaluation that have appeared in print leave much unsaid and it may be that a more detailed exposition of the work will alleviate some of the criticisms contained in this paper. The most detailed descriptions of the work available at the present time are Kristopher Kendall's BS/MS Thesis [6] and a paper [9] presented at DISCEX in January, 2000. In addition, the Lincoln Lab team has made presentations on the experiment at various meetings attended by the author. These include the August 1999 DARPA PI meeting in Phoenix, AZ and RAID 99. Presentations [8, 4] similar to ones given at those meetings also appear at the Lincoln Lab experiment site, http://ideval.ll.mit.edu[1].

According to the DISCEX paper [9], "The primary purpose of the evaluations is to drive iterative performance improvements in participating systems by revealing strengths and weaknesses and helping researchers focus on eliminating weaknesses." The experiment claims to provide "unbiased measurement of current performance levels." Another objective is to provide a common shared corpora of experimental data that is available to a wide range of researchers.

While these goals are laudable, it is not clear that the way in which the evaluation has been carried out is consistent with the goals. In section 3 we will discuss the adequacy of the data set used during the evaluation, suggesting that, at best, its suitability for this purpose has not been demonstrated. The way in which the results of the evaluation have been presented (through the use of ROC and ROC like curves as discussed in section 5.2) seems to demonstrate a bias towards systems that can be tuned to a known mix of signal and noise, even though the appropriate tuning parameters may not be possible to discover in the wild. Each of these factors will be discussed further in the appropriate sections.

Many of the systems evaluated by the Lincoln Lab group have been described in a variety of technical publications, some of which are cited in the DISCEX paper [9]. Each system under test was evaluated by its developers who adapted the data as necessary to fit the system in question [9, Section 7]. It is highly likely the disparate behaviors of the individual investigators introduced unintentional biases into the results of the evaluation, but there has been no discussion of this possibility in any of the presentations or in the DISCEX paper.

---

[1] This site is password protected. For information concerning access, contact intrusion@sst.ll.mit.edu.

3   The Evaluation Data

For reasons having to do with privacy and the sensitivity of actual data content, the experimenters chose to synthesize both the background data and the attack data used during the evaluation. There are problems with both components. The data also reflects problems that are inherent in the architecture used to generate it. The generated data is intended to serve as corpora for present and future experimenters in the field. As such, it may have a lasting impact on the way IDS systems are constructed. Unless the performance of an IDS system on the corpora can be related accurately to its performance in the wild, there is a risk that systems may be biased towards unrealistic expectations with respect to true detections, false alarms, or both. It is also necessary to ensure that the corpora are sufficiently large so that deviations from the desired norm do not alter evaluation results.

The data generated for the evaluation consists of two components, background data that is intended to be completely free of attacks and attack data that is intended to consist entirely of attack scenarios. The test stream results from simultaneously generating and interleaving of the two components. If we view background data as noise and attack data as signal, the IDS problem can be characterized as one of detecting a signal in the presence of noise. The evaluation produces two measures, one primarily a function of the noise, the other primarily a function of the signal embedded in noise. Given this approach, it is necessary to ensure that both the signal and the noise used for the evaluation affect the systems under test in a manner related to signals and noise that occur in real deployment environments.

3.1   Background Data

The process used to generate background data or noise is only superficially described in the thesis and presentations. The data is claimed to be similar to that observed during several months of sampling data from a number of Air Force bases, but the statistics used to describe the real traffic and the measures used to establish similarity are not given, except for the claim that word and word pair statistics of email messages match those observed. The DISCEX paper [9, Sections 3 and 4] devotes approximately a page to a discussion of this issue and makes a broad claim that the data is similar to that seen on operational Air Force bases. It has been observed that internet site behaviors differ greatly[2] and, while it is possible that Air Force bases form an exception, the notion of a typical mix of background traffic should be viewed with some skepticism. If this skepticism is justified, and if the nature of the background traffic is shown to have a substantial impact on IDS performance, we see no alternative to the provision of much more extensive corpora of evaluation data.

---

[2] This was pointed out by one of the anonymous reviewers for RAID 2000. Although it may not hold for Air Force bases, it is a factor to consider in extending the results of the evaluation to more general environments.

As far as can be determined from the record, neither analytical nor experimental validation of the background data's adequacy was undertaken prior to the evaluation. No rationale is given that would allow a reader to conclude that the systems under test should exhibit false alarm behaviors when exposed to the artificial background data that are similar to those that they exhibit when exposed to "natural" data. This is particularly troublesome since the metric used for the evaluation of the IDS systems under test is an operating point characterized by the percentage of detected intrusions at a given false alarm rate or percentage. False alarms should arise exclusively from the background data, and it would appear incumbent upon the evaluators to show that the false alarm behavior of the systems under test is not significantly different on real and synthetic data.

Real data on the internet is not well behaved. Bellovin reported on anomalous packets [2] some years ago. Observations by Paxson [12] indicate that the situation has become worse in recent years with significant quantities of random garbage being frequently observed on the internet. This internet "crud" consists of legitimate but odd looking traffic. Poor implementations of protocols often result in spontaneous packet storms that are indistinguishable from malicious attempts at flooding. Many of the packets that Bellovin and Paxson observe could (and probably should) be interpreted as suspicious. As far as we can tell, such packets were not included in the background traffic.

None of the sources that we have examined contain any discussion of the data rate and its variation with time is not specified. This may be another critical factor in performing an evaluation of an IDS system because it appears that some systems may have performance problems or may be subject to what are, in effect, denial of service attacks when deployed in environments with excessive data rates[3]. We have performed a superficial examination of several days of the tcpdump training data. The results indicate averages in the 10 to 50 kilobit per second range over the 22 hour period. Given that most of the activity occurs during working hours, the daylight rate may be 2 or 3 times this. In contrast, data rates at the Portland State University Computer Science department ($\approx$100 workstations) and Engineering school (several hundred) are 1 and 10 megabits per second respectively. Paxson indicates sustained data rates in excess of 30 megabits per second [12] on the FDDI link monitored by the Bro IDS. Since one would expect false alarm rates to be proportional the background traffic rate for a given mix, the false alarm rates reported by Lincoln Lab may need to be adjusted.

3.2 Attack Data

Similar arguments can be made about the synthetic attack data. The attacks used were implemented via scripts and programs collected from a variety of sources. As far as can be determined from the available descriptions, no attempt was made to ensure that the synthetic attacks were realistically distributed in

---

[3] This factor may not be relevant for an offline evaluation, but we would expect the evaluators to consider timing.

the background noise. This may or may not be significant, depending on several factors, including the use to be made of the evaluation results, but it raises several issues. Reporting an aggregate result over any mix requires a strong caveat to the effect that the results may not apply to other mixes. This is more important if the mix is atypical[4]. In addition, some systems that require training on a known mix of attack and background data may be sensitive to the mix and fail to perform as well on substantially different mixes.

Kendall [6, Section 12.2] describes the total number of attacks in various categories that were included in the training and test data sets. Some 300 attacks were injected into 10 weeks of data, an average of 3 to 4 attacks per day. Kendall gives a tabulation of the attack data in [6, Table 12.1]. In each of the major categories of the attack taxonomy (User to Root, Remote to Local User, Denial of Service, and Probe/Surveillance) the number of attacks is of the same order (114, 34, 99, and 64). This is surely unrealistic as current experience indicates that Probe/Surveillance actions are by far the most common attack actions reported.

An aggregate detection rate based on the experimental mix represented in the corpora is highly unlikely to reflect performance in the field. If a more detailed analysis and presentation of the data were to be used, the attack mix would be less significant, although the user of the evaluation results would have to invest more time and effort in understanding the results and their significance. Particular care would be needed to ensure that the presentation does not obscure the characteristics of the evaluated systems in this case. For example, the attack taxonomy used combines attacks that have widely differing manifestations. Reporting, for example, that a given system detected 60% of the denial of service attacks may reflect the system's ability to detect some kinds of manifestations and not others rather than reflecting on its ability to detect that taxonomic category of attack. Thus, even reporting performance by taxonomic attack category may be misleading if the distribution of attack manifestations is not explicitly considered.

The evaluation data represents an attempt at creating a somewhat realistic test environment in which known attacks are executed in a background of normal activity. A number of researchers have said that it would also be useful to present a variety of attacks under ideal conditions without background traffic so as to separate detection characteristics from the confounding effects of the background traffic. Providing attack data in this form was not one of the goals of the Lincoln effort.

---

[4] While it is clear that there is no such thing as a typical mix of attacks, experience over the past few years indicates that hacker activity on the internet (the attack population represented in the experimental mix) consists primarily of probe activities followed by fairly large numbers of the most recently popular attack *du jour*, followed by a sprinkling of less recently publicized attacks against well known vulnerabilities.

3.3   Eyrie AFB

The simulated data is said to represent the traffic to and from a typical Air Force Base, referred to as Eyrie AFB. The thesis [6, Figure 3-1] and the information available from the Lincoln Lab web site seem to differ on the details of the configuration. The host list for weeks 3-7 lists additional hosts linux1 – linux10 which are probably implemented on the additional Linux target mentioned in the thesis, but the week 3-7 network diagram does not show this host. The DISCEX paper [9, Section 3] is less specific.

The thesis contains a list of the attacks [6, Appendix A] from the test phase of the evaluation. 45 attacks target Pascal, 28 target Marx, 12 target Zeno, 10 target one of the virtual Linux machines, and 5 (all the same scenario) target the router. The only attacks that attempt to access any of the other simulated machines at Eyrie are probes or scans for which no response is necessary. The skewed nature of the attack distribution may affect the evaluation. By the end of the training period, it should have been clear to the testers that only a small subset of the systems are actually subject to interactive attacks. Tuning or configuring the IDS under evaluation to look only at these systems would be an effective way to reduce false alarms and might raise the true alarm rate by reducing noise. This appears to fall within the letter, if not the spirit, of the 1998 rules though there is no evidence that it was done by any of the participants.

Although it is claimed that the traffic used in the evaluation is similar to that of a typical Air Force base, no such claim is made for the internal network architecture used. The unrealistic nature of the architecture is implicitly acknowledged by Kendall [6, Section 6.8] where it is noted that the flat structure of the simulation network precluded direct execution of a "smurf" or ICMP echo attack. It is not known whether the flat network structure used in the experiment is typical of Air Force bases, but this seems doubtful as does the relatively small host population. Investigation of whether this as well as the limited number of hosts attacked affect the evaluation is needed. Certainly, intrusion detection systems that make a stateful evaluation of the traffic stream are less likely to suffer from resource exhaustion in such a limited environment.

3.4   Does It Matter?

Perhaps and perhaps not. Many experiments and studies are conducted in environments that are contrived. Usually, this is done to control for factors that might confound the results. When it is done, however, the burden is on the experimenter to show that the artificial environment did not affect the outcome of the experiment. A fairly common method of demonstrating that the experimental approach being used is sound is to conduct a controlled pilot study to collect evidence supporting the proposed approach. As far as we can tell, no pilot studies were performed either to validate the use of artificial data or to ensure that the data generation process resulted in reasonably error free data. The evaluators at Lincoln Lab have not shown that the test environment that they created does not confound the evaluation in ways that would affect its objectives.

3.5   Training and Test Data Presentation

The evaluators prepared datasets for the purposes of "training" and "test." The training set consists of seven weeks of data covering 22 hours per day, 5 days per week. As discussed in section 5.1 below, the training data contains attacks that are identified in the associated lists. It also contains examples of anomalies, here defined rather restrictively as departures from the normal behaviors of individual system users rather than the more common usage of abnormal or unusual events.

The apparent purpose of this data was to provide the researchers being evaluated with corpora containing known and identified attacks that could be used to tune their systems. For the systems based on the detection of anomalies, the training data was intended to provide a characterization of "normal," although the presence of attacks in the data renders it questionable from this standpoint. The question of the adequacy of this data for its intended purpose does not seem to have been addressed. There is no discussion, for example, of whether the quantity of data presented is sufficient to train a statistical anomaly system or other learning based system. Similarly, there is no discussion of whether the rates of intrusions or their relationship to one another is typical of the scenarios that such detectors might expect.

For systems using *a priori*, non parametric, rules for detecting intrusion manifestations, the training data provides a sanity check, but little more. If there are background manifestations that trigger the same rule as an identified intrusion in the training data, and the developer wishes to use the training data to guide development of his system he might attempt to refine the rules to be more discriminatory. The user could also change the way in which the system operates to make detections probabilistic, based on the relative frequencies of identified intrusion manifestations and background manifestations that trigger the same rule. As we will see later, the ROC analysis method is biased towards detection systems that use this kind of approach.

For systems that can be tuned to the mix of background and intrusions present in the training data, this bias may be inherent depending on whether the detection methods result in probabilistic recognitions of intrusions or whether internal thresholds are adjusted to achieve a similar effect. The problem with tuning the system to the data mix present in the training data is that transferring the system experience to the real world either requires demonstrating that the training mix is an accurate representation of real world data with respect to the techniques used by each system or it requires that accurate real world training data be available for each deployment environment. We claim that the former conditions have not been met and that the latter may not be possible. As far as we are aware, existing studies of network traffic patterns show a high degree of variability among sites as well as substantial changes with time at a given site. As we have noted earlier, unless the target environments, i.e. military installations, are atypical, it may be the case that there is no such thing as a "typical" traffic mix that is suitable for background data. If each deployment environment is characterized by a unique traffic mix and if the ability of an IDS to detect intrusions effectively depends on tuning it to match the mix under controlled conditions, the problem may well be intractable. More work on traffic characterization and the effects of traffic variability on the IDSs is clearly needed.

If one views the corpora of training data as a form of benchmark against which present and future IDS systems might be evaluated, there is also a risk that systems might be optimized for the benchmark at the expense of normal case behavior. This is a well known problem in the software evaluation field.

4   The Taxonomy of Attacks

Kendall's thesis uses a taxonomy of attacks that was originally developed by Weber [15]. The taxonomy describes intrusions from an intruder centric viewpoint based loosely on a user objective. For the purposes of the evaluation, the attacks used were characterized as

1. Denial of Service,
2. Remote to user,
3. User to Superuser, or
4. Surveillance/Probing

and were further characterized by the mechanism used. The mechanisms were characterized as

m Masquerading (stolen password or forged IP address)
a Abuse of a feature
b Implementation bug
c System misconfiguration
s Social engineering

While this taxonomy describes the kinds of attacks that can be made on systems or networks, it is not useful in describing what an intrusion detection system might see. For example, in the denial of service category, we see attacks against the protocol stack, against protocol services, against the mail, web, and syslog services, and against the system process table. The effects range from machine and network slowdowns to machine crashes. From the standpoint of a network or host observer (i.e. most intrusion detection systems), the attack manifestations have almost nothing in common. From this, it can be seen that the taxonomy used in the evaluation offers very little support for developing an understanding of intrusions and their detection. We suggest that the taxonomy used is not particularly supportive of the stated objectives of the evaluation and that one or more of the potential taxonomies discussed in the following section could be more useful in guiding the process.

The attacker centric taxonomy poses an additional problem. By tying attacks to overt actions on the part of a putative attacker, it creates a highly unrealistic evaluation bias. The treatment of probes is a case in point. Not all probes are hostile. They are a standard way of attempting to initiate internet communication, but communication does not always occur even when the probed host acknowledges that it provides the probed for service. As far as we have been able to tell, the 1998 background data does not contain this kind of benign probe activity, but the evaluation data contained at least one "attack" that consisted of a very small number of probes. We claim that, had the background data contained a typical mix of normal or benign probe data, these probes would have been distinguishable as attacks only if the intent of the prober were known. While this is possible in the evaluation context, it is generally not possible in the field.

4.1   An Alternative Taxonomy

Attacks could be classified based on the protocol layer and the particular protocol within the layer that they use as the vehicle for the attack. Under this approach, attacks such as "Land," "Ping of Death," and "Teardrop" are related because they never get out of the protocol stack. They are also similar in being detectable only by an external observer looking at the structure of the packets for the identifying characteristics. Smurf and UDPStorm attacks are even lower in the hierarchy because they affect the network and interface in the neighborhood of the victim. Also, they are detectable based on counting of packet occurrences which could be considered a lower level operation than examining packet structure. Attacks that involve altering the protocol stack state such as "SYNFlood" are higher since their detection either involves monitoring the state of the protocol stack internally, or modeling and tracking the state based on an external view. Attacks that require the protocol stack to deliver a message to an applications process (trusted or not) are still higher. Detecting such attacks requires either monitoring the messages within the host (between the stack and the application or within the application) or modeling the entire stack accurately, assembling messages externally and examining the interior data with respect to the view of the attacked application to determine the attack. Probes can take on a variety of forms, but are usually handled either within the stack (especially if the service sought is not supported) or via interaction with the application that supports the probed for service.

A strength of this taxonomic approach is that it leads to an understanding of what one must do to detect attacks. Within a particular higher level protocol or service this view may group attacks that exploit common vulnerabilities together, for example "Appache2" and "Back" exploit pathologies in the http specification while "phf" exploits a bug in the web server's implementation of CGI bin program handling.

Many other taxonomies are possible. The point is that the taxonomy must be constructed with two objectives in mind; describing the relevant universe and applying the description to gain insight into the problem at hand. Weber's taxonomy serves the first purpose fairly well, but fails to provide insights useful to understanding the detection of intrusions.

5   The Evaluation

The results of the evaluation and the way in which they have been presented by Lincoln Lab present a number of difficulties. We examine several of these, notably the problem of determining an appropriate "unit of analysis" and problems associated with the use of the ROC method of analysis. The unit of analysis problem arises whenever experimental results are reported as percentages. The evaluated IDS systems report detections which can be characterized as either correct, i.e. an attack was reported when one *was* present, or incorrect, i.e. a false alarm, an attack that was reported when one *was not* present. The ROC method requires both correct and incorrect detections to be reported as percentages of the possible cases in which the detection could have been made. In the case of the evaluation, successful detections can be reported as (number of attacks detected) / (number of attacks made), but no comparable denominator exists for reporting false alarms. The unit of analysis problem is well known in other fields [16] where it often results in ascribing more power than is appropriate to the results of certain statistical tests. While this is not the case here, the problem exists and its solution is a necessary prerequisite to performing meaningful comparisons among systems. For example, two sustems may raise the same number of false alarms and have different false alarm percentages if one bases its decisions on the examination of entire protocol sessions while the other examines individual packets.

ROC analysis is a powerful technique for evaluating detection systems, but there are a number of underlying assumptions that must be satisfied for the technique to be effective. It is not clear that these assumptions are or can be satisfied in the experimental context. In addition, ROC analysis is biased towards a classical detection approach not commonly used in IDS systems.

5.1   TCPdump Data and the Unit of Analysis Problem

The largest data set[5] made available to investigators for evaluating their systems consists of raw TCPdump data collected with a sniffer positioned on the network segment external to the Eyrie AFB router. This dataset should contain all the data generated inside the simulated base destined for the outside world and all the data generated outside the base destined for an inside location. Experience with TCPdump indicates that it can become overloaded and drop packets although the possibility of this is reduced by the apparently low data rates used. The thesis indicates that attacks were "verified" by hand and that this process was very labor intensive [6, Section 13.2.2], but it is unclear what verification means here.

Training data is accompanied by a list of the "sessions" that are present in the TCPdump data where a session is characterized by a starting time, duration, source, destination, and a protocol. If the session contained an attack, the list

---

[5] Solaris BSM audit data and file system dump data were also available. We have not looked at them.

identifies the attack. Examination of a sample of the TCPdump data indicates that it contains additional traffic, e.g. messages from ethernet hubs, that is not in the list.

The association of alarms with sessions is an instance of a more general unit of analysis problem. The question of an appropriate denominator for presenting the evaluation results is only superficially addressed. It may not be appropriate to use the same denominator for all systems and the choice of a denominator may vary from system to system or even from attack to attack within the same system. The appropriate unit of analysis is that body of information on which the system based its decision to raise or not raise an alarm. The denominator for the expression giving the percentage of true alarms is the number of cases when this decision point was reached and the body of data used to make the decision contained a manifestation of a real intrusion. Similarly, the appropriate denominator for false alarms is then the number of times that the system reached this decision point when the data on which the decision was based did not contain a manifestation of a real intrusion. These numbers are a function of the detection process and cannot be externally imposed unless the decision criteria are externally specified. Sessions may be the natural unit on which to base decisions in some systems and not for others and their use will bias the results when they are used as the unit of analysis where they are not appropriate.

The use of sessions as the unit of analysis presents other potential problems. Attacks are, of necessity, associated with a single session under this model, precluding the injection of coordinated attack behavior involving multiple sources and/or protocols. For example one could envision probes carried out from a large number of locations so that no single source address appears more than once. The session model seems to preclude this. Although the injected attacks are associated with sessions in the test data, nothing constrains the evaluated systems to use the session concept, and it is possible that alarms may be raised as a result of events contained in more than one session.

5.2   Scoring and the ROC

The Lincoln Lab team decided to use a technique known as the ROC[6] as the method for presenting their results and the use of this technique is claimed as one of the major contributions of their effort in the DISCEX paper [9, Section 2]. The ROC has its origin in radar signal detection techniques developed during World War II and was adopted by the psychological and psychophysical research communities during the early post war era [14]. Its adoption by the Lincoln Lab group is not surprising given that their background is in speech recognition (word spotting in particular). Much of the discussion that follows is due to Egan [3]. Signal detection theory was developed during the two decades following World War II to give an exact meaning, in a probabilistic sense, to the process of

---

[6] The term ROC originally stood for Receiver Operating Curve. Since the technique has been widely used to evaluate systems that do not have a recognizable receiver, ROC is commonly interpreted as Relative Operating Characteristic.

recognizing a wanted signal that has been degraded by noise. The methods took into account the relationship between the physical characteristics of the signal and the theoretically achievable performance of the observer. Later the concepts of signal detection theory were adapted to provide a basis for examining some problems in human perception. The basis for the ROC is given by Egan [3, P. 2]

> When the detection performance is imperfect, it is never assumed that the observer "detects the signal." Rather, it is assumed that the observer receives an input, and this input corresponds to, or is the equivalent of, the unique value of a likelihood ratio. Then, given other factors, such as the prior probability of signal existence, the observer makes the decision "Yes, the odds favor the event *signal plus noise*," or "No, the odds favor the event *noise alone*."

Egan goes on to note that signal detection theory consists of two parts, decision theory, which deals with the rules to be used in making decisions that satisfy a given goal, and distribution theory, dealing with the way in which the signals and noise are distributed. When the distributions are known (or can be assumed) the relationship between the distributions and possible performances is called ROC analysis.

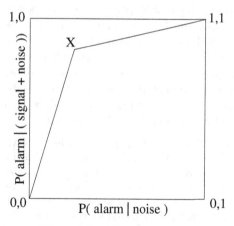

Fig. 1. A single point ROC

A typical ROC curve is a plot on two axes as seen in Figure 1. The vertical axis measures the true positive rate of the system (i.e. the Bayesian detection rate or the probability of a recognition given that signal plus noise is present). The horizontal axis gives the false positive rate (i.e. the probability that an alarm is raised given that only noise is present). An evaluation of a system provides estimates of these probabilities as the percentage of accurate and inaccurate recognitions in a series of trials under fixed conditions. By fixed conditions here, we mean constant distributions of signal plus noise and noise.

Note that there are two crucial aspects of the process. First, the observer receives an input and second, the observer makes a decision concerning that input. The observer thus controls the unit of analysis problem by defining the unit of analysis as the quantity of input on which a decision is made. Both positive and negative decisions must be recorded so that event counts for the denominators of the percentages used in ROC analysis will be available. Unless all the systems under evaluation are based on the same notion of an event on which a decision is to be made, choosing an arbitrary division in the input such as a packet or a session does not supply the necessary denominator.

Both parametric and non-parametric IDS detectors exist. Non parametric detectors have no provision for adjusting the sensitivity of the detection mechanism to effect a tradeoff between detection rates and false alarm rates. Examples include signature systems in which the attack signature is matched or it isn't and finite state approaches that raise an alert only if the underlying automata reaches an accepting state. Parametric systems have adjustable thresholds or are able to assign probabilities to alerts based, e.g., on a priori knowledge of signal and noise distributions[7] or on quantifiable uncertainties in the detection process. The later is more likely to be a property of anomaly detectors, especially those based on population or individual statistical properties.

If the ROC is an appropriate mechanism for presenting the results of an IDS evaluation in which non parametric, binary, decisions are made, the curve will consist of a single point that expresses the true positive and false positive percentages for the entire evaluation. The justification for drawing lines from the (0,0) coordinate to the point and from the point to the (1,1) coordinate is counterintuitive, imposing a probabilistic model where none is present. Nonetheless, the lines are usually presented as shown, and we follow the tradition in our presentation. In the environment in which most IDS systems operate, the signal percentage is very small[8] requiring very low false positive rates for useful detection as discussed in a recent paper by Axelsson [1].

---

[7] Suppose that we know that 0.1% of the probes for finger service are precursors to an attack, while 99.9% are benign. How should we deal with this situation? Assuming that we can detect the probe 100% of the time, we can raise an alert with a 0.1% probability that it represents an attack every time a finger probe occurs. The ROC method requires us to classify each alert as either a successful detection or as a false alarm, but allows us to vary the threshold for the decision. As we vary the threshold from 0.0% to 0.1% the curve will show 100% detection rate and 100% false alarm rate since both attacks and false alarms are assigned a probability above the threshold. Above a threshold of 0.1%, both the detection rate and false alarm rate drop to 0.0%. The problem here is that there is very little signal (attack instances) and a lot of noise (benign use of the finger service). In the absence of other factors that allow us to refine the probability assigned to a given probe, the a priori distribution does not help and we are left with two choices; ignore finger probes (missing a small number of attack indicators) or raise a large number of false alarms.

[8] This assumes that a small unit of analysis is chosen for computing the denominator of the false alarm rate.

As far as we are able to tell, none of the IDSs under evaluation use a likelihood ratio estimator that considers both the signal distribution and the noise distribution as their decision criteria and little is known about the *in vitro* distributions of intrusions and background activity that would make this fruitful. Most of the systems use only signal plus noise characteristics (signature based systems) or only noise characteristics (anomaly detection systems). The issue of tuning systems that use *a priori* distributions implicitly by learning or training procedures has been discussed above.

5.3   Errors per Unit Time

The DISCEX paper uses a non-standard variation of the ROC presentation [9, Figure 4] that labels the horizontal axis with false alarms per day rather than percent false alarms. A search of the traditional ROC literature [14, 3] shows no mention of this formulation. It does appear, without comment or justification in the word spotting literature where it is usually [7], but not always [5], referred to as a ROC curve.

Many of the corpora used for word spotting evaluations come from NIST, but researchers at NIST disavow the origin of the formulation saying that it was already in use when they entered the field. According to Alvin Martin of NIST, the earliest use of the formulation of which he is aware appeared in technical reports from Verbex Corporation in the late 1970s [10]. We were able to locate Stephen L. Moshier, one of the founders of Verbex and an author of some of the reports mentioned by Martin. He reported [11] that

> The military customer perceived that the user of a word spotter could cope with alarms (true or false) happening at a certain average rate but would becomes overloaded at a higher rate. So that is a model of the user, not a model of the incoming voice signals.

One of the more powerful features of the ROC analysis is its ability to abstract away certain experimental variables such as the rates at which detections are performed. The primary factors that influence ROC results are the detector characteristics and the distributions of signals and noise. If the latter are realistic, the ROC presentation of the detector characteristics should have good predictive power for detector performance in similar environments.

The pseudo-ROC, as we choose to call word spotting form, breaks these abstractions. By using incomparable units on the two axes, the results are strongly influenced by factors, such as data rate, that ought to be irrelevant. The form shown in the DISCEX paper is misleading for a number of reasons, notably because of its failure to present the relevant information. Using the data set as provided for the evaluation, but reassigning values to the time stamps attached to the data items, the false alarm rate per unit time can be manipulated to any degree desired by varying the total duration represented by the dataset[9]. At

---

[9] Changing the timestamps so as to give the appearance that a five day dataset represented a single day would raise the false alarms per day by a factor of five.

the very least, the pseudo-ROCs presented by Lincoln Lab [9, Figure 4] should be labeled with the data rate on which the false alarm axis is based. This is especially true given that the data rates used in the evaluation appear to be unrealistically low. Using the evaluated systems on data streams with megabit rates might result in a ten to hundredfold increase in the false alarm rate when reported per unit time.

6   Conclusions

The Lincoln Lab evaluation is a major and impressive undertaking, but its benefits seem to be far out of proportion with its costs and impacts on research programs. It is not clear that the results of the evaluation predict deployed performance. Reducing the performance of these systems to a single number or to a small group of numbers is not particularly useful to the investigators since the numbers have no explanatory power. While detection and false alarm rates are important at a gross level and might be a basis for comparing commercial products, the research community would benefit from an evaluation approach that would provide constructive advice for improvement.

It is hoped that this critique will either lead to a rethinking of the evaluation process and a recreation of it in a form that will help IDS development move forward. If the evaluation process cannot be modified so that it makes a substantial contribution to the improvement of the IDS state of the art, it would be better to abandon the evaluations for the present. Indeed, it appears that DARPA is currently rethinking its approach to evaluation in response to this and the other criticism[10] that it has received from other members of the IDS community.

Acknowledgments

I want to thank many members of the intrusion detection community for helpful comments on earlier versions of this paper. Some of them wish to remain anonymous and I respect those wishes. I also want to thank one of the anonymous reviewers for RAID 2000 who also provided numerous insightful and valuable comments. Roy Maxion of CMU has been a constant source of inspiration and support. Jim Jenkins of the Psychology Department of the University of South Florida provided help in tracking down the origins of the pseudo ROC curves as did Alvin Martin at NIST. Martin's efforts led me to Stephen L. Moshier, one of the founders of Verbex who was, in part, responsible for its introduction into

---

Similarly, increasing the generated background traffic from the average of 10Kb/s – 50Kb/s used in the evaluation to an average in the 50Kb/s – 250Kb/s rate should have the same effect.

[10] Criticisms similar to those presented in this paper were made in a presentation given by Brad Wood of Sandia National Laboratory at the DISCEX 2000 conference in January, 2000. Unfortunately, there is no corresponding paper in the DISCEX proceedings.

the word spotting arena. Stefan Axelsson provided valuable critiques of earlier versions of this paper. Julia Allen and Tom Longstaff of CERT have been most supportive and without their efforts, the paper would not exist. Jim Binkley of Portland State provided data on typical network traffic levels at the PSU School of Engineering.

References

[1] Stefan Axelsson. The base-rate fallacy and its implications for the difficulty of intrusion detection. In *6th ACM Conference on Computer and Communications Security*, pages 1–7, 1999. 158

[2] Steven M. Bellovin. Packets found on an internet. *Computer Communications Review*, 23(3):26–31, July 1993. 149

[3] James P. Egan. *Signal detection Theory and ROC Analysis*. Academic Press, 1975. 156, 157, 159

[4] Isaac Graf et al. Results of DARPA 1998 offline intrusion detection evaluation. Presentation at MIT Lincoln Laboratory PI Meeting (available at http://ideval.ll.mit.edu/results-html-dir/, 15 December 1998. 147

[5] D. A. James and S. J. Young. A fast lattice-based approach to vocabulary independent wordspotting. In *IEEE International Conference on Acoustics, Speech and Signal Processing*, pages 337–380, 1994. 159

[6] Kristopher Kendall. A database of computer attacks for the evaluation of intrusion detection systems. BS/MS thesis, Massachusetts Institute of Technology, June 1999. 147, 150, 151, 155

[7] Richard P. Lippmann, Eric I. Chang, and Charles R. Jankowski. Wordspotter training using figure-of-merit back propagation. In *IEEE International Conference on Acoustics, Speech and Signal Processing*, pages 385–388, 1994. 159

[8] Richard P. Lippmann et al. MIT Lincoln Laboratory offline component of DARPA 1998 intrusion detection evaluation. Presentation at MIT Lincoln Laboratory PI Meeting (available at http://ideval.ll.mit.edu/intro-html-dir/, 14 December 1998. 147

[9] Richard P. Lippmann et al. Evaluating intrusion detection systems: The 1998 DARPA off-line intrusion detection evaluation. In *DISCEX 2000*. IEEE Computer Society Press, January 2000. 147, 148, 151, 156, 159, 160

[10] Alvin Martin. Personal communications, January 2000. 159

[11] Stephen L. Moshier. Personal communications, January 2000. 159

[12] Vern Paxson. Bro: A system for detecting network intruders in real–time. *Computer Networks*, 31(23-24):2435–2463, December 1999. 149

[13] Stacy J. Prowell, Carmen J. Trammell, Richard C. Linger, and Jesse H. Poore. *Cleanroom Software Engineering: Technology and Process*. Addison–Wesley, Reading, Mass., 1998. 146

[14] John A. Swets. Measuring the accuracy of diagnostic systems. *Science*, 24(48):1285–1293, 3 June 1988. 156, 159

[15] Daniel Weber. A taxonomy of computer intrusions. MS thesis, Massachusetts Institute of Technology, 1998. 153

[16] Q. E. Whiting-O'Keefe, Curtis Henke, and Donald W. Simborg. Choosing the correct unit of analysis in medical care experiments. *Medical Care*, 22(12):1101–1114, December 1984. 155

Analysis and Results of the 1999 DARPA Off-Line Intrusion Detection Evaluation

Richard Lippmann, Joshua W. Haines, David J. Fried, Jonathan Korba, and
Kumar Das

MIT Lincoln Laboratory
244 Wood Street, Lexington, MA 02173-9108, USA
rpl@sst.ll.mit.edu
jhaines@sst.ll.mit.edu

Abstract. Eight sites participated in the second DARPA off-line intrusion detection evaluation in 1999. Three weeks of training and two weeks of test data were generated on a test bed that emulates a small government site. More than 200 instances of 58 attack types were launched against victim UNIX and Windows NT hosts. False alarm rates were low (less than 10 per day). Best detection was provided by network-based systems for old probe and old denial-of-service (DoS) attacks and by host-based systems for Solaris user-to-root (U2R) attacks. Best overall performance would have been provided by a combined system that used both host- and network-based intrusion detection. Detection accuracy was poor for previously unseen new, stealthy, and Windows NT attacks. Ten of the 58 attack types were completely missed by all systems. Systems missed attacks because protocols and TCP services were not analyzed at all or to the depth required, because signatures for old attacks did not generalize to new attacks, and because auditing was not available on all hosts.

1 Introduction

Computer attacks launched over the Internet are capable of inflicting heavy damage due to increased reliance on network services and worldwide connectivity. It is difficult to prevent attacks by security policies, firewalls, or other mechanisms. System and application software always contains unknown weaknesses or bugs, and complex often unforeseen interactions between software components and/or network protocols are continually exploited by attackers. Intrusion detection systems are designed to detect attacks that inevitably occur despite security precautions.

Discussions of alternate approaches to intrusion detection are available in [1,6,16]. Some approaches detect attacks in real time and can be used to monitor and possibly stop an attack in progress. Others provide after-the-fact forensic information about attacks and can help repair damage, understand the attack mechanism, and reduce the possibility of future attacks of the same type. More advanced intrusion detection systems detect never-before-seen, new, attacks, while the more typical systems detect previously seen, known attacks.

H. Debar, L. Mé, and F. Wu (Eds.): RAID 2000, LNCS 1907, pp. 162–182, 2000.

The widespread deployment and high cost of both commercial and government-developed intrusion detection systems has led to an interest in evaluating these systems. Evaluations that focus on algorithm performance are essential for ongoing research. They can contribute to rapid research progress by focusing efforts on difficult technical areas, they can produce common shared corpora or data bases which can be used to benchmark performance levels, and they make it easier for new researchers to enter a field and explore alternate approaches. A review of past intrusion detection evaluations is provided in [11].

The most comprehensive evaluations of intrusion detection systems performed to date were supported by DARPA in 1998 and 1999 [3,11,12]. These evaluations included research intrusion detection systems and attacks against UNIX, Windows NT, and Cisco Routers. They also used a relatively simple network architecture and background traffic designed to be similar to traffic on one Air Force base. The most recent 1999 evaluation included many novel aspects [11]. Both detection and false alarm rates were carefully measured for more than 18 systems. More than 56 attack types included stealthy and novel new attacks were used to measure detection rates and weeks of background traffic were used to measure false alarm rates. In addition, a unique intrusion detection corpus was created that includes weeks of background traffic and hundreds of labeled and documented attacks. This corpus has been widely distributed and is being used as a benchmark for evaluating and developing intrusion detection systems. Both 1998 and 1999 DARPA evaluations included two components. An off-line component produced labeled benchmark corpora that were used simultaneously at many sites to develop and evaluate intrusion detection systems [11,12]. The complementary real-time component [3] assessed only systems that had real-time implementations using fewer attacks and hours instead of weeks of background traffic. The remainder of this paper focuses on the off-line component of the 1999 evaluation. It provides a summary of this research effort, discusses details concerning the motivation and design of background traffic and stealthy attacks, and discusses an analytic approach that can be used to predict whether an intrusion detection system will miss a particular new attack. This paper complements [11], which provides further background and summary results for the 1999 off-line evaluation. Detailed descriptions of attacks in the 1999 evaluation are available in [2,8,9,13,14]. Further details and downloadable corpora are available at [14].

2   Overview of the 1999 Evaluation

The 1999 off-line evaluation included three weeks of training data with background traffic and labeled attacks to develop and tune intrusion detection systems and two weeks of test data with background traffic and unlabeled attacks. Techniques originally developed during the 1998 evaluation [12] were extended to more fully analyze system behavior and cover more attack types. Figure 1 shows the isolated test bed network used to generate background traffic and attacks. Scripting techniques, which extend the approaches used in [19], generate live background traffic similar to that which flows between the inside of one Air

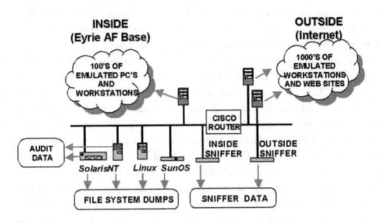

Fig. 1. Block diagram of 1999 test bed

Force base and the outside Internet. This approach was selected for the evaluation because hosts can be attacked without degrading operational Air Force systems and because corpora containing background traffic and attacks can be widely distributed without security or privacy concerns. A rich variety of background traffic that looks as if it were initiated by hundreds of users on thousands of hosts is generated in the test bed. The left side of Figure 1 represents the inside of the fictional Eyrie Air Force base created for the evaluations and the right side represents the outside Internet. Automated attacks were launched against four inside UNIX and Windows NT victim machines (Linux 2.0.27, SunOS 4.1.4, Sun Solaris 2.5.1, Windows NT 4.0) and a Cisco 2514 router. More than 200 instances of 58 different attacks were embedded in three weeks of training data and two weeks of test data. Inside and outside machines labeled sniffer in Figure 1 run a program named *tcpdump* [10] to capture all packets transmitted over the attached network segments. This program was customized to open a new output data file after the current active output file size exceeds 1 Gbytes. The status line printed when *tcpdump* was terminated each day never indicated that any packets were dropped. Data collected to evaluate intrusion detection systems include this network sniffing data, Solaris Basic Security Module (BSM) audit data collected from the Solaris host, Windows NT audit event logs collected from the Windows NT host, nightly listings of all files on the four victim machines, and nightly dumps of security-related files on all victim machines.

New features in the 1999 off-line evaluation include the Windows NT victim machine and associated attacks and audit data. These were added due to increased reliance on Windows NT systems by the military. Inside attacks, inside sniffer data to detect these attacks, and stealthy attacks were also added due the dangers posed by inside attacks and an emphasis on sophisticated attackers who can carefully craft attacks to look like normal traffic. In addition, an analysis of

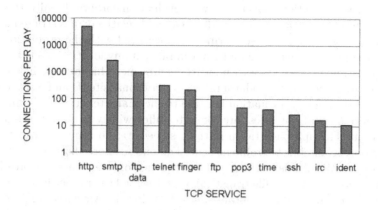

Fig. 2. Average connections per day for dominant TCP services

misses and high-scoring false alarms was performed for each system to determine why systems miss specific attacks.

The 1999 evaluation was designed primarily to measure the ability of systems to detect new attacks without first training on instances of these attacks. The previous 1998 evaluation had demonstrated that systems could not detect new attacks well. The new 1999 evaluation was designed to evaluate enhanced systems which can detect new attacks and to analyze why systems miss new attacks. Many new attacks were thus developed and only examples of a few of these were provided in training data.

3   Test Bed Network and Background Traffic

The test bed architecture shown in Figure 1 is a basic foundation that is becoming more complex as the evaluations progress. It was designed to simplify network administration and to support attack and background traffic generation and also instrumentation required to collect input data required by intrusion detection systems. This flat network architecture is not representative of an Air Force base. It is a minimal network designed to support intrusion detection systems that desired to participate in 1998 and 1999, attack types of interest, and most of the network traffic types seen across many Air Force bases. Future evaluations may include more complex networks including firewalls and other protective devices.

Background traffic was generated in the test bed for a variety of reasons. This traffic made it possible to measure baseline false alarm rates of evaluated intrusion detection systems and to deter the development of limited non-robust intrusion detection systems that simply trigger when a particular traffic type occurs. It also led to reasonably high data rates and a fairly rich set of traffic types that exercise traffic handling and analysis capabilities of network analysis and intrusion detection tools tested with evaluation corpora. Finally, the synthesized nature of the traffic allows widespread and relatively unrestricted access to the evaluation corpora. False alarm rates measured with the evaluation corpus may not represent operational false alarm rates at any location. As noted in [17], network traffic varies widely with location and time. This implies that it may be difficult to predict the false alarm rates at operational sites from false alarm rates measured during any evaluation because traffic characteristics, including details that affect false alarm rates, are likely to differ widely from those used in the evaluation. The approach taken in the test bed was to generate realistic traffic that is roughly similar to traffic measured on one Air Force base in early 1998. In addition, details of this traffic (e.g. the frequency of occurrence of words in mail, telnet sessions, and FTP file transfers) were designed to produce false alarm rates similar to operational rates obtained in 1998 using the Air Force ASIM intrusion detection system (ASIM is similar to the Network Security Monitor described in [5]). False alarm rates measured with this traffic can be used to benchmark or compare intrusion detection systems on reference evaluation background traffic corpora. They may not, however, be representative of false alarm rates on operational data. Supplementary measurements using restricted-access data are necessary to determine operational false alarm rates. Traffic characteristics of test bed background traffic that were similar to characteristics of measured Air Force base traffic include the following:

1. The overall traffic level in connections per day.
2. The number of connections per day for the dominant TCP services.
3. The identity of many web sites that are visited from internal users.
4. The average time-of-day variation of traffic as measured in 15-minute intervals.
5. The general purpose of telnet sessions.
6. The frequency of usage of UNIX commands in telnet sessions.
7. The use of the UNIX *time* command to obtain an accurate remote time reference.
8. The frequency of occurrence of ASIM keywords in telnet sessions, mail messages, and files downloaded using FTP.
9. The frequency of occurrence of users mistyping their passwords.
10. Inclusion of an SQL database server that starts up automatically after a user telnets to remote server.

Custom software automata in the test bed simulate hundreds of programmers, secretaries, managers, and other types of users running common UNIX and Windows NT application programs. Automata interact with high-level user application programs such as *Netscape, lynx, mail, ftp, telnet, ssh, irc,* and *ping* or they implement clients for network services such as HTTP, SMTP, and POP3. Low-level TCP/IP protocol interactions are handled by kernel software and are not simulated. The average number of background-traffic bytes transmitted per day between the inside and outside of this test bed is roughly 411 Mbytes per day, with most of the traffic concentrated between 8:00 AM and 6:00 PM. The dominant protocols are TCP (384 Mbytes), UDP (26 Mbytes), and ICMP (98

Table 1. Major types of network services and automaton session types generated to create background traffic in the test bed

Protocol	Session Type	Summary
Finger	Remote Work	Verify remote user name using *finger* before sending email.
FTP	FTP	Get/Put files on internal Eyrie FTP servers.
HTTP	Lynx Eyrie Browser	Browse Eyrie internal web servers using UNIX command-line *lynx* browser.
	Eyrie Browsers	Multi-browser automaton emulates users accessing Eyrie web sites with various browsers.
	Internet Browsers	Multi-browser automaton emulates users accessing Internet web sites with various browsers.
	Netscape Internet Browser	Windows NT user accesses external web sites using Netscape browser.
ICMP	Remote Work	Verify remote host is on line using *ping*.
IRC	IRC	Users participate in an IRC chat-room, external to Eyrie.
POP3	POP3	Internal users use POP3 to access their email from External mail servers.
SMTP	Sendmail	Individual, group, and global email messages to and from all users.
SSH	Remote Work	External users use *ssh* to connect to internal Eyrie hosts and perform daily, work-related, tasks.
SNMP	SNMP	External AF host monitors Eyrie router and hosts.
Telnet	Remote Work	External users telnet to internal Eyrie hosts to perform daily, work-related, tasks.
	Mailread	Users telnet to internal and external hosts to check their email using UNIX *mail* program.
	SQL	Users telnet to an internal Eyrie SQL server and query the database.
Time	Time	Periodic query to external time reference site.

Kbytes). These traffic rates are low compared to current rates at some large commercial and academic sites. They are representative of 1998 Air Force data and they also lead to sniffed data file sizes that can still be transported over the Internet without practical difficulties. Figure 2 shows the average number of connections per day for the most common TCP services. As can be seen, web traffic dominates but many other types of traffic are generated which use a variety of services.

Table 1 shows the many types of user sessions generated by automata and the types of network traffic these sessions create. As can be seen, user automata send and receive mail, browse web sites, send and receive files using the FTP protocol, use *telnet* and *ssh* to log into remote computers and perform work, monitor the router remotely using SNMP, and perform other tasks. For example, Table 1 shows that four different automata are used to generate HTTP traffic. The *lynx* command-line browser is used during telnet and console sessions to access internal Eyrie web sites, a multi-browser automaton which emulates many types of browsers including Netscape Navigator and Internet Explorer is used to browse both internal and external web sites, and a JavaScript browser that runs

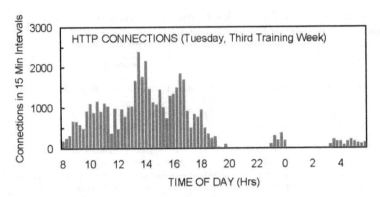

Fig. 3. Number of HTTP connections measured in 15 minute intervals generated by the four types of web automaton during Tuesday of the third week of training

inside Netscape Navigator browses external web sites from the internal Windows NT host.

Table 1 also shows that three automata are used to generate telnet sessions. First, remote programmers, secretaries, and administrators connect into internal Eyrie machines to work throughout the day using telnet or SSH. Characteristics of these work sessions including the frequency of occurrence of different UNIX commands issued, files accessed, the number of sessions per day, and the start time and duration of sessions are assigned probabilistically depending on the user type. A second telnet automaton simulates users who telnet to hosts to read and respond to mail using the UNIX *mail* program. The final telnet automaton simulates users who access an SQL database on an internal database machine. This machine automatically opens an SQL database server program, instead of a shell, after successful telnet logins. In addition to automatic traffic, the test bed allows human actors to generate background traffic and attacks when the traffic or attack is too complex to automate. For example, human actors performed attacks that included remote X-Windows Netscape browser displays.

Traffic varies over each simulation day to produce roughly the same average overall traffic rates in 15-minute intervals as measured in one week of operational Air Force traffic. Figure 3 shows the number of HTTP connections generated by the four browsing automata from Table 1 in one day of test bed traffic. Start times of browsing sessions are chosen using a Poisson process model with a time-dependent rate parameter and times between browsing actions within a session also have independent exponential distributions. Each browsing session accesses from 1 to 50 web pages. The model of human typing provided in expect is used for typing responses in telnet and other sessions where users normally provide responses from a keyboard. As can be seen in Figure 3, traffic rates are highest during the middle of the 8:00 AM to 6:00 PM workday and low after these hours. These plots vary with time in a similar manner for telnet and other session types, except the maximum number of sessions is scaled down.

Table 2. Probe and Denial of Service (DoS) attacks

	Solaris	SunOS	NT	Linux	All
Probe (37)	*portsweep* *queso*	*portsweep* *queso*	*ntinfoscan* portsweep	lsdomain mscan portsweep *queso* satan	*illegal-sniffer* *ipsweep* portsweep
DoS (65)	neptune pod processtable *selfping* smurf syslogd *tcpreset* warezclient	*arpoison* land mailbomb neptune pod processtable	*arpoison* *crashiis* *dosnuke* smurf *tcpreset*	apache2 *arpoison* back mailbomb neptune pod processtable smurf *tcpreset* teardrop udpstorm	

4 Attacks

Twelve new Windows NT attacks were added in 1999 along with stealthy versions of many 1998 attacks, new inside console-based attacks, and six new UNIX attacks. The 56 different attack types shown in Tables 2 and 3 were used in the evaluation. Attacks in normal font in these tables are old attacks from 1998 executed in the clear (114 instances). Attacks in italics are new attacks developed for 1999 (62 instances), or stealthy versions of attacks used in 1998 (35 instances). Details on attacks including further references and information on implementations are available in [2,8,9,13,14]. Five major attack categories and the attack victims are shown in Tables 2 and 3. Primary victims listed along the top of these tables are the four inside victim hosts, shown in the gray box of Figure 1, and the Cisco router. In addition, some probes query all machines in a given range of IP addresses as indicated by the column labeled "all" in Table 2.

The upper row of Table 2 lists probe or scan attacks. These attacks automatically scan a network of computers or a DNS server to find valid IP addresses (ipsweep, lsdomain, mscan), active ports (portsweep, mscan), host operating system types (queso, mscan), and known vulnerabilities (satan). All of these probes except two (mscan and satan) are either new in 1999 (e.g. ntinfoscan, queso, illegalsniffer) or are stealthy versions of 1999 probes (e.g. portsweep, ipsweep). Probes are considered stealthy if they issue ten or fewer connections or packets or if they wait longer than 59 seconds between successive network transmissions. The new "illegal-sniffer" attack is different from the other probes. During this attack, a Linux sniffer machine is installed on the inside network running the *tcpdump* program in a manner that creates many DNS queries from this new and illegal IP address.

The second row of Table 2 contains denial of service (DoS) attacks designed to disrupt a host or network service. New 1999 DoS attacks crash the Solaris operating system (selfping), actively terminate all TCP connections to a specific host (tcpreset), corrupt ARP cache entries for a victim not in others caches (arppoison), crash the Microsoft Windows NT web server (crashiis), and crash Windows NT (dosnuke).

The first row of Table 3 contains Remote to Local (R2L) attacks. In these attacks, an attacker who does not have an account on a victim machine gains local access to the machine (e.g. guest, dict), exfiltrates files from the machine (e.g. ppmacro), or modifies data in transit to the machine (e.g. framespoof). New 1999 R2L attacks include an NT PowerPoint macro attack (ppmacro), a man-in-the middle web browser attack (framespoof), an NT trojan-installed remote-administration tool (netbus), a Linux trojan SSH server (sshtrojan), and a version of a Linux FTP file access-utility with a bug that allows remote commands to run on a local machine (ncftp).

The second row of Table 3 contains user to root (U2R) attacks where a local user on a machine is able to obtain privileges normally reserved for the UNIX super user or the Windows NT administrator. All five NT U2R attacks are new this year and all other attacks except one (xterm) are versions of 1998 UNIX U2R attacks that were redesigned to be stealthy to network-based intrusion detection systems evaluated in 1998. These stealthy attacks are described below. The bottom row in Table 3 contains Data attacks. The goal of a Data attack is to exfiltrate special files, which the security policy specifies should remain on the victim hosts. These include "secret" attacks where a user who is allowed to access the special files exfiltrates them via common applications such as mail or FTP, and other attacks where privilege to access the special files is obtained using a U2R attack (ntfsdos, sqlattack). Note that an attack could be labeled as both a U2R and a Data attack if one of the U2R attacks was used to obtain access to the special files. The "Data" category thus specifies the goal of an attack rather than the attack mechanism.

4.1   Stealthy U2R Attacks

UNIX U2R attacks were made stealthy to network-based intrusion detection systems using a variety of techniques designed to hide attack-specific keywords from network-based sniffers [2,13]. Most stealthy U2R attacks included the components shown by the five columns in Figure 4. Attack scripts were first encoded, transported to the victim machine, and then decoded and executed. Actions such as altering or accessing secret or security-related files were performed and the attacker then removed files created for the attack and restored original permissions of altered or accessed files to clean up. The dark filled in actions in Figure 4 show one particular stealthy attack. In this attack, the clear-text attack script is encoded by "character stuffing" where extra unique characters (e.g. "AA") are added after every original character, the attack script is transported to the victim machine using FTP, the attack script is decoded using vi (not shown, but implicit), attack execution is hidden by generating screens full of chaff text directed to the standard output from a background process, and the attacker changes file permission on a secret file, displays the file, and then restores file permissions back to original settings and erases the attack script. As can be seen from Figure 4, there are many other possible variants of stealthy attacks. Five approaches were used to encode/decode and transport attack scripts and

Table 3. Remote to Local (R2L), User to Root (U2R), and Data attacks

	Solaris	SunOS	NT	Linux	Cisco
R2L (56)	dict ftpwrite guest httptunnel xlock xsnoop	dict xsnoop	dict framespoof netbus netcat ppmacro	dict imap named ncftp phf sendmail sshtrojan xlock xsnoop	snmpget
U2R (37)	eject fdformat ffbconfig ps	loadmodule	casesen ntfsdos nukepw sechole yaga	perl sqlattack xterm	
DATA (13)	secret		ntfsdos ppmacro	secret sqlattack	

to execute these scripts. The encode action "Octal Characters" refers to encoding binary files using the C *printf* octal backslash notation and then decoding the binary file using the *tcsh* builtin *echo* command. The execute action "Shell Variables" refers to encoding shell commands using shell variables to obscure the commands that are issued. The execute action "Delay Execution" refers to using *cron* or *at* to execute scripts at a later time after the session that created the attack script and "Multiple Sessions" refers to downloading, decoding, and running the attack script over multiple sessions. Further details and examples of other actions are available in [2,13].

Stealthy techniques that rely on packet fragmentation and other forms of packet manipulation [18] were implemented as part of the 1999 evaluation. Time constraints and the variety of victim operating systems used precluded extensive experimentation with these approaches. Preliminary exploratory results are provided in [2].

5   Participants and Scoring

Eight research groups participated in the evaluation using a variety of approaches to intrusion detection. Papers by these groups describing high-performing systems are provided in [4,7,15,20,21,22,23]. One requirement for participation in the evaluation was the submission of a detailed system description that was used for scoring and analysis. System descriptions described the types of attacks the system was designed to detect, data sources used, features extracted, and whether optional attack identification information was provided as an output. Most systems used network sniffer data to detect Probe and DoS attacks against all systems [7,15,21,23] or BSM Solaris host audit data to detect Solaris R2L and U2R attacks [4,15,23]. Two systems produced a combined output from both network sniffer data and host audit data [15,23]. A few systems used network sniffer data to detect R2L and U2R attacks against the UNIX victims [15,23]. One system used NT audit data to detect U2R and R2L attacks against the Windows NT victim [20] and two systems used BSM audit data to detect Data attacks against the Solaris victim [15,23]. A final system used information from a nightly

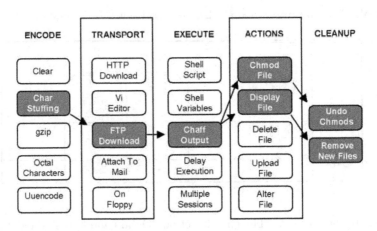

Fig. 4. Possible paths to generate stealthy user to root (U2R) attacks. Each attack requires selection of one or more of the alternate approaches shown in each column

file system scan to detect R2L, U2R, and Data attacks against the Solaris victim [22]. The software program that performs this scan was the only custom auditing tool used in the evaluation. A variety of approaches were employed including expert systems that use rules or signatures to detect attacks, anomaly detectors, pattern classifiers, recurrent neural networks, data mining techniques, and a reasoning system that performs a forensic analysis of the Solaris file system.

Three weeks of training data, composed of two weeks of background traffic with no attacks and one week of background traffic with a few attacks, were provided to participants from mid May to mid July 1999 to support system tuning and training. Only five weekdays of traffic were provided for each week. Locations of attacks in the training data were clearly labeled. Two weeks of unlabeled test data were provided from late September to the middle of October. Participants downloaded this data from a web site, processed it through their intrusion detection systems, and generated putative hits or alerts at the output of their intrusion detection systems. Lists of alerts were due back by early October. In addition, participants could optionally return more extensive identification lists for each attack.

A simplified approach was used in 1999 to label attacks and score alerts and new scoring procedures were added to analyze the optional identification lists. In 1998, every network TCP/IP connection, UDP packet, and ICMP packet was labeled, and participants determined which connections and packets corresponded to attacks. Although this approach pre-specifies all potential attack packets and thus simplifies scoring and analysis, it can make submitting alerts difficult because aligning alerts with the network connections and packets that generate alerts is often complex. In addition, this approach cannot be used with inside attacks that generate no network traffic. In 1999, a new simplified approach was adopted. Each alert only had to indicate the date, time, victim IP address, and score for each putative attack detection. An alert could also optionally indicate the attack category. This was used to assign false alarms to attack categories. Putative detections returned by participants were counted as true "hits" or true detections if the time of any alert occurred during the time of any attack segment and the alert was for the correct victim IP address. Alerts that occur outside all attack segments were counted as "misses" or false alarms. Attack segments generally correspond to the duration of all network packets and connections generated by an attack and to time intervals when attack processes are running on a victim host. To account for small timing inconsistencies across hosts, an extra 60 seconds leeway was typically allowed for alerts before and after the end of each attack segment. The analysis of each system only included attacks which that system was designed to detect, as specified in the system description. Systems werent penalized for missing attacks they were not designed to detect and false alarms that occurred during segments of out-of-spec attacks were ignored.

The score produced by a system was required to be a number that increases as the certainty of an attack at the specified time increases. All participants returned numbers ranging between zero and one, and many participants produced binary outputs (0s and 1s only). If alerts occurred in multiple attack segments of one attack, then the score assigned to that attack for further analysis was the highest score in all the alerts. Some participants returned optional identification information for attacks. This included the attack category, the name for old attacks selected from a list of provided names, and the attack source and destination IP addresses, start time, duration, and the ports/services used. This information was analyzed separately from the alert lists used for detection scoring. Results in this paper focus on detection results derived from the required alert lists. Information on identification results is provided in [11].

Attack labels were used to designate attack segments in the training data and also to score lists of alerts returned by participants. Attack labels were provided using list files similar to those used in 1998, except a separate list file was provided for each attack specifying all segments of that attack. Entries in these list files include the date, start time, duration, a unique attack identifier, the attack name, source and destination ports and IP addresses, the protocol, and details concerning the attack. Details include indications that the attack is clear or stealthy, old or new, inside or outside, the victim machine type, and whether traces of the attack occur in each of the different data types that were collected. Attack list files are available at [14].

6   Results

An initial analysis was performed to determine how well all systems taken together detect attacks regardless of false alarm rates. The best system was selected for each attack as the system that detects the most instances of that attack. The detection rate for these best systems provides a rough upper bound on compos-

Table 4. Poorly detected attacks where the best system for each attack detects half or fewer of the attack instances

Name	Category	Details	Total Instances	Instances Detected by Best System
Ipsweep	Probe	Stealthy	3	0
Lsdomain	Probe	Stealthy	2	1
Portsweep	Probe	Stealthy	11	3
Queso	Probe	New	4	0
Resetscan	Probe	Stealthy	1	0
Arppoison	DoS	New	5	1
Dosnuke	DoS	New-NT	4	2
Selfping	DoS	New	3	0
Tcpreset	DoS	New	3	1
Warezclient	DoS	Old	3	0
Ncftp	R2L	New	5	0
Netbus	R2L	New-NT	3	1
Netcat	R2L	New-NT	4	2
Snmpget	R2L	Old	4	0
Sshtrojan	R2L	New	3	0
Loadmodule	U2R	Stealthy	3	1
Ntfsdos	U2R	New-NT	3	1
Perl	U2R	Stealthy	4	0
Sechole	U2R	New-NT	3	1
Sqlattack	U2R	Stealthy	3	0
xterm	U2R	Old	3	1

ite system performance. Thirty seven of the 58 attack types were detected well by this composite system, but many stealthy and new attacks were always or frequently missed. Poorly detected attacks for which half or more of the attack instances were not detected by the best system are listed in Table 4. This table lists the attack name, the attack category, details concerning whether the attack is old, new, or stealthy, the total number of instances for this attack, and the number of instances detected by the system which detected this attack best. Table 4 contains 21 attack types and is dominated by new attacks and attacks designed to be stealthy to 1998 network-based intrusion detection systems. All instances of 10 of the attack types in Table 4 were totally missed by all systems. These results suggest that the new systems developed for the 1999 evaluation still are not detecting new attacks well and that stealthy probes and U2R attacks can avoid detection by network-based systems.

Further analyses evaluated system performance at false alarm rates in a specified range. The detection rate of each system at different false alarm rates can be determined by lowering a threshold from above 1.0 to below 0.0, counting the detections with scores above the threshold as hits, and counting the number of alerts above the threshold that do not detect attacks as false alarms. This results in one or more operating points for each system which trade off false alarm rate against detection rate. It was found that almost all systems, except some anomaly detection systems, achieved their maximum detection accuracy at or below 10 false alarms per day on the 1999 corpus. These low false alarm rates were presumably due to the low overall traffic volume, the relative stationarity of the traffic, and the ability to tune systems to reduce false alarms on three weeks of training data. In the remaining presentation, the detection rate reported for each system is the highest detection rate achieved at or below 10 false alarms per day on the two weeks of test data.

Table 5 shows average detection rates at 10 false alarms per day for each attack category and victim type. This table provides overall results and does not separately analyze old, new, and stealthy attacks. The upper number in a cell, surrounded by dashes, is the number of attack instances in that cell and the other entries provide the percent correct detections for all systems with detection rates above 40% in that cell. A cell contains only the number of instances if no system detected more than 40% of the instances. Only one entry is filled for the bottom row because only probe attacks were against all the victim machines and the SunOS/Data cell is empty because there were no Data attacks against the SunOS victim. High-performance systems listed in Table 5 include rule-based expert systems that use network sniffing data and/or Solaris BSM audit data (Expert-1 through Expert-3 [15,23,21]), a data mining system that uses network sniffing data (Dmine [7]), a pattern classification approach that uses network sniffing data (Pclassify), an anomaly detection system which uses recurrent neural networks to analyze system call sequences in Solaris BSM audit data (Anomaly [4]), and a reasoning system which performs a nightly forensic analysis of the Solaris file system (Forensics [22]).

No one approach or system provides the best performance across all categories. The best performance is provided for probe and denial of service attacks for systems that use network sniffer data and for U2R and Data attacks against the Solaris victim for systems that use BSM audit data. Detection rates for U2R and Data attacks are generally poor for SunOS and Linux victims where extensive audit data is not available. Detection rates for R2L, U2R, and Data attacks are poor for Windows NT, which was included in the evaluation for the first time this year.

Figure 5 shows the performance of the best intrusion detection system in each attack category at a false alarm rate of 10 false alarms per day. The left chart compares the percentage of attack instances detected for old-clear and new attacks and the right chart compares performance for old-clear and stealthy attacks. The numbers in parentheses on the horizontal axis below the attack category indicate the number of instances of attacks of different types. For example, in Figure 3A, there were 49 oldclear and 15 new denial-of-service attacks. Figure 3A demonstrates that detection of new attacks was much worse than detection of old-clear attacks across all attack categories, and especially for DoS, R2L, and U2R attacks. The average detection rate for old-clear attacks was 72% and this dropped to 19% for new attacks. Figure 3B demonstrates that stealthy probes and U2R attacks were much more difficult to detect for network-based intrusion detection systems that used sniffing data. User-to-root attacks against the Solaris victim, however, were accurately detected by host-based intrusion detection systems that used BSM audit data.

Attacks are detected best when they produce a consistent "signature," trace, or sequence of events in tcpdump data or in audit data that is different from

Table 5. Percent attack instances detected for systems with a detection rate above 40% in each cell and at false alarm rates below 10 false alarms per day

	DoS	Probe	R2L	U2R	Data
Solaris	-19- Expert-1: 63% Expert-2: 53%	-5- Expert-2: 60% Expert-3: 50%	-12- Expert-1: 50% Forensics: 50%	-11- Expert-1: 100% Expert-2: 100% Anomaly: 100% Forensics: 73%	-6- Expert-2: 100% Forensics: 83%
NT	-16- Expert-1: 69% Expert-2: 69%	-5- Expert-1: 80% Expert-2: 60%	-12-	-13-	-5-
SunOS	-8- DMine: 88% Expert-1: 63% Expert-2: 50%	-5- PClassify: 60%	-3- Expert-2: 67%	-3-	
Linux	-19- Expert-1: 84% DMine: 74% Expert-2: 68%	-8- Expert-3: 60% DMine: 50%	-25- Expert-2: 64% Expert-1: 44%	-10-	-4-
All		-11- Expert-1: 46%			

sequences produced for normal traffic. A detailed analysis by participants demonstrated that attacks were missed for a variety of reasons. Systems which relied on rules or signatures missed new attacks because signatures did not exist for these attacks, and because existing signatures did not generalize to variants of old attacks, or to new and stealthy attacks. For example ncftp a ls_domain attacks were visible in tcpdump data, but were missed because no rules existed to detect these attacks. Stealthy probes were missed because hard thresholds in rules were set to issue an alert only for more rapid probes, even though slow probes often provided as much information to attackers. These thresholds could be changed to detect stealthy probes at the expense of generating more false alarms. Stealthy U2R attacks were missed by network-based systems because attack actions were hidden in sniffer data and rules generated for clear versions of these attacks no longer applied. Many of the Windows NT attacks were missed due to lack of experience with Windows NT audit data and attacks. A detailed analysis of the Windows NT attacks [9] indicated that all but two of these attacks (ppmacro, framespoof) can be detected from the 1999 NT audit data using attack-specific signatures which generate far fewer than 10 false alarms per day.

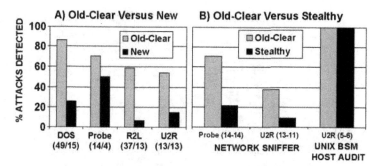

Fig. 5. Comparison of detection accuracy at 10 false alarms per day for (A) Old-Clear versus New attacks and (B) Old-Clear versus stealthy attacks

7   Predicting when New Attacks will Be Detected

Many network sniffer-based intrusion detection systems missed attacks because particular protocols or services were not monitored or because services were not analyzed to the required depth. This is illustrated in Figure 6. The horizontal axis in this figure shows the protocols and services that were used for many of the probe and DoS attacks and the vertical axis shows the depth of analysis required to reliably determine the action performed by an attack. Attacks near the top of Figure 6 require only lowlevel analysis of single or multiple packet headers. Attacks near the bottom of Figure 6 require understanding of the protocol used to extract the connection content and highlevel analysis of the content to determine the action performed. Well-known attacks can be detected at lower levels than shown when the attack produces a signature or trace at a lower level that is unique from background traffic. This approach is used in most signature-based intrusion detection systems. Determining the intended action of a new attack, however, requires the depth of analysis shown.

Attack names surrounded by white ovals in Figure 6 were detected well, while attacks surrounded by dark ovals were not. For example, many systems missed the "ARP Poison" attack on the bottom left because the ARP protocol was not monitored or because the attackers duplicate responses to arp-who-has requests were not detected. Many systems also missed the Illegal Sniffer and LS_DOMAIN attacks on the left middle because the DNS service was not monitored or because DNS traffic was not analyzed to determine either when an "ls" command is successfully answered by a DNS server or when a DNS request is sent from a new IP address. Many systems also missed the "SELF-PING" attack because telnet sessions were not reconstructed and commands issued in telnet sessions were not analyzed. Many of the attacks that were detected well required simpler high-level analysis of packet headers. For example, the "LAND" attack includes a UDP packet with the same source and destination IP address and the "TEARDROP" attack includes a mis-fragmented UDP packet. Other attacks that were detected well required sequential analysis of multiple packets

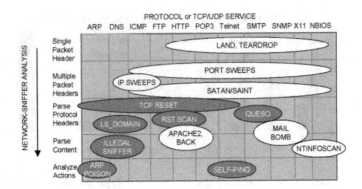

Fig. 6. Probe and DoS attacks displayed to show the services and protocols used and the maximum depth of analysis of network traffic required to reliably detect attacks. Attacks in white ovals were detected well by network-based systems, attacks in dark ovals were not

or deeper analysis of a particular protocol. For example, the "SATAN" and "NTINFOSCAN" attacks include a large variety of connections that occur in a short time interval, as do non-stealthy "IP SWEEPS" and "PORT SWEEPS".

The attack analysis shown in Figure 6 illustrates how two pieces of information are required to predict whether a new attack will be missed by network-based systems. Evidence of the attack or knowledge of where the attack manifests itself in data sources and also knowledge of input data and features used by the intrusion detection system are required. This analysis can be extended to other types of attacks and to host-based systems by analyzing the evidence an attack leaves on the victim host in audit records, log files, file system access times, and other locations. The general rule is that attacks will be missed if no evidence of the attack is available in data analyzed by the intrusion detection system or if necessary features are not extracted from this data. This may occur for many reasons. The required host-based data may not be available, network sensors may be in the wrong location to record attack trace components, required protocols or services may not be analyzed, a new attack may require a novel type of feature extraction which is not yet included, or a stealthy attack may leave no traces in information analyzed. If traces of an attack are processed by an intrusion detection system, then the attack may or may not be detected. Performance depends on the overlap with normal input features and details of the intrusion detection system. The analysis described above requires attack trace information and detailed intrusion detection system descriptions. It can be used as a preliminary analysis to determine which attacks an intrusion detection system may detect and can reduce the necessity of expensive experimentation. Network attack traces and system descriptions are available on the Lincoln Laboratory web site and included as part of the 1999 DARPA Intrusion Detection Evaluation corpus [14]. The traces list all network packets generated by each attack instance.

8   Discussion

The DARPA 1999 off-line intrusion detection evaluation successfully evaluated 18 intrusion detection systems from 8 sites using more than 200 instances of 58 attack types embedded in three weeks of training data and two weeks of test data. Attacks were launched against UNIX and Windows NT hosts and a Cisco router. Best detection was provided by network-based systems for old probe and old denial of service attacks and by host-based systems for Solaris user-to-root attacks launched either remotely or from the local console. A number of sites developed systems that detect known old attacks by searching for signatures in network sniffer data or Solaris BSM audit data using expert systems or rules. These systems detect old attacks well when they match known signatures, but miss many new UNIX attacks, Windows NT attacks, and stealthy attacks. Promising capabilities were provided by Solaris host-based systems which detected console-based and remote-stealthy U2R attacks, by anomaly detection systems which could detect some U2R and DoS attacks without requiring signatures, and by a host-based system that could detect Solaris U2R and R2L attacks without using audit information but by performing a forensic analysis of the Solaris file system.

   A major result of the 1998 and 1999 evaluations is that current research intrusion detection systems miss many new and stealthy attacks. Despite the focus in 1999 on developing approaches to detect new attacks, all systems evaluated in 1999 completely missed 10 out of 58 attack types and, even after combining output alerts from all systems, 23 attack types were detected poorly (half or fewer instances of an attack type detected). Detailed analyses of individual systems indicated that attacks were missed for many reasons. Input data sources that contained evidence of attacks were sometimes not analyzed or they werent analyzed to the required depth and rules, thresholds, or signatures created for old attacks often did not generalize to new attacks. This result is relatively independent of evaluation details because it depends only on attack traces and an analysis of why attacks were missed and how systems operate. An analysis of why attacks were missed suggested an analytic approach that can be used to predict whether an intrusion detection system will miss a particular new attack. It requires detailed attack traces and system descriptions to determine whether components of attack traces are contained in the inputs to an intrusion detection system and whether necessary features are extracted from these inputs. This analytic approach may be useful for designing future evaluations and reducing the need for experimentation.

   False alarm rate results of the 1999 evaluation should be interpreted within the context of the test bed and background traffic used. The evaluation used a simple network topology, a non-restrictive security policy, a limited number of victim machines and intrusion detection systems, stationary and low-volume background traffic, lenient scoring, and extensive instrumentation to provide inputs to intrusion detection systems. Most systems had low false alarm rates (well below 10 false alarms per day). As noted above, these low rates may be caused by the use of relatively low volume background traffic with a time varying, but relatively fixed proportion of different traffic types and by the availability of training data to tune or train systems.

Extensions to the current evaluation are planned to verify false alarm rates using operational network traffic and a small number of high-performing systems. Operational measurements will also be made to update traffic statistics and traffic generators used in the test bed. Further evaluations are also required to explore performance with commercial and updated research intrusion detection systems, with more complex network topologies, with a wider range of attacks, and with more complex background traffic. In addition, other approaches to making attacks stealthy should be explored including low-level packet modifications (e.g. [18]) and attacks which remove evidence from Windows NT and Solaris BSM audit records and other system audit logs before terminating.

Comprehensive evaluations of DARPA research systems have now been performed in 1998 and 1999. These evaluations take time and effort on the part of the evaluators and the participants. They have provided benchmark measurements that do not now need to be repeated again until system developers are able to implement many desired improvements. The current planned short-term focus in 2000 is to provide assistance to intrusion detection system developers to advance their systems and not to evaluate performance. System development can be expedited by providing descriptions, traces, and labeled examples of many new attacks, by developing threat and attack models, and by carefully evaluating COTS systems to determine where to focus research efforts.

A number of research directions are suggested by 1999 results. First, researchers should focus on anomaly detection and other approaches that have the potential of detecting new attacks. Second, techniques should be developed to process Windows NT audit data. Third, host-based systems shouldnt rely exclusively on C2-level audit data such as Solaris BSM data or NT audit data. Instead other types of host and network input features should also be explored. These could be provided by new system auditing software, by firewall or router audit logs, by SNMP queries, by software wrappers, by commercial intrusion detection system components, by forensic analysis of file-system changes as in [22], or by application-specific auditing. Fourth, research efforts should not overlap but should provide missing functionality. Finally, a greater breadth of analysis is required including a wider range of protocols and services.

Acknowledgements

This work was sponsored by the Department of Defense Advanced Research Projects Agency under Air Force Contract F19628-95-C-0002. Opinions, interpretations, conclusions, and recommendations are those of the author and are not necessarily endorsed by the United States Air Force. We would like to thank Sami Saydjari for supporting this effort. Many involved participants made this evaluation possible including Dick Kemmerer, Giovanni Vigna, Mabri Tyson, Phil Porras, Anup Ghosh, R. C. Sekar, and NingNing Wu. We would also like to thank Terry Champion and Steve Durst from AFRL for providing Linux kernel modifications that make one host simulate many IP addresses. Finally, we would like to thank others who contributed including Marc Zissman, Rob Cunningham, Seth Webster, Kris Kendall, Raj Basu, Jesse Rabek, and Simson Garfinkel.

References

1. E. G. Amoroso, Intrusion Detection: An Introduction to Internet Surveillance, Correlation, Trace Back, Traps, and Response, Intrusion.Net Books, 1999. 162
2. K. Das, The Development of Stealthy Attacks to Evaluate Intrusion Detection Systems, S. M. Thesis, MIT Department of Electrical Engineering and Computer Science, June 2000. 163, 169, 170, 171
3. R. Durst, Terrence Champion, Brian Witten, Eric Miller and Luigi Spagnuolo, Testing and evaluating computer intrusion detection systems, Communications of the ACM, 42, 1999, 53-61. 163
4. A. K. Ghosh and A. Schwartzbard, A Study in Using Neural Networks for Anomaly and Misuse Detection, in Proceedings of the USENIX Security Symposium, August 23-26, 1999, Washington, D.C, http://www.rstcorp.com/~anup. 171, 175
5. T. Heberlein, T., Network Security Monitor (NSM) - Final Report, U. C. Davis: February 1995, http://seclab.cs.ucdavis.edu/papers/NSM-final.pdf 166
6. K. Jackson, Intrusion Detection System (IDS) Product Survey, Los Alamos National Laboratory, Report LA-UR-99-3883, 1999. 162
7. S. Jajodia, D. Barbara, B. Speegle, and N. Wu, Audit Data Analysis and Mining (ADAM), project described in http://www.isse.gmu.edu/~dbarbara/adam.html, April, 2000. 171, 175
8. K. Kendall, A Database of Computer Attacks for the Evaluation of Intrusion Detection Systems, S. M. Thesis, MIT Department of Electrical Engineering and Computer Science, June 1999. 163, 169
9. J. Korba, Windows NT Attacks for the Evaluation of Intrusion Detection Systems, S. M. Thesis, MIT Department of Electrical Engineering and Computer Science, June 2000. 163, 169, 176
10. Lawrence Berkeley National Laboratory Network Research Group provides tcp-dump at http://www-nrg.ee.lbl.gov. 164
11. R. P. Lippmann, Joshua W. Haines, David J. Fried, Jonathan Korba, and Kumar Das, The 1999 DARPA Off-Line Intrusion Detection Evaluation, Computer Networks, In Press, 2000. 163, 173
12. R. P. Lippmann, David J. Fried, Isaac Graf, Joshua W. Haines, Kristopher R. Kendall, David McClung, Dan Weber, Seth E. Webster, Dan Wyschogrod, Robert K. Cunningham, and Marc A. Zissman, Evaluating Intrusion Detection Systems: the 1998 DARPA Off-Line Intrusion Detection Evaluation, in Proceedings of the 2000 DARPA Information Survivability Conference and Exposition (DISCEX), Vol. 2, IEEE Press, January 2000. 163
13. R. P. Lippmann and R. K. Cunningham, Guide to Creating Stealthy Attacks for the 1999 DARPA Off-Line Intrusion Detection Evaluation, MIT Lincoln Laboratory Project Report IDDE-1, June 1999. 163, 169, 170, 171
14. MIT Lincoln Laboratory, A public web site http://www.ll.mit.edu/IST/ ideval/index.html, contains limited information on the 1998 and 1999 evaluations. Follow instructions on this web site or send email to the authors (rpl or jhaines@sst.ll.mit.edu) to obtain access to a password-protected site with more complete information on these evaluations and results. Software scripts to execute attacks are not provided on these or other web sites. 163, 169, 173, 178

15. P. Neumann and P. Porras, Experience with EMERALD to DATE, in Proceedings 1st USENIX Workshop on Intrusion Detection and Network Monitoring, Santa Clara, California, April 1999, 73-80, http://www.sdl.sri.com/emerald/index.html. 171, 175

16. S. Northcutt, Network Intrusion Detection; An Analysis Handbook, New Riders Publishing, Indianapolis, 1999. 162

17. V. Paxson, "Empirically-Derived Analytic Models of Wide-Area TCP Connections", IEEE/ACM Transactions on Networking, Vol. 2, No. 4, August, 1994, ftp://ftp.ee.lbl.gov/papers/WAN-TCP-models.ps.Z. 166

18. T. H. Ptacek and T. N. Newsham, Insertion, Evasion, and Denial of Service: Eluding Network Intrusion Detection, Secure Networks, Inc. Report, January 1998. 171, 180

19. N. Puketza, M. Chung, R. A. Olsson, and B. Mukherjee, A Software Platform for Testing Intrusion Detection Systems, IEEE Software, September/October, 1997, 43-51. 163

20. A. Schwartzbard and A. K. Ghosh, A Study in the Feasibility of Performing Host-based Anomaly Detection on Windows NT, in Proceedings of the 2nd Recent Advances in Intrusion Detection (RAID 1999) Workshop, West Lafayette, IN, September 7-9, 1999. 171

21. R. Sekar and P. Uppuluri, Synthesizing Fast Intrusion Prevention/Detection Systems from High-Level Specifications, in Proceedings 8th Usenix Security Symposium, Washington DC, Aug. 1999, http://rcs-sgi.cs.iastate.edu/sekar/abs/usenixsec99.htm. 171, 175

22. M. Tyson, P. Berry, N. Williams, D. Moran, D. Blei, DERBI: Diagnosis, Explanation and Recovery from computer Break-Ins, project described in http://www.ai.sri.com/~derbi/, April. 2000. 171, 172, 175, 180

23. G. Vigna, S. T. Eckmann, and R. A. Kemmerer, The STAT Tool Suite, in Proceedings of the 2000 DARPA Information Survivability Conference and Exposition (DISCEX), IEEE Press, January 2000. 171, 175

Using Rule-Based Activity Descriptions to Evaluate Intrusion-Detection Systems

Dominique Alessandri

IBM Research, Zurich Research Laboratory
CH–8803 Rüschlikon, Switzerland,
dal@zurich.ibm.com

Abstract. After more than a decade of development, there are now many commercial and non-commercial intrusion-detection systems (IDSes) available. However, they tend to generate false alarms at high rates while overlooking real threats. The results described in this paper have been obtained in the context of work that aims to identify means for supporting the analysis, evaluation, and design of large-scale intrusion-detection architectures. We propose a practical method for evaluating IDSes and identifying their strengths and weaknesses. Our approach shall allow us to evaluate IDSes for their capabilities, unlike existing approaches that evaluate their implementation. It is furthermore shown how the obtained knowledge can be used to analyze and evaluate an IDS.

1 Introduction

In the past few years, an increasing number of intrusion-detection systems (IDSes) have become available [1]. This development has been driven by the growing number of computer security incidents [2,3,4,5,6,7,8] that demonstrate the need for organizations to protect their network against adversaries [9]. The issue of protecting networks and making them secure and reliable has been addressed in many publications that have analyzed the problems and made pertinent recommendations [10,11]. Intrusion detection (ID) is widely regarded as being part of the solution for protecting today's networks. However, IDSes may fail by generating false alarms or not recognizing attacks. This, together with the fact that today's networks are not only distributed but also highly heterogeneous, makes it desirable to deploy multiple instances of different types of IDSes in order to achieve adequate protection of such networks. Last but not least such an *ID architecture* embodying multiple IDSes has to achieve adequate compliance with an organization's security policy.

The work described in the following is motivated by the fact that IDSes tend to generate large amounts of *alarms* (reports of suspicious activities) that need to be collected and interpreted. This is an issue because a substantial number of these alarms (up to 90% for some IDSes) may be false alarms, whereas these IDSes may still miss real attacks [12,13]. Our experience has shown that the processing of IDS alarms becomes even more challenging when considering a large-scale deployment of IDSes.

H. Debar, L. Mé, and F. Wu (Eds.): RAID 2000, LNCS 1907, pp. 183–196, 2000.
© Springer-Verlag Berlin Heidelberg 2000

Like systems in general, IDSes can be evaluated in various ways, such as benchmarking or modeling. As we feel that benchmarking real IDSes [12,13] is not generic and systematic enough [14] for our evaluation needs, we investigated another approach, namely testing for IDS capabilities and not the implementation of IDSes. One of the advantages of our approach is that we believe it enables us to evaluate a given IDS for its ability to detect a given attack even in the case where the corresponding attack signature has not yet been written for the IDS considered. Furthermore our approach is more generic and requires a relatively limited effort.

1.1 Scope

The long-term goal of this work is to provide a framework that allows the efficient operation of a large-scale ID architecture. This paper describes a first step towards evaluating IDSes in terms of their strengths and weaknesses. These evaluation results will allow us to validate and to improve ID-architecture designs and to identify measures to process and interpret IDS alarms.

Our approach describes IDSes and their environment by formalizing their characteristics. We do not try to describe the implementation of the ID algorithms used. Rather, our approach focuses on the description of attacks and activities in general. That is to say we are describing attacks in terms of the IDS characteristics required for their detection.

In this first step we describe a Boolean-only approach, which is based on rules that express IDS characteristics required for the generation of an alarm. We claim that this approach enables us to analyze an IDS systematically by the output expected for a given input. The output we consider is the list of alarms and the set of diagnostic information (IP source address, user ID etc.) an IDS potentially generates for a given input.

In order to limit the scope of this paper, we focus on *network-based* and *knowledge-based* IDSes as defined in [15]. Network-based IDSes are IDSes that monitor the traffic on a network, whereas knowledge-based IDSes monitor their information source for known suspicious activities [15]. Furthermore we restrict ourselves to a Boolean representation of IDS characteristics. The expansion to a non-Boolean notion of IDS characteristics and other types of IDSes is subject to further research.

1.2 Outline

We start this work by introducing an example in Section 2. In Section 3 we identify the IDS and environment characteristics relevant to describing the characteristics of IDSes. Based on these IDS characteristics we then discuss in Section 4 how attacks and non-attacks can be described so they can be used to analyze an IDS. In Section 5 we propose a mechanism to evaluate IDSes, which uses IDS characteristics and activities identified in the preceding sections. Section 6 concludes this work with a proposal of avenues for future work.

2   Simple Example

Our approach describes attacks and non-attacks, i.e. *activities* in general, in terms of the IDS characteristics required for them to be reported by an IDS. Activities can be defined as a sequence of events that may lead to a system state transition.[1]

As we need to formalize the description of IDS characteristics in order to describe activities, we propose that IDS characteristics be expressed by means of Boolean *properties*. These properties describe the various characteristics, capabilities, configuration settings etc. that are inherent to a given IDS.

In order to illustrate our notion of properties we introduce the following example of a well-known *sendmail* (a Unix mail system) vulnerability to which we are going to refer in further sections. An ancient version of sendmail allowed the unauthorized execution of arbitrary commands on the target host [16]. This was possible by supplying a UNIX command preceded by the pipe symbol "|" within the "from" field of a mail message sent over *SMTP* (simple mail transfer protocol). If at the same time an invalid destination address was supplied, which caused the message to bounce, sendmail executed the offending command while trying to deliver the bounced message to the mail folder of the sender (specified in the "from" field) of the message. Considering network-based IDSes, we can identify the following characteristics and capabilities required for detecting this attack on the network:

- Pattern recognition algorithm – the IDS must be capable of recognizing the offending character sequence.
- SMTP *awareness* – basic capability to treat SMTP traffic. We consider the awareness of a protocol to be an IDS's capability to recognize a given protocol based on protocol identifiers, layer 4 port numbers etc. This does not necessarily mean that the IDS is capable of verifying the correctness of the protocol sequence observed or to perform any further analysis of the protocol sequence.
- TCP awareness – basic capability to treat TCP traffic.
- IP awareness – basic capability to treat IP traffic.

Furthermore, the following configuration characteristics appear to be required:

- Known attack – the characteristics of the attack must be known to the IDS.
- Enabled alarm – the reporting of this attack must be enabled in the IDS's configuration.

Having identified all these characteristics, the knowledgeable reader might argue that the use of such an IDS might result in *false negatives*. A false negative is a non-event that is an instance of *failure* of the IDS. Such a failure manifests itself in the fact that the alarm describing an attack launched against the system

---

[1] Note that activities do not necessarily represent an attack. In fact, most activities observed are completely normal.

to be protected is not generated. The term failure has been defined by the dependability community [17] and represents in our case the fact that an IDS did not fulfill the requirements concerning the generation of alarms. The threat of false negatives becomes clearer when considering the following issues:

- Attack variation – knowing the definitions of the IDS's set of known attacks, the adversary may launch *subterfuge attacks* (slightly modified attacks [18]), which do not match any of the attack descriptions. An example of such a variation is IP fragmentation. Adversaries may send attack sequences in a fragmented IP PDU (protocol data unit). To detect such an attack the IDS must be able to reassemble IP fragments, which is a functionality not commonly implemented by IDSes. Further examples of attack variations, not related to the SMTP one, such as TCP stream slicing or hexadecimal encoding of URLs can be found when looking at tools such as whisker [19].
- Overload situation – the machine monitoring the information source, e.g. the network, may be overwhelmed by the amount of information to be inspected. This may occur applications are draining resources from the machine hosting the IDS or if the network is heavily loaded.
- Information loss – Information to be examined may be lost, e.g. a network interface may lose PDUs owing to misreception. If this occurs to the packet containing the offending sequence, the IDS will not recognize this attack.

As mentioned in the introduction, IDSes may also fail by generating false alarms—also called *false positives.* In the context of this work a false positive can be defined as an alarm with an erroneous semantic.[2] This issue can be illustrated by considering a variation of the SMTP example where the pipe symbol appears within the mail body instead of within the mail header. In this case the IDS can only function correctly if it is capable of performing

- State-full protocol analysis – simply checking the TCP stream for the pipe symbol is not enough. The pipe symbol can only be considered an instance of an attack if it appears in the "from" field of the mail message. State-full protocol analysis requires the IDS to implement a finite state machine.

IDS Failures

This example has outlined a few causes for IDS failures. The operation of IDSes is rather costly in terms of resources. This often results in IDSes with limited functionality so they can cope with the amount of data they need to examine, e.g. TCP sessions may be analyzed on a per-packet basis instead of a stream basis [18,19]. In addition the information source used may limit the IDS's view of an activity, e.g. the TCP source port number of a connection does not show up in a web-server log file [20].

---

[2] Having defined false positives and false negatives, it may be worthwhile to mention that they may occur concurrently. This corresponds to a *false recognition*, i.e. the required alarm is missing and a false alarm is generated.

3 IDS Characteristics

Looking at this discussion of IDS failures we realize that there may be a large number of properties that we need to identify and define in order to describe IDSes to an adequate level of detail.

We can distinguish among the characteristics of an IDS according to two orthogonal classification schemes. The first scheme separates properties according to the level of detail of the characteristics they describe. The more generic group of properties can usually be derived from IDS taxonomies such as [15]. The more detailed group of properties describes characteristics related to a specific protocol, applications etc.

The second classification scheme separates properties based on building blocks. We can distinguish among the IDS core, the information source, and the IDS configuration. As the IDS configuration usually does not influence IDS characteristics as they can be derived from IDS taxonomies, we were not able to identify properties representing generic configuration characteristics.

We trust that these two classification schemes facilitate the definition of properties by simplifying the identification of IDS and environment characteristics.

3.1 Generic Properties

Generic properties may be derived from an IDS taxonomy [15]. These properties are independent of specific protocols, applications etc.

Information Source

The information source serves primarily to distinguish between host-based and network-based IDSes. Besides its type, further details are required in order to characterize the information source:

- Type – One can distinguish between information sources that are based on the network, e.g. sniffers (network-based IDS), and those based on system and application logs, e.g. web server logs (host-based IDS).
- Information loss – Risk (approximated with high, medium and low) of missing an information unit (e.g. PDU).
- Information suppression – Possibility of an adversary to suppress information used by the IDS.
- Information modification – Possibility of an adversary to modify information used by the IDS.
- Information insertion – Possibility of an adversary to insert information used by the IDS.

IDS Core

Without going to detail one can identify the following sets of generic properties, which are not bound to any specific application or protocol:

- Context awareness – Context awareness is used to describe an IDS' ability to analyze distributed actions, e.g. split routing [18], actions executed under differing user IDs on behalf of a single person etc.
- Location awareness – The location of an IDS in the network is relevant because it influences the set of activities that an IDS can observe. In addition it influences the value of activity attributes such as the source MAC address of an Ethernet frame. This may be used to determine whether the frame source is located on the local subnet, which may be of importance for recognizing spoofed IP PDUs.
- Techniques available – Various techniques are required for the recognition of activities. Regular expression matching is required for string-based attacks; state machines are required for protocol analysis etc.
- Delay – The delay introduced between the occurrence of an activity and the generation of an alarm can be approximated to high, medium and low, e.g. an IDS.
- Load treatable – Depending on the techniques used by the IDS and the available resources, the network and machine load that can be sustained by an IDS varies and determines the risk of not recognizing an activity due to an overload situation [13].

3.2   Low-Level Properties

Again considering our SMTP example it becomes clear that the generic properties identified above are not fine-grained enough to represent an IDS. Its awareness of a given protocol or application may vary, which influences the quality of the output generated.

Information Source

The information source may be refined by a set of properties describing the activity attributes that the information source provides to the IDS, e.g. IP source address etc.

IDS Core

One can identify lower-level IDSM properties describing application, operating system or protocol-specific IDS characteristics.

IDS Configuration

Another set of properties may be used to specify the set of enabled alarms. A set of properties may be used to represent the set of attacks known to an IDS. These properties are important because an IDS may fulfill requirements such as TCP stream reassembly, but if it does not provide a description of how to detect a given attack, it may never generate the corresponding alarm.

4 Activities

Based on the two property classification schemes just introduced we can characterize IDSes in suitable way to define activities proposed in the following.

The definition of activities we are proposing is based on rules expressed by properties and other rules. So to speak, an activity is defined by a set of rules, whereas these rules describe the IDS characteristics required for the generation of a given alarm.

An example (derived from the SMTP example introduced above) of such a rule describing the condition for the generation of the alarm `alarm.SMTP.pipe` in the case that an IDS observes the activity `A.SMTP.pipe` on the network could look as follows:

> *A.SMTP.pipe->r.alarm.SMTP.pipe* = p.infoSrc.type.net &
>   r.tech.patRec & r.prot.SMTP.aware &
>   p.sign.alarm.SMTP.pipe & p.conf.alarm.SMTP.pipe

The rule can be read as "the activity `A.SMTP.pipe` may cause an IDS to generate the alarm `alarm.SMTP.pipe` if the information source used is network-based and a pattern recognition algorithm is available etc." To further elucidate the example, the semantics of the properties used can be described as follows:

- `p.infoSrc.type.net` – true if the information source is the network.
- `r.tech.patRec` – true if any type of pattern recognition algorithm is provided by the IDS.
- `r.prot.{SMTP|TCP|IP}.aware` – true if the IDS has basic capabilities to treat the protocols listed.
- `p.sign.alarm.SMTP.pipe` – true if the IDS is capable of generating the SMTP pipe alarm.
- `p.conf.alarm.SMTP.pipe` – true if the SMTP pipe alarm is enabled.

Note that to improve the readability, we suppress `p.infoSrc.type.net`, `p.sign.alarm.SMTP.pipe` and `p.conf.alarm.SMTP.pipe` in the following discussions. This is possible because they are not relevant to the principles to be introduced.

4.1 Notation of Activities and Rule Groups

Considering the example rule above, one notices that every term has a one-character prefix. The semantics of this notation is used to indicate the type and complexity of terms. Lower case characters indicate a simple property or rule. Upper case characters indicate complex constructs such as activities that may consist of several rules and properties. In the context of this work we use the following prefixes:

p.*   Previously defined properties.
r.*   Rules that may be composed of simple properties, rules or the somewhat more complex rule groups.

G.*   Rule groups are used as a writing convention and shall help us define activity variations. We use the rule groups to indicate that the rule within which they are used has to be expanded to a list of rules, i.e. they can be considered place holders. For each group member a list element, i.e. rule, is created, whereas the place holder is replaced with the corresponding group element. Using a C-like language, such a construct would be implemented as a loop over an array, whereas in prolog one would take advantage of the inference engine to expand the group.

A.*   Activities are a construct that may consist of several rules or lists of rules expressing conditions an IDS has to fulfill to be able to generate a given alarm.

4.2   Activity Variations

Adversaries often try to circumvent detection by slightly modifying their attacks. A typical example is IP fragmentation. One could envisage defining a separate activity for every variation that seems possible. However, this does not seem to be advisable because the number of activity variations may be very high—especially when considering the fact that an adversary may combine several variations at once.

As mentioned above, activity variations are the main motivation for the introduction of rule groups. The use of rule groups can be demonstrated by developing the simplified SMTP pipe example activity introduced earlier:

$A.SMTP.pipe$->$r.alarm.SMTP.pipe$ =
          `r.tech.patRec` & `r.prot.SMTP.aware`

In this example we define the two remaining terms as follows:

`r.tech.patRec`[3] = `p.tech.stringMatch` | `p.tech.regexp`
`r.prot.SMTP.aware` = `p.prot.SMTP.aware` & `G.prot.TCP.aware`

The first term was easily developed to simple properties representing an IDS's capability of performing either simple string matching or more complex regular expression matching. The second term has not yet been extended to simple properties. `G.prot.TCP.aware` stands for a group of the various degrees of TCP awareness. The resulting list represents the activity variations that may be created by an adversary by playing around with TCP-specific features. An example is the slicing of the TCP data stream into very small byte sequences, which may be used to circumvent detection by IDSes that do not fully reconstruct TCP streams [18,19]. One could argue that a property expressing the fact that an IDS is SMTP-aware implicitly also requires TCP awareness and that therefore the additional term `G.prot.TCP.aware` is not required. This not quite correct because the degree of TCP awareness influences the activity variations an IDS is able to cope with—which we try to represent with the term `G.prot.TCP.aware`.

---

[3] As this is an example, the list of the group members does not aim to be complete.

The terms above can be further developed as follows:

```
G.prot.TCP.aware = {r.prot.TCP.aware,
      r.prot.TCP.streamReassembly}
r.prot.SMTP.aware[] = {
    p.prot.SMTP.aware & r.prot.TCP.aware,
    p.prot.SMTP.aware & r.prot.TCP.streamReassembly
    }
A.SMTP.pipe->r.alarm.SMTP.pipe[] = {
    (p.tech.stringMatch | p.tech.regexp) & p.prot.SMTP.aware &
    r.prot.TCP.aware,
    (p.tech.stringMatch | p.tech.regexp) & p.prot.SMTP.aware &
    r.prot.TCP.streamReassembly
    }
```

This expansion results in two variations of the SMTP pipe attack—one of them requiring the IDS to be capable of reassembling TCP streams. However, the activity has yet not been developed into a property-only representation. The next step would now be to expand `r.prot.TCP.aware` and `r.prot.TCP.streamReassembly` according to their definition, which could be made as follows:

```
r.prot.TCP.aware = p.prot.TCP.aware & G.prot.IP.aware
r.prot.TCP.streamReassembly = p.prot.TCP.streamReassembly &
    r.prot.TCP.aware & r.prot.IP.fragmentReassembly⁴ &
    r.tech.statefull⁵
G.prot.IP.aware = {
    r.prot.IP.aware, r.prot.IP.fragmentReassembly
    }
```

We are not going to exercise the further expansion here because this can be done in a similar way as the previous expansion steps. However, one might want to note that further activity variations are created by the term `G.prot.IP.aware`.

4.3   Activity Groups

By introducing the notion of activity groups (`AG.*` prefix) whose member activities are similar in the sense that an IDS may confuse them, we hope to facilitate the finding and definition of activities. Once activity groups have been defined, IDSes can be evaluated on a per-activity group basis, which should result in a simplified evaluation procedure.

---

[4] `r.prot.IP.fragmentReassembly` stands for the IDS's capability to reassemble fragmented IP traffic.

[5] `r.tech.statefull` represents the group of techniques that allow an IDS to perform a state-full analysis of the activities observed. Those techniques are typically finite state machines, Petri nets, etc.

The systematic identification of suspicious activities that an IDS should report is subject to ongoing research and is outlined in the outlook section (Section 6). However, for the following we assume that a suspicious activity that may potentially cause an IDS to generate alarms has been identified.

Along with the definition of the activity describing an attack, we propose a search for non-attack activities based on common knowledge about IDS failures as outlined in Section 2.

In order to facilitate the definition of activity group members, i.e. activities, we introduce a rule describing the characteristics commonly required from an IDS so it is able to cope with this group of activities. Reconsidering the SMTP pipe example we could define the activity group and the activity as follows:

```
AG.SMTP.pipe->r.common = r.tech.patRec & r.prot.SMTP.aware
A.SMTP.pipe->r.alarm.SMTP.pipe = AG.SMTP.pipe->r.common
```

The group `AG.SMTP.pipe` can now be used to define further activities such as the non-malicious activity where a message containing the pipe symbol within the message body is transferred over SMTP. Although this is not an attack, an IDS may generate an alarm (false positive) if it is performing pattern matching on the SMTP data stream only. In order to recognize the situation correctly, the IDS needs the ability to analyze SMTP at the protocol level, i.e. the IDS must be able to identify the beginning and the end of the message body. The corresponding activity `A.SMTP.pipe.body` could be defined as follows:

```
A.SMTP.pipe.body->r.alarm.SMTP.pipe =
        AG.SMTP.pipe->r.common &
        ! r.prot.SMTP.cmdAware[6]
r.prot.SMTP.cmdAware = p.prot.SMTP.cmdAware
        & r.tech.statefull & r.prot.SMTP.aware
```

Having identified such an activity group one can evaluate the behavior of an IDS with respect to this group of activities. We expect the evaluation to provide information about the activity variations that are detected or ignored correctly along with the false positives and the false negatives that a given IDS might generate.

It is further noteworthy that we expect the definition of activities to be reasonably scalable. We believe that the rules that have been identified once can be reused within the definition of other activities, e.g. once we have specified the rule that represents the IDS capabilities required for treating TCP traffic, this rule can be reused when specifying SMTP activities, HTTP activities etc.

5   IDS Evaluation

Having identified all the IDS characteristics and activity definitions we propose a simple model that allows us to evaluate a given IDS based on its characteristics.

The IDS evaluation model as proposed in Figure 1 can be used to evaluate IDSes systematically with respect to a given list of activities, i.e. activity groups.

---

[6] `r.prot.SMTP.cmdAware` represents the IDS's capability to recognize SMTP commands and to treat the corresponding data in the appropriate context.

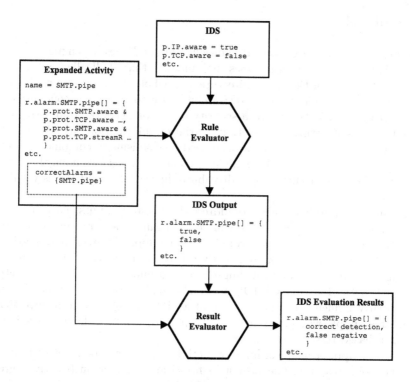

Fig. 1. Evaluation of an IDS for a given activity

Once an activity has been analyzed with respect to the IDS characteristics one obtains a list of activity variations associated with values that indicate whether an alarm would have been generated (IDS output). In order to know which of those results represent correct detection, correct non-detection, false positives or false negatives, one has to cross-validate (result evaluator) these results. This cross-validation is done with the knowledge of whether the activity represents an attack and, if so, which (`correctAlarms`) alarms one would expect the IDS to generate (IDS evaluation results).

5.1 Finding Strengths and Weaknesses

Let us assume one has characterized a number of IDSes and defined a set of activity groups that shall be used to evaluate the IDSes. If we evaluate every IDS for every activity defined, we should obtain a clear picture about the types of activities a given IDS masters well and the types of activities that cause an IDS to fail. Also we hope to be able to compare IDSes based on the number and types of failures one can expect on a per-activity basis. We hope that this knowledge will enable us to analyze, evaluate and improve more complex ID-architectures consisting of several diverse IDSes.

6 Outlook

The long-term goal of collecting knowledge about IDSes' strengths and weaknesses is to combine several IDSes in a manner that shall allow us to reduce of the failure rate of the ID-architecture as a whole. Furthermore we hope this knowledge will enable such an IDS-architecture to present a condensed view of security-related activities to a security officer or network administrator. We hope that this structured, per-activity variation information has adequate level of detail that we can derive good rules and mechanisms to combine the output of different IDSes to reach the goals just mentioned. Also we hope that this information helps us decide how to distribute different types of IDSes within the network.

However, before being able to address these issues, we first have to validate the proposed approach, which we will do by means of an implementation using a rule-based language such as prolog. Also the approach itself may need to be extended as we have not yet sufficiently taken the influence of the environment into account and are not providing diagnostic information about the activity observed by the IDS and the IDS itself. The load on the network, for instance, may greatly influence the failure rate of an IDS. Finally we have investigated whether a simple way exists to extend this proposal to behavior-based IDSes and host-based IDSes.

Also the approach concerning how activity groups can be identified is a subject of ongoing research. The most straightforward way to identify activity groups is probably to take a list of advisories (CERT etc.) and start defining activities that cover the vulnerabilities they describe. Whereas this seems to be a valid approach [21], it is not particularly systematic. We are considering exploring a more formal approach based on so-called fault assumptions [22] as used in the dependability research field [17]. In a nutshell the idea is first to identify a list of systems and subsystems (network elements, services, applications, middleware, files etc.). Then, considering systems as objects, we identify a list of high-level operations (methods) that can be executed in the context of a system, e.g. reading an object attribute etc. We hope to find a common set of methods that could then be extended with system-specific operations as required. Finally, we plan to consult a classification of vulnerabilities [4,23] and to extract a list of attack types (buffer overflow, meta-character tricks, privilege abuse, spoofing etc.). We then try to identify attack scenarios that apply for a given method defined for a given object, which we hope will allow us to find an adequate set of activity groups that can be used to evaluate IDSes.

7 Conclusion

In this paper we described an approach that will hopefully allow us to obtain a unified, in-depth understanding of the strengths and weaknesses of a given IDS. The main objective we addressed is the description of activities by the combination of IDS characteristics required for generating the corresponding alarms.

Furthermore the approach was illustrated by the definition of an activity that represents an SMTP attack, along with a nonmalicious activity that potentially may cause an IDS to generate a false alarm for the very same attack.

In addition we described the scope within which this work was conducted and outlined our future plans.

References

1. Michael Sobirey, "Michael Sobirey's Intrusion Detection Systems page," http://www-rnks.informatik.tu-cottbus.de/~sobirey/ids.html, November 1998. 183

2. CERT Coordination Center, "CERT Incident Note IN-99-07 - Distributed Denial of Sevice Tools," CERT Coordination Center, Pittsburgh, Incident Note IN-99-07, 1996. 183

3. Andrew H. Gross, "Analyzing Computer Intrusions," Ph.D. Thesis, San Diego: University of California, San Diego Supercomputer Center, 1997, pp. 233. 183

4. Sandeep Kumar, "Classification and Detection of Computer Intrusions," Ph.D. Thesis, Purdue, IN: Purdue University, Computer Sciences Department, August 1995. 183, 194

5. Peter G. Neumann and Donn B. Parker, "A Summary of Computer Misuse Techniques," presented at 12th National Computer Misuse Techniques, October 1989. 183

6. Peter A. Loscocco, Stephen D. Smalley, Patrick A. Muckelbauer, Ruth C. Taylor, S. Jeff Turner, and John F. Farrell, "The Inevitability of Failure: The Flawed Assumptions of Security in Modern Computing Environments," National Security Agency, 1998. 183

7. Peter G. Neumann, "Illustrative Risks to the Public in the Use of Computer Systems and Related Technology," Computer Science Laboratory, SRI International, Menlo Park, CA, Technical Report, October 1998. 183

8. John D. Howard, "An Analysis Of Security Incidents On The Internet," Ph.D. Thesis, Pittsburgh: Canegie Mellon University, Engineering and Public Policy, 1997, pp. 292. 183

9. Aurobindo Sundaram, "An Introduction to Intrusion Detection," COAST Laboratory, Purdue University, Purdue, IN. 183

10. R. Benjamin, B. Gladman, and B. Randell, "Protecting IT Systems from Cyber Crime," Imperial College, London, Technical Report, 1998. 183

11. Peter G. Neumann, "Practical Architectures for Survivable Systems and Networks," Computer Science Laboratory, SRI International, Menlo Park, CA, Technical Report, October 1998. 183

12. R. Lippmann, D. Fried, I. Graf, J. Haines, K. Kendall, D. McClung, D. Weber, S. Webster, D. Wyschogrod, R. Cunningham, and M. Zissman, "Evaluating Intrusion Detection Systems: The 1998 DARPA Off-Line Intrusion Detection Evaluation," presented at DISECEX'00 – DARPA Information Survivability Conference & Exposition, Hilton Head, SC, 2000. 183, 184

13. Robert Durst, Terrence Champion, Brian Witten, Eric Miller, and Luigi Spanguolo, "Testing and Evaluating Computer Intrusion Detection Systems," Commun. of ACM, vol. 42, July 1999. 183, 184, 188

14. J. McHugh, "The Lincoln Laboratories Intrusion Detection System Evaluation: A Critique," presented at DISCEX'00 - DARPA Information Survivability Conference & Exposition, Hilton Head, SC, 2000. 184

15. Hervé Debar, Marc Dacier, and Andreas Wespi, "Towards a Taxonomy of Intrusion Detection Systems," Computer Networks, vol. 31, pp. 805-822, 1999. 184, 187
16. CERT Coordination Center, "Sendmail v.5 Vulnerability," CERT Coordination Center, Pittsburgh, Advisory CA-95.05, 1995. 185
17. J. C. Laprie, A. Avizienis, and H. Kopetz, "Dependability: Basic Concepts and Terminology, vol. 5: Springer Verlag, 1992. 186, 194
18. Vern Paxson, "Bro: a system for detecting network intruders in real-time," Computer Networks, vol. 31, pp. 2435-2463, 1999. 186, 188, 190
19. Rain Forest Puppy <rfp@wiretrip.net>, "A look at whisker's anti-IDS tactics - Just how bad can we ruin a good thing?",
    http://www.securityfocus.com/templates/forum_message.html?forum=2&
    head=670&id=670, 2000. 186, 190
20. William E. Weinman, "About Web Server Logs: Common Log Format,"
    http://www.weinman.com/wew/log-talk/clf.html, 1998. 186
21. Taimur Aslam, "A Taxonomy of Security Faults in the UNIX Operating System," Master's thesis, Purdue, IN: Purdue University, Computer Sciences Department, 1995, pp. 120. 194
22. David Powell, "Failure Mode Assumptions and Assumption Coverage," presented at 22nd Int. Symp. on Fault-Tolerant Computing (FTCS-22), Boston, MA, 1992. 194
23. Carl E. Landwehr, Alan R. Bull, John P. McDermott, and William S. Choi, "A Taxonomy of Computer Program Security Flaws," Information Technology Division, Naval Research Laboratory, Washington, D. C. 20375-5337, 1994. 194

LAMBDA: A Language to Model a Database for Detection of Attacks

Frédéric Cuppens[1] and Rodolphe Ortalo[2]

[1] ONERA, Centre de Toulouse
2, avenue Edouard Belin, 31055 Toulouse cedex 4, France
cuppens@cert.fr
[2] NEUROCOM, Ter Sud A – Z.I. La Plaine
5, avenue Marcel Dassault, 31500 Toulouse, France
roo@neurocom.com

Abstract. This article presents an attack description language. This language is based on logic and uses a declarative approach. In the language, the conditions and effects of an attack are described with logical formulas related to the state of the target computer system. The various steps of the attack process are associated to events, which may be combined using specific algebraic operators. These elements provide a description of the attack from the point of view of the attacker. They are complemented with additional elements corresponding to the point of view of intrusion detection systems and audit programs. These detection and verification aspects provide the language user with means to tailor the description of the attack to the needs of a specific intrusion detection system or a specific environment.

1 Introduction

In this article, we study the definition of an attack description language which could be used in a diagnosis program to model the various alerts raised by one or several Intrusion Detection Systems (IDS), and to reason about the behaviour of a potential computer system intruder. This topic is related to several independent previous work. For example, CISL [1] is a language that aims at representing specific instances of an intruder attack. Similarly, work currently in progress at IETF [2,3,4] proposes a language to describe the alerts raised by different IDS in a common framework. These languages focus on the description of specific occurrences of some type of attack or alert. They also address data communication issues, and offer a common basis to exchange information between, for example, various intrusion detection systems and system administration consoles.

In our work, we focus on the problem of describing attacks themselves. The language we present allows us to define a generic description of an attack operation, independently of a specific intrusion detection process in a specific computer system. The generic description is then complemented by additional elements related to the intrusion detection operation, and verification of the feasibility of the attack in the actual computer system target of the attack. This should allow

H. Debar, L. Mé, and F. Wu (Eds.): RAID 2000, LNCS 1907, pp. 197–216, 2000.
© Springer-Verlag Berlin Heidelberg 2000

us to take into account the specificities of a particular computer system and of the IDS used.

The work performed on CISL and at IETF offers the opportunity to exchange information concerning specific attacks or alerts raised by IDS. One objective of our approach is to define a language in a syntactic framework compatible with the common framework under development at IETF. Furthermore, the language should provide means that could be used by a reasoning program. This program could provide a detailed and sensible diagnosis concerning a (potential) intrusion occurring in the computer system under analysis.

The structure of this article is the following: Section 2 presents the context of our study and various definitions. Section 3 details the requirements we adopt for an attack description language. Section 4 defines the attack description language proposed in this paper. Section 5 presents an example of a multiple steps attack described with this language. Section 6 describes some of the possible applications of the attack formalisation. Finally, Section 7 concludes.

2   Context and Definitions

Figure 1 presents a high level overview of the various elements appearing in the intrusion detection framework and the way they interact with each other.

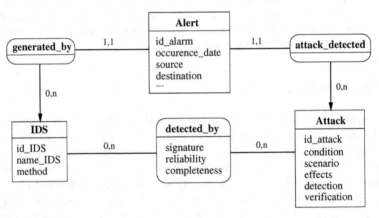

Fig. 1. Conceptual model

In the remaining of this section, we present in more detail some of the components of Fig. 1, with respect to the attack process in the first part, and then with respect to the intrusion detection process in the second part.

2.1   Attack Process

Overview. In the language, we essentially describe an attack as a combination of actions, complemented by several statements in relation with the target com-

puter system. (We add IDS-related issues to this description in a later step.)
The core components of an attack description are:

- A set of *conditions* to be satisfied in the system target of the attack for this
  attack to succeed, or to be satisfied by the attacker (for instance, specific
  access rights the attacker needs to perform the attack).
- The *effects* of a successful attack are the consequences of its performance in
  the system. Such effects can be associated with the occurrence of a damage
  in the system (e.g. data destruction, service disruption) or a gain for the
  attacker (for instance the acquisition of knowledge concerning the target
  system).
- A *scenario* describes how an attacker combines different actions in order to
  perform the attack described. These actions are associated to the different
  attack steps. One attack step can be an elementary operation performed by
  the attacker, either in the target computer system or in the systems under
  the attacker control. Such step can also correspond to the execution of other
  lower-level attacks.

With these elements, we address the description of the attack from the point
of view of the attacker. We describe the attack *scenario* the attacker should
perform against a computer system satisfying the *conditions* of the attack when
his intention is to bring about the *effects* of the attack.

Malicious and Suspicious Actions. We introduce a distinction between two
kind of attacks: *malicious* actions and *suspicious* actions.

We define malicious actions with respect to the security policy of the system. Malicious actions are attacks whose effects lead to direct violation of the
security policy of the computer system target of the attack. Such attacks are an
immediate security concern when successful.

Suspicious actions are defined with respect to malicious actions. We say an
action is suspicious if such action may be used as a step of the scenario of a
malicious action. Therefore, an action is suspicious when it can contribute to
the execution of a malicious action.[1]

2.2   Detection Process

Intrusion Detection Issues. In order to account for the attack from the point
of view of an intrusion detection system, we describe separately what should be
done to detect the occurrence of an attack. Therefore, we describe additionally:

---

[1] In this case, it may be inappropriate to designate the suspicious actions with the
term "attack" – this word usually *implies* a malicious intention. In this paper, we use
such a terminology as it seems to us that the word "attack" is used commonly in the
computer security field to designate the special combination of both malicious and
suspicious actions we want to designate, and does not necessarily imply a relation
with the security objectives of a specific environment.

- The *detection* process, i.e. the elementary actions that should be performed in order to detect an attack. Several operations may be needed to complete the detection. These detection operations are closely related to the actions performed by the attacker, but they are clearly not identical. For example, some of the attack actions may be performed on the attacker local computer and are not observable by the IDS of the target computer system. In this case, the action associated with the detection of such a non observable attack would be the empty action (denoted *noop* in the following).
- We also describe how these detection actions are combined. Such description is similar to the description of the attack scenario, but the action types involved are distinct: only detection actions are involved in the detection scenario, while only attack actions are involved in the attack scenario.
- Finally, we want to complement detection actions with verification actions. These actions aim at evaluating the impact of an attack on the computer system. For instance, system checks may indicate if an attack was successful or not. Similarly, audit scripts may indicate if the system exhibits a known vulnerability.

For convenience, we use the same word "action" for describing detection, verification and attack actions in this text. However, notice that, even though we represent them in the same way in the formalism, there are clearly three distinct types of actions involved.

IDS Signatures. In order to identify an attack, scenario-based IDS often rely on attack *signatures*. Such signatures are related to detection actions, but often they correspond to more pragmatic representations guided by operational concerns (e.g. performance). Attack signatures incorporate information related to all or a subset of the detection actions. Signatures should be directly usable by the IDS to examine the events monitored in the computer system.

Further in the intrusion detection process, the detection of such a signature in the flow of events monitored by the IDS lead to the generation of an alert.

An additional objective of our attack description language is to establish a link between the abstract representation of a detection scenario included in the attack process, and the signatures used in practice by IDS to recognise attacks. However, it is not the purpose of this paper to develop a language to represent attack signatures.

Notice that the attack signature is one attribute of the **detected_by** relationship between the **Attack** and **IDS** entities (see Fig. 1). Other attributes may be **reliability** and **completeness**. These attributes are used respectively to represent how the IDS is reliable (resp. complete) with respect to the detection of a given attack.

Alerts. The terms *alarm* and *alert* are often used to refer to the informative actions performed by IDS when they identify attack actions regarding the system they monitor. In this article, we consider that both terms are equivalent. We will only use the term *alert* in the rest of this paper.

Ideally, an alert should be raised by the IDS only when it detects the execution, or the execution attempt, of a malicious action. Indeed, either successful or unsuccessful, an intention to violate the system security policy requires the IDS to actively request the attention of the security administrator (who is responsible for the enforcement of the security policy and possibly specified this policy in the first place).

In practice, suspicious actions frequently lead IDS to raise alerts, even though the actions detected do not relate directly to the security policy. Of course, suspicious actions may be related to potential violations of the security policy. As such they clearly require attention from the part of the IDS. For example, the suspicious nature of an action is clearly a logging criteria. We think it should be up to the security administrator to decide if he wants to receive an alert when such attacks are detected.

Providing a common framework for the description of alerts is currently one of the objectives of the IETF [2,3]. As mentionned in the introduction, our goal in this paper is different but we aim at defining a language that is compatible with the IETF framework.

3 Requirements

3.1 Expressive Power

First, the language we study should allow us to describe attacks in conformance with the different aspects identified in Section 2.

Furthermore, we follow a *declarative* approach for the language definition. A requirement is to provide a language that allows the definition of the different components of an attack description in a declarative manner. Therefore, we see that :

Pre-condition and post-condition. The conditions that should be satisfied by the computer system for an attack to be feasible are associated to a *pre-condition* of the attack. The effects of the successful execution of this attack are associated to a *post-condition*. These pre-condition and post-condition are described by *logical conditions*. These logical conditions deal with the states of the computer systems corresponding to the potential targets of the attack (the computer system to protect) and with a representation of the attacker (its knowledge or its rights). Notice that we can assume that a given attack may have one or several potential targets.

Scenario. The scenario of the attack from the point of view of the attacker is described as a combination of events as well as a description of the various events involved in this scenario. Specifically, the action associated to each event of the scenario should be identified.

Detection. The actions to perform in order to detect the attack are described in a similar language, but while the attack scenario contains the actions of the attacker, the detection scenario only contains detection actions. According to the various attacks we studied, the two scenarios frequently differ. As an example, this is the case when some of the attacker actions are not observable by the IDS.

Verification. Generally, the effects of an attack are observable in the computer system. Similarly, it is possible to use audit programs [5,6] to test the existence of vulnerabilities in the system. We would like to include events associated to such verification in the attack description. For example, such events correspond to a system failure detection procedure or a specific vulnerability test program.

The scenario-related, detection-related and verification-related parts of one attack description correspond to distinct parts of the description. Most noticeably, we do *not* intend to deduce automatically the detection or verification actions from the attack scenario. Similarly, the pre-condition and post-condition clauses do *not* directly correspond to some (logic-based) description of the attack scenario.

With our approach, the occurence of attack actions is deduced from detection actions. Similarly, the truth value of the pre-condition and post-condition is derived from the verification actions. Furthermore, the pre-condition and post-condition induce constraints on the description of a high-level attack as the combination of several low-level attacks.

3.2   Modularity

We require the language to offer the opportunity to describe an attack scenario using actions corresponding to other, different, lower-level attacks. This modularity requirement correspond to the need to describe high-level attacks using previously defined attacks. Additionally, a high-level attack may also involve several steps related to practical basic operations.

Indeed, in practice, an attacker is often required to perform several successive attacks in order to cause real damage to a computer system, or obtain a significant profit. The description language should be modular to offer some way to combine attacks as well as basic operations in order to describe such a high-level scenario.

3.3   Deduction

Finally, as our language is based on a logical representation, it should offer some deductive capabilities. More precisely, deduction procedures may be helpful for several reasons:

- Deductive reasoning offer the opportunity to help the user to express the pre-condition and post-condition of a high-level scenario, using the pre-conditions and post-conditions of the lower level attacks involved in this scenario.

- If two different attack scenarios are detected by one or several IDS, logical reasoning may allow us to take into account directly the fact that these combined tools have also detected a high-level scenario. This high-level scenario composed of the combination of two scenarios may correspond to another attack (or to some steps of it), that may be taken care of automatically (see also [7] for a similar idea). Such automatic deduction could complement the atomic detection capabilities of the intrusion detection tools used. The attack description language should allow us to perform such deductions with respect to stand-alone attacks as well as complex attacks. However, this reasoning may necessitate a new additional component in the IDS to manage the information delivered by the detection tools. (The software architecture of such a deduction module is not further studied in this article.)

4   Language

4.1   System Model

Our system model is presented in Fig. 2. The information associated to system states is represented in first order logic using logical predicates. The information associated to system transitions is modelled using events, according to the approach presented in [8].

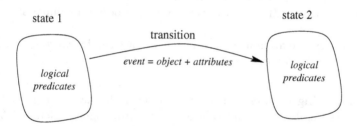

Fig. 2. System model

L_1 – **State Description.** State descriptions correspond to the definition of the pre-condition and post-condition of an attack. We use a language, denoted L_1, which is simply the logic of predicates.

Predicates are used to describe properties of the state relevant to the description of an attack. For example, for network-related attacks, interesting predicates may be : $port(telnet, 23, tcp)$, $local\_access(S, U)$ or $active\_service(S, telnetd)$ (where S and U are logical variables denoting respectively a computer system and a user).

These predicates are combined using the usual logical connectives ¬, ∨, ∧ to build the pre-condition and post-condition denoting the conditions and effects of an attack on the system state. For example, a pre-condition of the form $active\_service(s, telnetd) \land port(telnet, 23, tcp)$ denotes the fact that the *telnet* network service should be available in the target system on the standard TCP port for the attack to be performed successfully.

Sometimes, the effect of an attack is simply a knowledge gain for the attacker about the target system. In order to represent a knowledge gain, we also assume that language L_1 includes a meta-predicate *knows*. For instance, if A is the attacker, then $knows(A, active\_service(S, telnetd))$ means that A knows that *telnet* is an active service of system S.

L_2 – **Transition Description.** In our system model, we associate transitions to the occurrence of events, and we provide a language for combining these events in ways similar to event calculus.

We consider that events are objects [8]. These objects are collections of attributes. Events are defined in a language, denoted L_2, based on the logical operators $\neg$ and $\wedge$ plus the equality operator $=$ and a set A of attribute names, with $A = \{attribute_1, attribute_2, ...\}$. If e is an event, $attribute_1(e) = v$ denotes the fact that the value of attribute $attribute_1$ of e is v.

In the following, we will commonly use the set $A = \{action, actor, date\}$ to define the possible attributes of an event.

Attribute *action* is associated to an attack action (e.g. command `finger`). Attribute *actor* is associated to a set $\{s_1, ..., s_n\}$ of users performing the action. When a single user s is involved, we will follow the convention that $s = \{s\}$ for convenience. Attribute *date* corresponds to a time interval $[t_1, t_2]$ associated to event e. Similarly, we write t instead of $[t, t]$ for convenience. We assume that language L_2 includes the predicates $\leq$ and $<$ to perform comparisons between times.

In summary, the attributes of a specific event e can be expressed in L_2 with:
$action(e) = a \wedge actor(e) = u \wedge date(e) = [t_1, t_2]$

L_3 – **Combining Events.** Then, the events calculus algebra that may be used to combine several events is introduced via a third language, denoted L_3. In L_3, we provide the following operators to combine two events e_1 and e_2:

1. $e_1 ; e_2$: designates the sequential composition of events e_1 then e_2;
2. $e_1 \mid e_2$: designates the parallel unconstrained execution of e_1 and e_2;
3. $\overline{e_1}$: indicates the absence of e_1 in the event flow;
4. $e_1 ? e_2$: represents the non deterministic choice between e_1 and e_2;
5. $e_1 \& e_2$: designates the synchronised execution of both events e_1 and e_2 (order is not significant) – we have: $e_1 \& e_2 = (e_1 ; e_2) ? (e_2 ; e_1) ? (e_1 \mid e_2)$.

Finally, it is possible to include optional events in the attack specification. We note $[e]$ the fact that e is an optional event. To define $[e]$, first we define the event constant *noevent*, corresponding to a null event, such that $action(noevent) = noop$, where *noop* is a no-operation action. Then, we state: $[e] = e ? noevent$.

4.2   Full Attack Description

We use the following notation to define all the elements of an attack description:

> **attack** $attack\_name(arg_1, arg_2, ...)$
>   **pre** : $cond \in L_1$
>   **post** : $cond \in L_1$
>   **scenario** : $expr \in L_3$
>   **where** $cond \in L_2$
>   **detection** : $expr \in L_3$
>   **where** $cond \in L_2$
>   **verification** : $expr \in L_3$
>   **where** $cond \in L_2$

By convention, inside the description of an attack, names spelled in lower case or numbers designate *constants* (e.g. 21, $fingerd$). Names starting with a capital letter designate *variables* (e.g. U, $Host$, E_i). Variables are local variables: their scope is limited to the attack description where they appear. Variables declarations are omitted.

Attack names may be used as event actions. Therefore, the *action* attribute of one event e appearing in the scenario of an attack named $attack_1$ may correspond to another lower-level attack $attack_2$. For instance, we indicate this by stating $action(e) = attack_2(...)$ in the **where** clause of the definition of the scenario of $attack_1$.

The conditions appearing in **where** clauses of an attack description are used to formulate constraints between the various attributes of the events of the description and the variables used in the pre-condition or post-condition. For example, if e is an event of the scenario of the attack, e' a detection event, and e'' a verification event, we may express the following constraints between the attributes of e, e' and e'':

> **scenario** : e
>   **where** $action(e) = sniffer(TargetHost, FromHost)$
> $\wedge\ actor(e) = User \wedge date(e) = [t_1, t_2]$
> **detection** : e'
>   **where** $action(e') = detect\_sniffer()$
> $\wedge\ actor(e') = FromHost \wedge date(e') = [t_1, t_2]$
> **verification** : e''
>   **where** $action(e'') = failed\_login(TargetHost)$
> $\wedge\ actor(e'') = User \wedge date(e'') = t_3 \wedge t_2 \leq t_3$

The language L_2 used to describe the attributes of events aims at describing these events as data objects. The alert and attack description language currently under development at IETF shows similar objectives [3,4]. Furthermore, the effort of IETF should provide a more detailed and standard language for describing the various attributes associated to occurrences of attacks and alerts.

Such a language could be used to extend L_2 in the future to describe with more details the components of the events appearing in the attack description.

The detection-specific and verification-specific parts of the attack description (indicated by keywords **detection** and **verification**) reveal some redundancy in the description. The **detection** clause describing the actions an IDS should perform to detect the attack execution is linked to the **scenario** part of the attack description (i.e. the view of a potential attacker). Similarly, the **verification** clause is used to check the truth value of a subset of the information provided by the **pre** and **post** clauses. These pre-condition and post-condition model the required opportunities and possible effects of the attack execution respectively. A system verification tool should execute audit actions corresponding to these formulas to check if a specific computer system is vulnerable to such an attack or if a (previously detected) occurrence of this attack has succeeded. Therefore, for a given system, actions mentioned in the **verification** clause should correspond to pre-condition or post-condition checking test.

As mentioned previously, these additional components of the attack description exist for specific reasons. First, they identify *explicitly* the aspects related either to an IDS, or to an audit tool that could be used to assess the feasibility of an attack in a specific computer system, or the impact of a detected attack. Furthermore, these components identify *actions* that should be performed either to detect the occurrence of such attack or to analyse the existing vulnerabilities of a computer system. They correspond to an operational view, with respect to a security audit or to intrusion detection.

5   Example

As an example, we present the description of a simple attack that can be performed against a computer system whose security configuration is too permissive. This example illustrates the use of the language and illustrates the potential differences between the various parts of an attack description.

5.1   Overview

The attack we want to describe involves several steps corresponding to the following commands:

1. `rpcinfo -p` *Target-IP*
2. `showmount -e` *Target-IP*
3. `showmount -a` *Target-IP*
4. `finger @`*Target-IP*
5. `adduser --uid` *Userid Username*[2]
6. `mount -t` *Target-partition* `/mnt`

---

[2] Alternatively, `vi /etc/passwd` and editing actions may be used instead of the common **adduser** script.

In this attack, steps 1, 2, 3 and 4 correspond to knowledge acquisition: the attacker obtain information concerning the various hard disk partitions exported by the target computer system using the NFS protocol. Step 5 is a local action from the point of view of the attacker: he creates a new user account on his own computer with specific parameters matching those identified in the previous steps. Finally, in step 6 the attacker mounts the target partition on his computer and obtains access to its content. This last step will succeed only if the target computer configuration is somehow permissive (some method of *host* authentication could prevent such an attack).

5.2 Partial High-Level Description

In an initial phase, the attack is modelled by combining the various steps identified previously. Attack events, noted $A_1, A_2, ..., A_6$ are introduced for each step of the attack. The actions associated to these events are enumerated. These actions correspond to lower-level attacks, which are modelled in the next section.

> **attack** $NFS\_abuse(Target\text{-}IP)$
>   **pre** :
>   **post** :
>   **scenario** : $((A_1 ; (A_2 \& A_3)) \& A_4 \& A_5) ; A_6$
>   **where** $action(A_1) = rpcinfo(Target\text{-}IP)$
> $\wedge\ action(A_2) = showmount\_e(Target\text{-}IP)$
> $\wedge\ action(A_3) = showmount\_a(Target\text{-}IP)$
> $\wedge\ action(A_4) = finger(Target\text{-}IP)$
> $\wedge\ action(A_5) = create\_account(Username, Userid)$
> $\wedge\ action(A_6) = mount(/\mathtt{mnt})$
>   **detection** :
>   **where**
>   **verification** :
>   **where**

At this step, the description is still incomplete. Most notably, the precise pre-condition and post-condition of the attack are not easy to determine directly given that the attack involve several steps. We show in the following how these elements are related to the pre-condition and post-condition of lower-level attacks. Such logical relations allow us to complete the description later in Sect. 5.4.

Similarly, the **detection** and **verification** clauses are also left unspecified in this initial sketch of the attack description.

5.3 Elementary Steps

In this section, we describe the basic steps of the complex attack sketched previously. In these descriptions, several kind of events are used: attack events are noted E_i, detection events are noted F_i and system verification events are noted G_i.

Step 1.

attack $rpcinfo(Target\text{-}IP)$

$$pre : \overbrace{remote\_access(A, H)}^{C_1} \wedge \overbrace{ip\_address(H, Target\text{-}IP)}^{C_2}$$
$$\wedge \underbrace{use\_service(H, portmapper)}_{C_3} \wedge \underbrace{use\_service(H, mountd)}_{C_4}$$

$$post : \underbrace{knows(A, C_3)}_{P_1} \wedge \underbrace{knows(A, C_4)}_{P_2}$$

scenario : E_1
    where $action(E_1) = $ `rpcinfo -p` $Target\text{-}IP$
    $\wedge\ actor(E_1) = A$
detection : F_1
    where $action(F_1) = detect(E_1)$
verification : G_1
    where $action(G_1) = test\_service(portmapper)$

Pre-conditions and post-conditions of the attack are expressed using :

- $C_1 : remote\_access(A, H)$ which means that attacker A has a remote network access to the target host H.
- $C_2 : ip\_address(H, Target\text{-}IP)$ which means that the IP address of host H is $Target\text{-}IP$.
- $C_3 : use\_service(H, portmapper)$, the $portmapper$ network service is active on host H.
- $C_4 : use\_service(H, mountd)$, the NFS service (daemon program $mountd$) is active on host H.
- $P_1 : knows(A, use\_service(H, portmapper))$ which means that the attacker learns that host H uses the network service $portmapper$.
- $P_2 : knows(A, use\_service(H, mountd))$ the attacker learns that host H uses an NFS daemon.

Step 2.

attack $showmount\_e(Target\text{-}IP)$

$$pre : C_1 \wedge C_2 \wedge C_4 \wedge \overbrace{exported\_partition(H, P)}^{C_5}$$
$$post : \underbrace{knows(A, C_5)}_{P_3}$$

scenario : E_2
    where $action(E_2) = $ `showmount -e` $Target\text{-}IP$
    $\wedge\ actor(E_2) = A$
detection : F_2
    where $action(F_2) = detect(E_2)$
verification : G_2
    where $action(G_2) = \underbrace{test\_service(mountd)}_{V_1}$

- C_5 means that host H exports the hard disk partition P via NFS.
- P_3 means that the attacker A knows that C_5 is true.

Step 3.

    attack $showmount\_a(Target\text{-}IP)$

$$\mathbf{pre} : C_1 \wedge C_2 \wedge C_4 \wedge \overbrace{mounted\_partition(H, P)}^{C_6}$$

$$\mathbf{post} : \underbrace{knows(A, C_6)}_{P_4}$$

    scenario : E_3
        where $action(E_3) = $ showmount -a $Target\text{-}IP$
        $\wedge \ actor(E_3) = A$
    detection : F_3
        where $action(F_3) = detect(E_3)$
    verification : G_3
        where $action(G_3) = V_1$

- C_6 means that the partition P is also a partition locally mounted by host H.
- P_4 knows that the attacker A knows that C_6.

Step 4.

    attack $finger(Target\text{-}IP)$

$$\mathbf{pre} : C_1 \wedge C_2 \wedge \overbrace{connected\_user(U, H)}^{C_7} \wedge \overbrace{userid(U, H, Userid)}^{C_8}$$
$$\wedge \ \underbrace{use\_service(H, fingerd)}_{C_9}$$

$$\mathbf{post} : \underbrace{knows(A, C_7)}_{P_5} \wedge \underbrace{knows(A, C_8)}_{P_6}$$

    scenario : E_4
        where $action(E_4) = $ finger @$Target\text{-}IP$
        $\wedge \ actor(E_4) = A$
    detection : F_4
        where $action(F_4) = detect(E_4)$
    verification : G_4
        where $action(G_4) = test\_service(fingerd)$

- C_7 means that user U is currently connected to host H.
- C_8 means that the user ID associated to the target user name U is $Userid$ on host H.
- C_9 means that host H provides the $finger$ service.
- P_5 means that the attacker A knows that C_7.
- P_6 means that the attacker A knows that C_8.

Step 5.

> **attack** $create\_account(U, Uscrid)$
>
> $\overbrace{}^{C_{10}}$
>
> **pre** : $root\_user(A, H_A)$
>
> **post** : $\underbrace{userid(U, H_A, Userid)}_{P_6} \wedge \underbrace{knows(A, P_6)}_{P_7}$
>
> **scenario** : E_5
>
> **where** $action(E_5) = $ adduser --uid $Userid\ U$
>
> $\wedge\ actor(E_5) = A$
>
> **detection** : $noevent$
>
> **where** $True$
>
> **verification** : $noevent$
>
> **where** $True$

- C_{10} means that the attacker A is a super-user on the attack host H_A.
- P_6 means the user U is now a user of the attack host H_A with a user ID equal to $Userid$.
- P_7 means the attacker A knows that P_6 is now true.

Step 6.

> **attack** $mount(Mount\text{-}point)$
>
> **pre** : $C_1 \wedge C_2 \wedge C_5 \wedge C_6 \wedge C_8 \wedge P_6 \wedge$
>
> $\underbrace{connected\_user(A, H_A)}_{C_{11}} \wedge \underbrace{owner(Directory, U)}_{C_{12}}$
>
> **post** : $\underbrace{can\_access(A, Directory)}_{P_8}$
>
> **scenario** : E_6
>
> **where** $action(E_6) = $ mount -t nfs $P\ Mount\text{-}point$
>
> $\wedge\ actor(E_6) = A$
>
> **detection** : F_5
>
> **where** $action(F_5) = detect(E_6)$
>
> **verification** : G_5
>
> **where** $action(G_5) = V_1$

- C_{11} means that A is connected to the attack host H_A.
- P_6 was described at step 5.
- C_{12} means that the user U is the owner of some $Directory$, contained in the exported partition P.
- P_8 means that the attacker A can now access the $Directory$ of U.

5.4 Full Description

Thanks to the description of the basic attacks presented in the previous section, we can now complement the partial description given in Sect. 5.2.

More precisely, we see that the pre-condition and post-condition mentioned in the descriptions of *rpcinfo*, *showmount_e*, *showmount_a*, *finger*, *mount* and *create_account* can be used to propose automatically to the user valid pre-condition and post-condition for attack *NFS_abuse*.

This process can be repeated to identify precisely the events appearing in the scenario of the attack. This leads to a detailed description of the **scenario** clause (compared to the equivalent one shown in Sect. 5.2). Taking into account the description of the low-level attacks, the high-level events $A_1, A_2, ..., A_6$ used in Sect. 5.2 are mapped to the actual commands corresponding to events $E_1, E_2, ..., E_6$. Detection and verification events ($F_1, ..., F_5$ and $G_1, ..., G_5$) omitted in the partial description of Sect. 5.2 are also extracted from the low-level attacks.

> **attack** *NFS_abuse*(*Target-IP*)
>   **pre** : $C_1 \wedge C_2 \wedge C_3 \wedge C_4 \wedge C_5 \wedge C_6 \wedge C_7 \wedge C_8 \wedge C_9 \wedge C_{10} \wedge C_{11} \wedge C_{12} \wedge P_6$
>   **post** : P_8
>   **scenario** : $((E_1 \, ; \, (E_2 \, \& \, E_3)) \, \& \, E_4 \, \& \, E_5) \, ; \, E_6$
>   **where** $action(E_1) = $ `rpcinfo -p` *Target-IP*
> $\wedge \ action(E_2) = $ `showmount -e` *Target-IP*
> $\wedge \ action(E_3) = $ `showmount -a` *Target-IP*
> $\wedge \ action(E_4) = $ `finger` @*Target-IP*
> $\wedge \ action(E_5) = $ `adduser --uid` *Userid U*
> $\wedge \ action(E_6) = $ `mount -t nfs` *P* `\mnt`
> $\wedge \ actor(E_1) = A \ \wedge \ actor(E_2) = A$
> $\wedge \ actor(E_3) = A \ \wedge \ actor(E_4) = A$
> $\wedge \ actor(E_5) = A \ \wedge \ actor(E_6) = A$
>   **detection** : $((F_1 \, ; \, (F_2 \, \& \, F_3)) \, \& \, F_4) \, ; \, noevent \, ; \, F_5$
>   **where** $action(F_1) = detect(E_1)$
> $\wedge \ action(F_2) = detect(E_2)$
> $\wedge \ action(F_3) = detect(E_3)$
> $\wedge \ action(F_4) = detect(E_4)$
> $\wedge \ action(F_5) = detect(E_6)$
>   **verification** : $((G_1 \, ; \, (G_2 \, \& \, G_3)) \, \& \, G_4) \, ; \, noevent \, ; \, G_5$
>   **where** $action(G_1) = test\_service(portmapper)$
> $\wedge \ action(G_2) = test\_service(mountd)$
> $\wedge \ action(G_3) = test\_service(mountd)$
> $\wedge \ action(G_4) = test\_service(fingerd)$
> $\wedge \ action(G_5) = test\_service(mountd)$

It is possible to simplify the description produced by a systematic examination of the low-level steps of the attack. Events *noevent* may be removed from the **detection** or **verification** clauses. We can note also that P_6, which appear in the pre-condition of *NFS_abuse* due to the fact that it appears in the pre-condition of the low-level attack *mount*() (step 6), appears also in the post-condition of *create_account*(). (In fact, step 5 exists for this purpose.) Therefore, P_6 is obtained during the attack process and may be eliminated from the pre-condition of NFS_abuse entirely. We integrate these simplifications in the operational description of the attack presented in the next section.

5.5   Operational Description

The full description presented in the previous section may not be the best suitable for an operational implementation of either the detection of the attack or the audit of the vulnerability of a computer system to this attack.

We present now the detailed attack specification that we adopt for attack NFS_abuse in this example. Manual modifications of the description provided automatically in Sect. 5.4 are done in this operational description. These modifications are detailed in the following.

attack NFS_abuse(Target-IP)
    pre : $remote\_access(A, H) \ \wedge \ ip\_address(H, Target\text{-}IP)$
        $\wedge \ use\_service(H, portmapper) \ \wedge \ use\_service(H, mountd)$
        $\wedge \ exported\_partition(H, P) \ \wedge \ mounted\_partition(H, P)$
        $\wedge \ connected\_user(U, H) \ \wedge \ userid(U, H, Userid)$
        $\wedge \ use\_service(H, fingerd) \ \wedge \ root\_user(A, H_A)$
        $\wedge \ connected\_user(A, H_A) \ \wedge \ owner(Directory, U)$
    post : $can\_access(A, Directory)$
    scenario : $((E_1 \ ; \ (E_2 \ \& \ E_3)) \ \& \ E_4 \ \& \ E_5) \ ; \ E_6$
        where $action(E_1) = $ `rpcinfo -p` $Target\text{-}IP$
        $\wedge \ action(E_2) = $ `showmount -e` $Target\text{-}IP$
        $\wedge \ action(E_3) = $ `showmount -a` $Target\text{-}IP$
        $\wedge \ action(E_4) = $ `finger @`$Target\text{-}IP$
        $\wedge \ action(E_5) = $ `adduser --uid` $Userid \ U$
        $\wedge \ action(E_6) = $ `mount -t nfs` P `\mnt`
        $\wedge \ actor(E_1) = A \ \wedge \ actor(E_2) = A$
        $\wedge \ actor(E_3) = A \ \wedge \ actor(E_4) = A$
        $\wedge \ actor(E_5) = A \ \wedge \ actor(E_6) = A$
    detection : $((F_1 \ ; \ (F_2 \ \& \ F_3)) \ \& \ F_4) \ ; \ F_5$
        where $action(F_1) = detect(E_1)$
        $\wedge \ action(F_2) = detect(E_2)$
        $\wedge \ action(F_3) = detect(E_3)$
        $\wedge \ action(F_4) = detect(E_4)$
        $\wedge \ action(F_5) = detect(E_6) \ \wedge \ date(F_5) = t$
    verification : W_1
        where $action(W_1) = foreign\_mount() \wedge date(W_1) = t'$
        $\wedge \ t \le t'$

In the operational description, we see that – even if six attack steps are identified – it is desirable that only five detection events $F_1, F_2, ..., F_5$ be included in the description of the attack. Such difference is due to the remote and undetectable nature of attack step E_5: the creation of an account on a foreign computer. No detection event is associated to E_5. Such situation demonstrates the need to provide a separate description of the detection-related or verification-related events in the attack description language. The IDS and attacker point of view may diverge concerning the events associated to an attack.

Furthermore, the **detection** or **verification** clauses focus on operational issues. They may differ from the clauses deduced logically from the low-level attacks description due to system observability or to design choices. Detection or verification events may be omitted or changed by the language user.

Such attitude was adopted for the definition of the **verification** clause in the above description. Instead of enumerating the verification events $G_1, ..., G_5$ identified in the basic attacks, we introduced a single system verification event W_1 specific to the description of attack NFS_abuse. In our example, W_1 is related to an hypothetical test check, denoted $foreign\_mount()$. This test program is supposed to determine the success of the attack by checking directly if a foreign computer (out of the local network) successfully obtained access to some local partition of a local computer. Finally, to indicate that $foreign\_mount()$ should be run only after an attack of type NFS_abuse is detected, we introduce a constraint concerning the date of the test event W_1 with respect to the last detection event F_5.

A similar decision could be made with respect to the deduced detection events $F_1, F_2, ..., F_5$. In fact in practice, for operational or performance reasons, most scenario-based IDS do not monitor *all* the events associated to an attack, but only a specific and significant subset which constitutes the *signature* of the attack. The event(s) composing the signature are chosen in order to correspond unambiguously to the occurrence of events $F_1, F_2, ..., F_5$, but they may be less numerous. Practical detection events may even include totally different events, for example if user profiles modifications are included among the events mentioned in the **detection** clause.

These examples show that a separate description of detection-related or verification-related events allows greater flexibility and specialisation of the attack description with respect to a specific environment. However, the language may also be used to deduce these components from lower-level attacks using an automatic procedure similar to the one used for the pre-condition and the post-condition.

6   Potential Applications

The attack descriptions written with the language presented in Sect. 4 may be used to perform further analysis of an attack process.

When an IDS raises an alert due to the occurence of a combination of actions associated to a specific attack, it is not always possible to decide if the attack failed or succeeded. Verification actions described in the **verification** clause of an attack description may be used to check the success of an occurence of this attack by observing its effects. Such verification actions could be triggered by the alert generated by the IDS. Like IDS alerts, the results of these checks may not be totally reliable or complete (e.g. if the attacker hide some of the effects of the attack, or when the target host availability is compromised).

The logical formulas describing the conditions and effects of one attack may be related to the security properties expected from the system described in the security policy. Similarly, the chaining and correlation between two attacks A_1 and A_2 can be studied in more detail. For example, we can say that A_1 and A_2 are chained if the post-condition of attack A_1 logically implies the pre-condition of attack A_2. Two attacks A_1 and A_n are defined as correlated if there exist some attacks $A_2, ..., A_{n-1}$ such that $\forall i \in [1, n-1]$, A_i and A_{i+1} are chained.[3]

If the post-condition of an attack A corresponds to a direct violation of the properties defined in the security policy, we say that this attack A is *malicious* (see Sect. 2.1). Furthermore, we say that an attack A is a *suspicious* action if attack A is correlated to a malicious action A'.[4] Hence, in the above example, if the post-condition of A_n corresponds to a violation of the security policy, A_n is a malicious action, and $A_1, A_2, ..., A_{n-1}$ are suspicious actions.

The combination of events appearing in the **detection** clause of a high-level attack – deduced from the description of lower level attacks – could be used to create IDS signatures. If an IDS is configurable enough, such automatically generated signatures may enable an IDS to detect multiple steps attacks when it can recognise the individual steps composing them.

Similarly, the events that appear by default in the **verification** clause of a complex attack could be used to drive an audit tool in order to find existing vulnerabilities in the computer system based on simpler system checks.

The logical formulation of the pre-condition and post-condition of attack descriptions can be used to build new complex scenario. For example, if two attacks A_1 and A_2 are chained (as defined previously), it is possible to build a new high-level attack A based on A_1 and A_2. This allows to consider automatically multiple steps attacks based on known low-level steps.

The information provided by the detection-specific and verification-specific parts of an attack description further complements the logical information provided by the pre-condition and post-condition. Given a suitable notion of corre-

---

[3] In practice, such a definition of correlation is a strong property, that we call strong correlation. Weaker definitions can be adopted. For instance, let us consider the attacks $rpcinfo(Target\_IP)$ (see step 1) and $showmount\_e(Target\_IP)$ (see step 2). One of the effect of attack $rpcinfo(Target\_IP)$ is that the attacker knows that the target system uses an NFS daemon: $knows(A, C_4)$. But, since condition C_4 appears in the pre-condition of attack $showmount\_e(Target\_IP)$, we can consider that step 1 and step 2 are correlated. This simulates the following reasoning: the attacker has performed step 1 in order to acquire knowledge useful to perform step 2 of the NFS_abuse attack. The definitions of weak and strong correlation will be presented in a forthcoming paper.

[4] Therefore, the definition of a suspicious attack depends on the notion of correlation adopted.

lation between attacks, these various elements may also be used in a deduction system to build and check potential intruder plans. Connected with one or several IDS, such deduction module could build some of the possible plans of an attacker, using the alerts generated by the IDS and the possible correlations between the attacks corresponding to the alerts. Such plans could be revised dynamically according to the information later provided by the IDS. Furthermore, the verification process mentioned in the attack descriptions may be used by such deduction module to drive automatic audit tools in order to check the absence or the existence of a vulnerability in the computer system [5,6,9,10]. The results could be used to validate or reject possible plans of the attacker, or to assess the gravity of an intrusion with respect to the security objectives of the target computer system.

7 Conclusion

The attack description language we study in this article shares many common elements with the languages defined in the USTAT [11] and IDIOT [12] intrusion detection systems. USTAT focuses on state transition analysis, whereas IDIOT detects intrusion by pattern-matching a signature against audit records. The former is based on finite state machine graphs, while the latter uses a variation of Coloured Petri Nets. The intrusion detection system IDES [13] relies also on a general rule-based expert system to propose a description of the attacks it detects, and follows a declarative approach.

The main difference of the language we propose with these systems resides in the integration in the attack description language of specific components dedicated to the description of the intrusion detection and system verification processes. These descriptions are separated from the actual description of the attack process. This separation provides additional degrees of freedom to the language used to describe the attack signatures by the operational IDS, or the results made available by specific audit programs.

Notice also that a new component may be added to the attack description language to describe the possible *reactions* to a detected attack (either successful or not). This reaction may involve several actions. The event algebra described previously may be suitable to describe these events. Such events may correspond to passive actions, such as the reconfiguration of the IDS or audit programs, or active actions, such as connection termination, etc.

Finally, the description of the attack process itself incorporates information concerning the conditions and the effects of the attack using a logical language. This language offers the opportunity to build a deduction module that could complement the detection capabilities of IDS with respect to multiple steps intrusions and analysis of the behaviour and intentions of an intruder.

Acknowledgements

This work was funded by the CELAR/CASSI as a part of the Mirador project. The authors want to thank all the members of this project: Jacques Capoulade,

Patrice Carle, Ewan Cochevelou, Mammadou Diop, Aldric Feuillebois, Sylvain Gombault, Ludovic Mé and Cédric Michel.

The authors would also like to thank Nora Cuppens and Marie Ortalo for their helpful comments on early versions of this paper.

References

1. Feiertag, R., Kahn, C., Porras, P., Schnackenberg, D., Staniford-Chen, S., Tung, B., "A Common Intrusion Specification Language (CISL)", Common Intrusion Detection Framework (CIDF) working group, June 11, 1999. 197
2. Debar, H., Huang, M. and Donahoo, D., "Intrusion Detection Exchange Format Data Model", draft-ietf-idwg-data-model-02.txt, *Internet Draft*, IDWG, Internet Engineering Task Force, March 7, 2000, *work in progress*. 197, 201
3. Wood, M., "Intrusion Detection Message Exchange Requirements", draft-ietf-idwg-requirements-02.txt, *Internet Draft*, IDWG, Internet Engineering Task Force, October 21, 1999, *work in progress*. 197, 201, 205
4. Curry, D., "Intrusion Detection Message Exchange Format Extensible Markup Language (XML) Document Type Definition", draft-ietf-idwg-idmef-xml-01.txt, *Internet Draft*, IDWG, Internet Engineering Task Force, March 15, 2000, *work in progress*. 197, 205
5. W. Baldwin Robert, *Su-Kuang: Rule-based Security Checking*, Technical report, Programming Systems Research Group, Lab. for Computer Science, MIT, May 1994. 202, 215
6. Zerkle, D. and Levitt, K., "NetKuang – a Multi-Host Configuration Vulnerability Checker", in *6th USENIX Security Symposium*, San Jose, CA, USA, July 1996. 202, 215
7. Ming-Yuh Huang, Thomas W. Wicks, "A Large-scale Distributed Intrusion Detection Framework Based on Attack Strategy Analysis", *First International Workshop on the Recent Advances in Intrusion Detection (RAID'98)*, Louvain-la-Neuve, Belgium, September 14-16, 1998. 203
8. Sadri, F. and Kowalski, R., "Variants of the event calculus", *Proc. of ICLP*, MIT Press, 1995. 203, 204
9. A. Mounji and B. Le Charlier, "Continuous Assessment of a Unix Configuration: Integrating Intrusion Detection and Configuration Analysis", in *Proceedings of the ISOC'97 Symposium on Network and Distributed System Security*, San Diego, USA, February 1997. 215
10. A. Mounji, *Languages and Tools for Rule-Based Distributed Intrusion Detection*, PhD thesis, Computer Science Institute, Université de Namur, Belgium, September 1997. 215
11. Ilgun, K., "USTAT: A real-time intrusion detection system for Unix", in *IEEE Symposium on Security and Privacy*, pp. 16-29, 1993. 215
12. Sandeep Kumar, *Classification and Detection of Computer Intrusion*, Ph. D. thesis, Department of Computer Science, Purdue University, West Lafayette, IN, USA, August 1995. 215
13. Teresa Lunt, "IDES: An intelligent system for detecting intruders", in *Computer Security, Threats and Countermeasures*, November 1990. 215
14. Hervé Debar, Marc Dacier and Andreas Wespi, *A Revised Taxonomy for Intrusion-Detection Systems*, Research Report RZ 3176 (#93222), IBM Research, Zurich Research Laboratory, 23 p., October 25, 1999.

Target Naming and Service Apoptosis

James Riordan and Dominique Alessandri

IBM Research Zürich Laboratory
CH-8803 Rüschlikon, Switzerland
{rij,dal}@zurich.ibm.com

Abstract. The volume of traffic on security mailing lists, bulletin boards, news forums, *et cetera* has grown so sharply in recent times that it is no longer feasible for a systems administrator to follow all relevant news as a background task; it has become a full-time job. Even when relevant information does eventually reach the systems administrator, there is, often a dangerous window between public knowledge of a vulnerability and the administrators ability to correct it. Automated responses mechanisms are the key to closing these vulnerability windows. We propose a database of likely areas of vulnerability, called targets, in a machine readable and filterable manner so that administrators can greatly reduce the amount of security mail to be read. We then propose a cryptographically secure service with which semi-trusted third parties can act in a manner limited by the system administrator, say shutting down a specific service while not allowing general access, to diminish the window of vulnerability.

1 Introduction

Reading of Bugtraq [1] and other sources of security-relevant news and information [4,10,2,9,8], one notices that the amount of information published on a daily basis is increasing continuously and rapidly. A few years ago it was possible to read and act in response to the complete stream of commonly available security news. Doing so was one of the many background tasks done by a competent systems administrator. Today, by contrast, it is difficult for any one individual even to read all security news.

Systems administrators are generally quite busy. The result is a dangerous window between public announcement of a vulnerability and the system administrator's ability either to update the service, hopefully eliminating the vulnerability, or disable the service until an update is available. The fact that vulnerabilites are often published at night and over the weekends makes response time yet longer. Even security services and compacted security news sources have the disadvantage of offering too much information and often have significantly longer time delays. Automated response mechanisms can help to reduce these time delays thereby effectively making systems more secure.

It is tempting to equate the danger of this window of vulnerability with the physical analog of leaving house or office window unlocked and, accordingly, to

H. Debar, L. Mé, and F. Wu (Eds.): RAID 2000, LNCS 1907, pp. 217–225, 2000.

consider that the chances of attack quite low. Unfortunately this thinking is incorrect. System crackers build large databases of which versions and revisions of various software systems are running [6]. It is often possible to use search engines to locate certain classes of vulnerability (e.g. the presence of vulnerable CGI programs). Announcement of a vulnerability is generally followed by immediate wide- scale exploitation of vulnerable systems.

There is often a time delay between discovery of a vulnerability and the availability of a patch. For many varieties of system, such as embedded cryptographic devices, upgrades are prohibitively expensive. In these cases it would be useful to be able to trigger an automatic fall-back behavior in case of discovery of catastrophic vulnerability (such as cryptanalysis of the underlying algorithms). For example, if a block cipher is discovered to be insecure *after* deployment, the scheme could trigger systems to revert to (presumably secure) triple DES without costly servicing and down time.

Additional problems are posed by consumer devices which effectively have no systems administrator. Current multi-function consumer devices, such as PCs running Windows 98, Macintoshes, and Win CE and PalmOS PDAs, offer no or little security. If the next generation of devices are to provide a foundation for e-commerce and e-society, significantly higher levels of security will be necessary. Automated response mechanisms will play a key role in attaining these levels of security.

We propose the creation of a database of likely areas of vulnerability and introduce a scheme with which system administrators can use this database to reduce greatly the amount of security mail to be read. We further introduce mechanisms to allow systems administrators to automate reactions to vulnerability announcements in a configurable manner based upon the authenticated announcements by a semi- trusted third party.

Although one wants to allow semi-trusted outside agents to alter the behavior of internal services, one does not wish to enable new attacks. The ability to shut down a service is the ability to stage a denial-of-service attack. More powerful remote abilities compromise to more powerful attacks. As such, careful consideration must be given to enable apoptosis services.

The simplest form of the idea is publication of a collection of pairs (name,token) where token is the image of a nonce secret under a one- way hash function. Should a vulnerability be found in name, secret is released into the environment to trigger various preconfigured responses (presumably to shut down name or to warn a responsible party).

2   Apoptosis and Naming

The term *apoptosis* comes from biology and it refers to the programmed self-destruction of cells. Apoptosis is often initiated when a cell detects that it has become a threat to the health of the organism, although it has many other functions.

We propose programmed death for computational services when these services have been fount to threaten the health/security of the entire system (e.g. when a vulnerability has been found). Cryptographic de/activation and alteration of mobile agents is proposed in [7], where the term *cluelessness* is introduced. The idea is developed, again in the context of mobile agents, in [11], where the biological analogy is explained.

In apoptosis, unlike necrosis, cells are killed in a controlled manner. Similarly, in service apoptosis, services should be shut down in a controlled manner. This shutdown would involve sending appropriate warning messages, logging active connections, putting up an "out of service" banner, *et cetera*.

The important difference between biological and computational apoptosis is that the computational variety must be secure against abuse and should maintain a limited trust model. In the biological setting, there is no value to abusing an apoptosis mechanism. Evil harmful agents, such as viruses, need a cell to function properly in order to propogate themselves. In the computational setting, the situation is very different. More sophisticated control leads to the possibility of more damaging forms of attack.

The ideal situation, as always, limits trust as much as possible. Use of an apoptosis service should not grant general access to system, leak information from the system, or even grant knowledge of a system's existence. Schemes such as debian's [5] automatic udpate mechanism are extremely powerful[1] but are vulnerable to abuse.

2.1   Naming

Experience has demonstrated that one of the most difficult problems in computer science, and in many other fields, is that of *naming* [3]. Many services have canonical names such as `wu-ftpd-2.6.0(1)`. Unfortunately, security announcements related to this daemon might refer to the daemon as any of

- `wu-ftpd-2.6.0(1)`
- `wu ftpd-2.6.0(1)`
- `wu ftpd 2.6.0(1)`
- `wu-ftpd 2.6.0(1)`
- `wu-ftpd-2.6.0.1`
- `WASHINGTON UNIVERSITY FTP SERVER, RELEASE 2.6.0(1)`
- `WASHINGTON UNIVERSITY ftpd 2.6.0(1)`
- *et cetera.*

This multiplicity of names makes writing filters that pass on only relevant messages to a system administrator very difficult.

It is moreover the case that many vulnerabilities are not properties of the services themselves but of their configuration.[2] In these cases, whereas delivery of

---

[1] The debian package management systems allows to configure a system to upgrade its packages in an automated fashion from a trusted system not requiring a system-administrators interaction.

[2] We are not speaking of *incorrect* configuration, which can always turn a service into a vulnerable service, but of proper configuration with vulnerable subservices (as with the optional `mime` decoding with `sendmail` [10]).

security (CERT-97-05: CA-97.05.sendmail) announcements is relevant, one does not wish to disable the entire service but only relevant subservice. Consideration must be made as to an appropriate limited execution environment in which detection scripts may be run. This would require further research and is not discussed in this work.

3   Terminology

A *security threat*[3] is any kind of security problem one can encounter on the Internet or intranets - including the e-business arena. We distinguish among the following levels of security threats:

- Level 1: Service degradation. Any kind of vulnerability that allows an adversary to impair the performance of the system significantly.
- Level 2: Denial of service. Any kind of vulnerability that allows an adversary to tamper with the system such that it becomes unavailable.
- Level 3: Information theft. Any kind of vulnerability that allows an adversary to obtain supposedly secret information (privacy issues).
- Level 4: Information manipulation. Any kind of vulnerability that allows an adversary to manipulate or inject data into a system (integrity issues).
- Level 5: Control of system. Any kind of vulnerability that allows an adversary to execute arbitrary code on a system and therefore to compromise a system.

An *apoptosis service* (AS) consists of publishing a list of selected products (commercial, any kind of freeware or open source), following closely any available publications concerning security issues of the selected products. Once a previously unknown security threat has been discovered, this information is published in a cryptographically secure manner.

The *apoptosis service provider* (ASP) is an organization that selects a list of products for which it offers an apoptosis service AS to its customers.

The *apoptosis customer* (AC) is the receiver of the AS as it is offered by the ASP. The AC aims to protect itself by signing an AS contract with its ASP. Consequently the AC is required to semi-trust the ASP as the AC grants the ASP the power of actively influencing services offered by the AC.

An *apoptosis activation key* (AAK) is a secret random string (nonce). It should be long enough to render brute force attack intractable.

An *apoptosis token* (AT) consists of the image of an AAK under a cryptographic one-way function Htogether with a complete description of a particular service or subservice instance. This description should include version, platform, and configuration information. The token will generally be signed to bind the AAK.

An *apoptosis activation token* (AAT) consists of the AAK together with a complete description of a particular service or subservice instance. This description should include version, platform, and configuration information. The token will generally be signed to bind the AAK.

---

[3] It is worth mentioning that the list provided below serves as an example to facilitate understanding of the remaining document.

4   Architecture

The most basic form of fully functional apoptosis built into a daemon might look like:

```
// apoptosis token AT
at = read_my_AT_from_cfg_file();
// verify AT signature
if (!verify_sign(at)) {
  send_warn("AT signature incorrect.");
  exit();
}
// extract activation key hash from AT
akh = extract_ak_hash(at);

while (true) {
  // receive an apoptosis activation token
  aat = receive_aat();
  if (!verify_sign(aat)) {
    send_warning("AAT signature incorrect. \
                  Possible DoS attack.");
  }
  // extract the apoptosis activation key
  aak = extract_aak(aat);
  if (hash(aak) == akh) {
    disable_daemon();
    send_warning("Daemon received valid \
                  AAT. Daemon stopped.");
    exit();
  }
  act_daemonically();
}
```

As with many password schemes, the important feature is that complete knowledge of the above code fragment, and in particular of the AT, does not give one the ability to trigger the shutdown behavior due to the one-way nature of the one way hash function. One- way hash functions, digital signatures, secret sharing, and the constructions from [7] allow us to configure apoptosis services according to arbitrary trust models.

The above configuration places the service in the daemon itself. Naturally the services could be implemented in a number of different ways, several of which do not require modification of the daemons themselves. A special apoptosis service could manage all other daemons on the system. This could naturally be combined with the meta-daemon inet. Alternatively, tcp-wrappers [12], rpcbind or a subsystem management system could easily be modified to implement such functionality.

4.1 Apoptosis Token Distribution

In the interest of privacy and anonymity, the apoptosis customer AC should be able to obtain ATs without providing the information about which ATs he or she is actually interested in. This can be achieved by any of the following distribution channels:

- Public data repository: Typically the world wide web (http, ftp, *et cetera*) or services similar to antivirus products. In order to guarantee the property mentioned above (not providing information about the exact product versions installed), the entire list of recently published ATs (including those of interest) has to be downloaded by the customer.
- Public forum: New ATs are published in public forums such as mailing lists or news groups.
- Product vendor: The vendor of a product may provide this service and distribute the appropriate ATs along with every product item shipped. If a vendor releases a patch or a new version a new AT is supplied as well.
- Any other broadcast system.
- An oblivious transfer mechanism.

4.2 Distribution of Apoptosis Activation Tokens

The goal of an AAK once it has been released by the ASP is to reach every AC subscribed with the ASP. In order to guarantee a secured distribution the AAK will be encapsulated in an AAT. The distribution can be achieved by various means:

- Apoptosis publication protocol: The ASP publishes the AAK in the AAT by a special purpose protocol. (This would mean that ASP establishes a connection to every of its ACs and transfers the AAK.)
- Mailing list: The ASP publishes the AAT on a mailing list. These messages could then be treated on the AC site in an automated fashion.
- Use of an existing service: The AAT can be distributed by reusing an existing service such as http or ftp. (The AAT could be transferred by means of a specific URL or by uploading a specific file.)
- Polling: The AC queries the ASP on a regular basis for newly published AATs. (This introduces a possibly dangerous delay between the publication of an AAT and the customers' reactions.)

4.3 Customer Apoptosis Functionality

On the customer side the following functionality must be provided:

- Reception and verification of AATs,
- Reaction to AATs,
- Update of apoptosis configuration.

Receipt of AATs There are two different ways to implement apoptosis functionality on the customer side. In the first approach the apoptosis functionality is distributed in the products themselves. This means for instance that a web server (e.g. httpd) interprets arriving AATs by itself and takes appropriate action (e.g. shuts itself down). The second approach is to introduce an apoptosis subsystem. This subsystem receives AATs by any of the means listed above and takes appropriate action such as shutting services down. This subsystem can be realized by any combination of means such as a separate daemon, a kernel module, a modified inittab, a modified inetd, modified tcp-wrappers, a modified rpcbind, *et cetera*. Before taking any action the receiver of the AAT has to verify the ASP's signature and compute the hash portion of the AT based on the AAK received within the AAT, go through its configuration and verify whether any actions have been defined for the hash portion of the AT just computed.

Reaction to AATs The most obvious action to be taken in case of a matching AT is to shut down the respective service. However any combination of other actions can also be taken:

- Shut a service down,
- Reconfigure a service (e.g. disable a certain functionality, *et cetera*),
- Install a patch,
- Alarm the systems administrator,
- Execute any customized set of commands.

If the notion of security threat level is used, one can configure separate actions depending on the level of the threat to which the AAT is refers.

It is important to note that the AC is free to configure the manner in which its systems react upon the reception of an AAT as desired. The AC may wish to configure its systems differently depending on

- Their importance for business operations,
- The sensitivity of the information they host,
- The environement in which the systems are operated,
- The degree to which ASP is trusted,
- Daytime,
- Weekdays,
- *et cetera*.

The important features are that the reaction is triggered automatically and that it is completely customizable by the owner of the system.

Update of Apoptosis Configuration An update of the apoptosis configuration is required only if a new product or a new version of a product is installed, or the ASP has started to support a product (installed on the customer system) it has not been supporting before. The update procedure has to add the AT for a specific version of a specific product to the apoptosis configuration. Along with the AT the various actions to be taken in case the appropriate AAT is received have to be defined. The update of the apoptosis configuration can be done either manually or in an automated fashion. In any case the ASP's signature should be verified first for obvious reasons.

4.4 Apoptosis Service Provider

The apoptosis service provider has two main functionalities to offer:

- Publication of ATs,
- Publication of AATs.

Publication of ATs Whenever a vendor releases a new product, a new version of a product, or a security- related fix for a product the, ASP has to generate a new AAT which is kept secret, and release the new AT to the public.

Publication of AATs Once the ASP has released a new AT, it commits to releasing the corresponding AAT to the public in case a security problem in that version of a product has been discovered.

5   Conclusion

The apoptosis scheme presented can significantly diminish the window of vulnerability of deployed systems, thereby making them more secure. It is arbitrarily configurable, which allows the use of one of several apoptosis service providers with varying degrees of trust. We feel that its utility of constructions will be increasingly useful as computing devices become ever more pervasive and system administrators become increasingly occupied, as with most corporate or educational systems, or nonpresent, as with home systems and PDAs.

References

1. bugtraq community. bugtraq archive. Mailing list. http://www.securityfocus.com/. 217
2. Computer Incident Advisory Capability. Ciac advisory mailing list. Email News Bulletin. http://www.ciac.ORG/. 217
3. Saul A. Kripke. *Naming and Necessity*. Harvard Universit Press, 1982. ISBN 0674598466. 219
4. COAST Lab. Computer operations, audit, and security technology web site. Web Site. http://www.cs.purdue.edu/coast/. 217
5. Debian Security Page. Debian project community. Web Site. http://www.debian.org/security/. 219
6. James Riordan. Patterns of network intrusion. In Günter Müller and Kai Rannenberg, editor, *Multilateral Security in Communications*, Information Security, pages 173–186. Addison-Wesley, 1999. 218

7. J. Riordan and B. Schneier. Environmental key generation towards clueless agents. In G. Vigna, editor, *Mobile Agents and Security*, volume 1419 of *LNCS*, pages 15–24. Springer, 1998. http://www.counterpane.com/clueless-agents.html. 219, 221

8. Bruce Schneier. Cryptogram. Email News Bulletin. http://www.counterpane.com/. 217

9. Australian Computer Emergency Response Team. Auscert news letter. Email News Bulletin. http://www.auscert.org.au/. 217

10. Computer Emergency Response Team. Cert news letter. Email News Bulletin. http://www.cert.org/. 217, 219

11. C. Tschudin. Apoptosis - the programmed death of distributed services. In In J. Vitek and C. Jensen, editors, *Secure Internet Programming - Security Issues for Mobile and Distributed Objects*, pages 253–260. Springer, 1999. 219

12. Wietse Venema. tcp-wrappers-7.6.blurb. anonymous FTP. ftp://ftp.porcupine.org/pub/security/. 221

Author Index

Lecture Notes in Computer Science

For information about Vols. 1–1856
please contact your bookseller or Springer-Verlag

Vol. 1893: M. Nielsen, B. Rovan (Eds.), Mathematical Foundations of Computer Science 2000. Proceedings, 2000. XIII, 710 pages. 2000.

Vol. 1894: R. Dechter (Ed.), Principles and Practice of Constraint Programming – CP 2000. Proceedings, 2000. XII, 556 pages. 2000.

Vol. 1895: F. Cuppens, Y. Deswarte, D. Gollmann, M. Waidner (Eds.), Computer Security – ESORICS 2000. Proceedings. 2000. X, 325 pages. 2000.

Vol. 1896: R. W. Hartenstein, H. Grünbacher (Eds.), Field-Programmable Logic and Applications. Proceedings, 2000. XVII, 856 pages. 2000.

Vol. 1897: J. Gutknecht, W. Weck (Eds.), Modular Programming Languages. Proceedings. 2000. XII, 299 pages. 2000.

Vol. 1898: E. Blanzieri, L. Portinale (Eds.), Advances in Case-Based Reasoning. Proceedings, 2000. XII, 530 pages. 2000. (Subseries LNAI).

Vol. 1899: H.-H. Nagel, F.J. Perales López (Eds.), Articulated Motion and Deformable Objects. Proceedings. 2000. X, 183 pages. 2000.

Vol. 1900: A. Bode, T. Ludwig, W. Karl, R. Wismüller (Eds.), Euro-Par 2000 Parallel Processing. Proceedings, 2000. XXXV, 1368 pages. 2000.

Vol. 1901: O. Etzion, P. Scheuermann (Eds.), Cooperative Information Systems. Proceedings, 2000. XI, 336 pages. 2000.

Vol. 1902: P. Sojka, I. Kopeček, K. Pala (Eds.), Text, Speech and Dialogue. Proceedings, 2000. XIII, 463 pages. 2000. (Subseries LNAI).

Vol. 1903: S. Reich, K.M. Anderson (Eds.), Open Hypermedia Systems and Structural Computing. Proceedings, 2000. VIII, 187 pages. 2000.

Vol. 1904: S.A. Cerri, D. Dochev (Eds.), Artificial Intelligence: Methodology, Systems, and Applications. Proceedings, 2000. XII, 366 pages. 2000. (Subseries LNAI).

Vol. 1905: H. Scholten, M.J. van Sinderen (Eds.), Interactive Distributed Multimedia Systems and Telecommunication Services. Proceedings. 2000. XI, 306 pages. 2000.

Vol. 1906: A. Porto, G.-C. Roman (Eds.), Coordination Languages and Models. Proceedings, 2000. IX, 353 pages. 2000.

Vol. 1907: H. Debar, L. Mé, S.F. Wu (Eds.), Recent Advances in Intrusion Detection. Proceedings. 2000. X, 227 pages. 2000.

Vol. 1908: J. Dongarra, P. Kacsuk, N. Podhorszki (Eds.), Recent Advances in Parallel Virtual Machine and Message Passing Interface Proceedings, 2000. XV, 364 pages. 2000.

Vol. 1910: D.A. Zighed, J. Komorowski, J. Żytkow (Eds.), Principles of Data Mining and Knowledge Discovery. Proceedings, 2000. XV, 701 pages. 2000. (Subseries LNAI).

Vol. 1912: Y. Gurevich, P.W. Kutter, M. Odersky, L. Thiele (Eds.), Abstract State Machines. Proceedings, 2000. X, 381 pages. 2000.

Vol. 1913: K. Jansen, S. Khuller (Eds.), Approximation Algorithms for Combinatorial Optimization. Proceedings, 2000. IX, 275 pages. 2000.

Vol. 1914: M. Herlihy (Ed.), Distributed Computing. Proceedings, 2000. VIII, 389 pages. 2000.

Vol. 1917: M. Schoenauer, K. Deb, G. Rudolph, X. Yao, E. Lutton, J.J. Merelo, H.-P. Schwefel (Eds.), Parallel Problem Solving from Nature – PPSN VI. Proceedings, 2000. XXI, 914 pages. 2000.

Vol. 1918: D. Soudris, P. Pirsch, E. Barke (Eds.), Integrated Circuit Design. Proceedings, 2000. XII, 338 pages. 2000.

Vol. 1919: M. Ojeda-Aciego, I.P. de Guzman, G. Brewka, L. Moniz Pereira (Eds.), Logics in Artificial Intelligence. Proceedings, 2000. XI, 407 pages. 2000. (Subseries LNAI).

Vol. 1920: A.H.F. Laender, S.W. Liddle, V.C. Storey (Eds.), Conceptual Modeling – ER 2000. Proceedings, 2000. XV, 588 pages. 2000.

Vol. 1921: S.W. Liddle, H.C. Mayr, B. Thalheim (Eds.), Conceptual Modeling for E-Business and the Web. Proceedings, 2000. X, 179 pages. 2000.

Vol. 1922: J. Crowcroft, J. Roberts, M.I. Smirnov (Eds.), Quality of Future Internet Services. Proceedings, 2000. XI, 368 pages. 2000.

Vol. 1923: J. Borbinha, T. Baker (Eds.), Research and Advanced Technology for Digital Libraries. Proceedings, 2000. XVII, 513 pages. 2000.

Vol. 1924: W. Taha (Ed.), Semantics, Applications, and Implementation of Program Generation. Proceedings, 2000. VIII, 231 pages. 2000.

Vol. 1925: J. Cussens, S. Džeroski (Eds.), Learning Language in Logic. X, 301 pages 2000. (Subseries LNAI).

Vol. 1926: M. Joseph (Ed.), Formal Techniques in Real-Time and Fault-Tolerant Systems. Proceedings, 2000. X, 305 pages. 2000.

Vol. 1927: P. Thomas, H.W. Gellersen, (Eds.), Handheld and Ubiquitous Computing. Proceedings, 2000. X, 249 pages. 2000.

Vol. 1931: E. Horlait (Ed.), Mobile Agents for Telecommunication Applications. Proceedings, 2000. IX, 271 pages. 2000.

Vol. 1766: M. Jazayeri, R.G.K. Loos, D.R. Musser (Eds.), Generic Programming. Proceedings, 1998. X, 269 pages. 2000.

Vol. 1791: D. Fensel, Problem-Solving Methods. XII, 153 pages. 2000. (Subseries LNAI).

Vol. 1932: Z.W. Raś, S. Ohsuga (Eds.), Foundations of Intelligent Systems. Proceedings, 2000. XII, 646 pages. (Subseries LNAI).

Vol. 1933: R.W. Brause, E. Hanisch (Eds.), Medical Data Analysis. Proceedings, 2000. XI, 316 pages. 2000.

Vol. 1934: J.S. White (Ed.), Envisioning Machine Translation in the Information Future. Proceedings, 2000. XV, 254 pages. 2000. (Subseries LNAI).

Vol. 1937: R. Dieng, O. Corby (Eds.), Knowledge Engineering and Knowledge Management. Proceedings, 2000. XIII, 457 pages. 2000. (Subseries LNAI).

Vol. 1938: S.Rao, K.I. Sletta (Eds.), Next Generation Networks. Proceedings, 2000. XI, 392 pages. 2000.

Vol. 1939: A. Evans, S. Kent (Eds.), «UML» – The Unified Modeling Language. Proceedings, 2000. XIV, 572 pages. 2000.